PUBLISHED AS A SPECIAL EDITION OF THE UNIVERSITY OF QUEENSLAND LAW JOURNAL

Editors
Margaret Stephenson, Lecturer in Law, T.C. Beirne School of Law, University of Queensland
Clive Turner, Senior Lecturer in Law, T.C. Beirne School of Law, University of Queensland

Editorial Advisory Board
Professor Geoffrey de Q. Walker, Dean, T.C. Beirne School of Law, University of Queensland
Professor R.D. Lumb, T.C. Beirne School of Law, University of Queensland
Professor Alan Fogg, T.C. Beirne School of Law, University of Queensland
Professor Sir William Wade, University of Cambridge
Professor Douglas Kmiec, University of Notre Dame, Indiana
Professor R. Van Caenegem, University of Ghent
Professor N.R.M. Menon, National Law School of India University, Bangalore
Professor G.L. Peiris, University of Colombo
Professor Michael Pryles, Bond University
Professor David Link, University of Notre Dame, Indiana

Editorial Advisers to the Special Edition
Gabriël Moens, Associate Professor of Law, T.C. Beirne School of Law, University of Queensland
Darrell Lumb, Professor of Law, T.C. Beirne School of Law, University of Queensland

Editorial Assistants
Alexander Bates
Jane Hunter
Caroline Jobbins

The University of Queensland Law Journal has been published since 1948, making it one of the oldest and most prestigious law journals in Australia. It publishes scholarly articles on Queensland law, Commonwealth law, international and comparative law and jurisprudence. The journal is fully refereed and is produced by editors appointed by the Law Faculty Board. The journal is served by an Editorial Advisory Board consisting of eminent Australian and overseas legal scholars.

REPUBLIC OR MONARCHY?

Legal and Constitutional Issues

Edited by M.A. Stephenson and Clive Turner

University of Queensland Press

First published 1994 by University of Queensland Press
Box 42, St Lucia, Queensland 4067 Australia

© University of Queensland Law Journal 1994
Copyright in the individual contributions remains with the authors

This book is copyright. Apart from any fair dealing
for the purposes of private study, research, criticism
or review, as permitted under the Copyright Act, no
part may be reproduced by any process without written
permission. Enquiries should be made to the publisher.

The typeset text for this book was supplied by the editors
Printed in Australia by McPherson's Printing Group, Victoria

Distributed in the USA and Canada by
International Specialized Book Services, Inc.,
5804 N.E. Hassalo Street, Portland, Oregon 97213-3640

Cataloguing in Publication Data
National Library of Australia

Australia, republic or monarchy?

    1. Republicanism — Australia. 2. Australia — Constitutional
law. 3. Australia — Politics and government — 1990– .
I. Stephenson, M.A. (Margaret Anne), 1954– . II. Turner,
Clive, 1942– . III. Title: University of Queensland law
journal.

342.9403

ISBN 0 7022 2718 8

Contents

Acknowledgments *vii*
Contributors *ix*
Foreword *xiii*
Introduction *xvii*

The Australian Constitution and Australian Constitutional Monarchy
   The Right Honourable Sir Harry Gibbs 1
The Constitutional Implications of a Republic
   George Winterton 15
A Civic Identity—Not A National Identity
   Donald Horne 34
A History of the Inevitable Republic
   Mark McKenna 50
'Mañana'—The Politics of Becoming a Republic
   T. Abbott 72
The Republic and the Issues of 2001
   Kenneth Wiltshire 84
Monarchy: Mystery and Practicality
   Gareth Grainger 96
The British Influence on the Australian Constitution
   A.A. Preece 132
The American Republic
   Keith A. Cline 146
The German Republic
   Isolde Turwitt–Fieber 158
Representative Democracy, Federalism and Constitutional Revision
   R.D. Lumb 165
Republicanism and State Constitutions
   Gerard Carney 183
The Other Road to the Republic: the Separation of Powers
   Suri Ratnapala 211
The Wrongs of a Constitutionally Entrenched Bill of Rights
   Gabriël A. Moens 233
The Status of Aborigines and Torres Strait Islanders in an Australian Republic
   Frank Brennan SJ 257

Appendix I—
 The Report of the Republic Advisory Committee: Summary of
 Conclusions and Options   286
Appendix II—
 The States and a Republic: A Legal Opinion by Sir Harry Gibbs
 and the Legal Committee of Australians for Constitutional
 Monarchy in Response to the Republic Advisory Committee
 Report   298

Acknowledgments

Margaret Stephenson initiated and compiled this publication. It has been edited by Margaret Stephenson and Clive Turner.

The willingness of the authors to participate in this project and their valuable contributions in this important debate are appreciated.

Thanks are due to Betty Rogan and Kim Coram for their excellent secretarial assistance, and to Alexander Bates, Jane Hunter and Caroline Jobbins, editorial assistants, for their diligent efforts. Thanks also go to Barry Maher for typesetting the manuscript.

Special thanks and appreciation are due to the Editorial Board, in particular to Professor Darrell Lumb; and also to Associate Professors Gabriël Moens and Caroline Sappideen for their continued guidance, encouragement and advice. The constitutional advice given by Professor Lumb and Associate Professor Moens in the preparation of this work is gratefully acknowledged.

Publication was made possible by the resources of the T.C. Beirne School of Law, University of Queensland. Thanks are also due to the Dean, Professor Geoffrey de Q. Walker for his active support. The staff of the University of Queensland Press, especially Robert Brown and Judy MacDonald, were most helpful at all stages of the project.

Contributors

Tony Abbott is Executive Director of Australians for Constitutional Monarchy. Previously he was Political Adviser to the Leader of the Federal Opposition and a journalist with The Australian and The Bulletin. He studied politics and philosophy at Oxford University (where he was a Rhodes Scholar) and law and economics at Sydney University.

Father Frank Brennan, SJ is both a Jesuit priest and lawyer. He graduated LL.B. from the University of Queensland and LL.M. from the University of Melbourne and obtained a Bachelor of Divinity from the Melbourne College of Divinity. He was founding Director of Uniya—a Christian Centre for Social Research and Action based at Kings Cross, and for many years was the Aboriginal Affairs consultant to the Australian Catholic Bishops. He is a member of the Council of the Constitutional Centenary Foundation. He has written extensively on Aboriginal Land Rights and is the author of a number of books including *Land Rights Queensland Style* and *Sharing the Country* and is the co-author of *Finding Common Ground* and *Reconciling our Differences*. In 1989 he won the United Nations Association of Australia Media Peace Award. The National Australia Day Council selected him as an Outstanding Achiever in 1993 for his contribution to the Aboriginal Community. He is presently a Visiting Fellow with the 'Reshaping Australian Institutions: Towards and Beyond 2001' project in the law program at the Research School of Social Sciences at the Australian National University in Canberra.

Gerard Carney holds the degrees of LL.B. (Hons) and LL.M. (London). He is an Associate Professor of Law at Bond University where he teaches Constitutional and Administrative Law. He has a particular interest in the field of State Constitutional Law, as well as in the parliamentary system and public integrity. His publications include articles in those areas, and a major comparative study for the Commonwealth Secretariat, London, *Conflict of Interest: A Commonwealth Study of Members of Parliament* 1992.

Keith Cline obtained a B.A. from the University of Indianapolis and a J.D. (*summa cum laude*) from the University of Notre Dame, Indiana, U.S.A. He was awarded an Overseas Postgraduate

Research Scholarship and is currently researching in the area of Comparative Constitutional Law for a Master of Laws degree at the University of Queensland.

The Right Honourable Sir Harry Gibbs was Chief Justice of the High Court of Australia from 1981 to 1987, having become a member of that Court in 1970. Previously he had served on the bench of the Federal Court of Bankruptcy, the Supreme Court of the Australian Capital Territory and the Supreme Court of Queensland. Sir Harry chaired the Review into Commonwealth Criminal Law 1987–1990 as well as other major commissions of inquiry in New South Wales and Queensland. He holds the degrees of B.A., LL.B., LL.M. and honorary LL.D. from the University of Queensland and lectured in Evidence and Personal Property at the Law School between 1948 and 1959. He was admitted to the Queensland Bar in 1939.

Gareth Grainger, at the time of writing his paper, was a visiting Associate Professor of Law at Bond University. He is a Sydney solicitor, academic and author who has worked both in private practice and in senior positions in the New South Wales and Commonwealth public sector.

Donald Horne opened up wide public discussion on the republican issue in his book, *The Lucky Country* in 1964. He has written on the subject regularly since, most recently in *The Coming Republic*. He has also contributed to books and conferences on more general constitutional reform. He was a member, 1985-87, of the Executive Government Committee of the Constitutional Commission and co-convener of the *National Campaign for Democratic Constitution Conference*, 1977, and co-convener of the *Change the Rules Conference*, 1977.

Professor R. D. Lumb has been a member of the academic staff of the T.C. Beirne School of Law, University of Queensland since 1958 when he was appointed after completing his doctorate at Oxford. Professor Lumb has researched and published in the area of *Australian Constitutional Law* for several decades. He is the author of *The Constitutions of the Australian States* (5th ed., 1991), *The Constitution of Australia Annotated* (4th ed., 1986) and *Australian Constutionalism* (1983), as well as being the author of many articles in the *Australian Law Journal*, the *University of Queensland Law Journal* and other legal journals.

Mark McKenna currently teaches Australian Studies within the Centre for Liberal and General Studies at the University of New South Wales. Mark McKenna's book on the history of republicanism in Australia will be published by Allen and Unwin later this year.

Gabriël A. Moens is an Associate Professor of Law at the University of Queensland. He obtained law and philosophy degrees from the University of Leuven (Belgium) and a postgraduate degree in law from Northwestern University (Chicago). He holds a Ph.D. from the University of Sydney. He co-authored with Professor David Flint, a book entitled *Business Law of the European Community* published by DataLegal Publications in 1993. Also in 1993, he contributed to SBS's television production of *The Republic—Court in the Act*.

Alun Preece has degrees in mathematics and law from Cambridge University, and a Masters degree in law from the University of Queensland. He has held lecturing positions at the University of Wales, the Queensland University of Technology, and since 1990 at the University of Queensland. He served as a full-time member of the Queensland Law Reform Commission from 1987-90. He has published numerous articles in the fields of Land Law, Succession and in areas related to Constitutional Law.

Suri Ratnapala is a senior lecturer in law at the University of Queensland. Before migrating to Australia, he served as a Senior State Counsel in the Attorney-General's Department of Sri Lanka, where, as a specialist in Constitutional Law, he was involved in that country's republican constitution. He is the author of *Welfare State or Constitutional State* (Centre for Independent Studies, 1990) and co-author of *The Illusions of Comparable Worth* (Centre for Independent Studies, 1992).

Isolde Turwitt-Fieber is a German lawyer who worked with the Ministry for Foreign Affairs in Bonn, Germany, and at the United Nations in Geneva, Switzerland. She studied law at the University of Bonn, the University of Tennessee Law School, Knoxville, U.S.A., and the University of Munich before becoming a

Referendarin in Lower Saxony, Oberlandesgericht Celle. She spent three months in 1993 at the Supreme Court of Queensland.

Professor Kenneth Wiltshire is J.D. Story Professor of Public Administration at the University of Queensland. He is the author of several texts and numerous articles on comparative federalism and government in Australia, Europe and North America. Professor Wiltshire has served as consultant to Commonwealth and State Governments, government business enterprises and private sector groups. He is currently Chair of a number of Commonwealth and State statutory bodies and is a Board member of the Constitutional Centenary Foundation.

Professor George Winterton is a Professor of Law at the University of New South Wales, specialising in Constitutional Law and Comparative Law. He was a member of the Republic Advisory Committee (1993), and served on the Executive Government Advisory Committee of the Constitutional Commission (1986–87). Professor Winterton is the author of *Monarchy to Republic: Australian Republican Government* (Oxford University Press, 1986) and *Parliament, the Executive and the Governor-General* (Melbourne University Press, 1983), and co-edited *Australian Constitutional Perspectives* (Law Book Company, 1992). He published a draft republican constitution in the *Independent Monthly* in March 1992.

Foreword

The Right Honourable Sir Zelman Cowen AK GCMG GCVO GCOMRI DCL
Former Governor-General of Australia

In this last decade of the twentieth century we approach the centenary of the Commonwealth of Australia which was proclaimed to come into existence on 1 January 1901. The years which take us to that date have been styled the Constitutional Decade because they commemorate events, a hundred years past, which were milestones on the road to Australian federation. The first of these was the National Australasian Convention of 1891 which debated and adopted the first text of a Commonwealth constitution.

Since that time many great changes have taken place in our Australian lives, and the commemoration of the centenary of the Convention of 1891 was seen as an occasion for an independent non-governmental initiative to bring together a widely representative group of Australians in March 1991. The Conference identified twelve issues which were seen as significant for the Australian polity on the threshold of the twenty-first century. It also proposed the establishment of a Constitutional Centenary Foundation to assist in a public process of education, review and development of the Australian constitutional system in the interests of all Australians, to be completed by the year 2000. Under the Chairmanship of Sir Ninian Stephen it was to consider not only the Constitution, but the whole constitutional system of Australia. Twelve key issues were identified by the Conference of 1991 as an agenda for the constitutional decade, and the Head of State was placed first. Sir Ninian Stephen spoke of the issue of the monarchy as 'engaging the attention of the Australian public more than at any time in the past'.

This has come upon us with a sudden urgency, or so it seems. The Constitutional Commission, which was established in 1985 by the Australian Government to undertake a comprehensive review of our constitutional system, reported in 1988 that it had accepted the advice of its Constitutional Committee on the Executive that there was no prospect of success for any constitutional amendment to establish a republic in Australia. I was Chairman of that Committee, and in its meetings the matter of a republic was actively considered and there was, indeed, significant support for such a change. Two of the contributors to this edition of the University of Queensland Law Journal were members of that advisory committee: Professor George Winterton and Donald Horne. They shared the view that there was insufficient public support for a republic to lead to success in a constitutional referendum.

In light of this, I confess myself a little surprised by the seeming strength of the republican movement very few years later. It has the support of the contemporary national political leadership which hitherto was content to leave the issue on the backburner; now it is said by the Prime Minister that it is incompatible with full independence that the monarchical link, however formal and attenuated, should continue to exist. It is said with not a little passion by the writer Tom Keneally that 'if we cannot discover loyalty, sanity, human decency and leadership among our own people then we are finished as a nation'. This is said in the specific context of the republic.

For whatever reason, the republic as an issue has come to occupy the foreground. The Prime Minister established a committee under the chairmanship of a declared republican, Malcolm Turnbull, to explore a variety of questions, which necessarily arise in the creation of an Australian republic. That committee was required to take the establishment of a republic as given and within the framework of a 'minimalist' change in our political and legal system, it explored a variety of issues some of them very complex, which were involved in bringing a republic into being.

This special edition of the University of Queensland Law Journal examines in detail a variety of questions bearing on the issue of an Australian republic. The contributors include supporters and opponents of that change, and the focus is on constitutional and legal issues and upon the major problems which would have to be tackled in the transfer to a republican system of government.

The contributors to the issue include lawyers and non-lawyers some of whom have been active in the debate, and there is impressive coverage of the issues. The editorial board is to be congratulated on the planning and production of this important publication.

I am pleased to be invited to write this foreword to the volume. I was Vice Chancellor of the University of Queensland from 1970 to 1977, and it was from St Lucia that I went early in December 1977 to become the nineteenth Governor-General of Australia.

Introduction

In the early to mid-nineteenth century, as the various Australian colonies moved toward responsible government, voices were raised seeking freedom from control of the British Parliament. Some equated freedom with republicanism and thus advocated that the colonies should become republics. The republic/monarchy debate pre-dated Federation and was highlighted in the 1852 works of John Dunmore Lang, a strong advocate of a republic. The shadow of the struggle for independence of the American colonies loomed large. With the British genius for compromise, the Australian colonies became self-governing in the mid-1850s with the advent of responsible government, although this occurred towards the end of the nineteenth century for Western Australia. After thorough analysis of a draft of a new constitution by an elected Constitutional Convention in the mid 1890s, the several colonies in 1901 federated in the Commonwealth of Australia. As the twentieth century advanced each of the Dominions of the British Commonwealth of Nations became *de facto* and *de jure* (in fact and in law), less dependent upon the Imperial Parliament. Federation in 1901 did not create an independent Australian nation; this did not occur until, arguably, the adoption in Australia in 1942 of the British *Statute of Westminster* 1931, which gave the Commonwealth legislative independence from Britain. Further constitutional links were severed in 1986 when the *Australia Acts* were passed by the United Kingdom and Australian Parliaments. This legislation completed the abolition of appeals from Australian courts to the Privy Council and terminated remaining Imperial controls on State laws. Few would doubt the reality of Australia's independence today.

As the century of the Australian Federation approaches it is an appropriate time to raise the question whether all remaining constitutional links with Britain should be severed by Australia becoming a republic, or whether by so doing an important part of our history would be denied and the potential for political instability created. In passing, it should be noted that the severing of constitutional links with Britain would not preclude a republican Australia from remaining a member of the Commonwealth of Nations.

The Australian constitutional system has been based to a large extent on the British 'Westminster' model of responsible government. The Constitution provides for a system of representative democracy where the people elect representatives to Parliament to make decisions on their behalf. Although the Australian Constitution is a written constitution it is not an exhaustive text. Under the Constitution the Governor-General, as representative of the Queen, is the Head of State. The Governor-General appears to have extensive powers under the wording of the Constitution. However, except for certain reserve powers, which allow the Head of State (the Governor-General) to act without, or contrary to, ministerial advice, the Governor-General acts on the advice of the Government and has little real power. Constitutional conventions or customs have developed in relation to the exercise of the reserve powers which, although not enforceable as laws, are regarded as binding by those to whom they apply. The allocation of powers between the Governor-General, as the representative of the Queen, the Senate and the House of Representatives has served the nation well since 1901. However, in times of crisis, such as in 1975 when the Governor-General dismissed the Whitlam Government, this allocation of power has been questioned. Such questioning has led, no doubt, to different views being taken about the Constitutional system and has assisted in the revival of the republican debate.

The key issues in this debate include questions as to the style of government with which Australia should enter the second century of Federation and whether the present Commonwealth Constitution is satisfactory, and if not, whether the changes needed are major or minor. An important question is whether a republican constitution should be adopted with an elected Head of State or whether the monarchy should be retained. Accordingly, if the republican option is chosen, the central question would relate to the nature of the powers which would be vested in a republican Head of State. Before a republic could be achieved a referendum, for the people to approve the necessary constitutional amendments, would be required to be held pursuant to section 128 of the Constitution. It appears that this would require approval by the majority of voters in a majority of States. However, as far as the States are concerned, section 15 of the *Australia Acts* 1986 (UK and Cth) appears to impose certain limitations on the process of amendment.

These and other issues are dealt with by the contributors to this book. The Right Honourable Sir Harry Gibbs in his paper 'The

Australian Constitution and Australian Constitutional Monarchy' considers that a republican form of government has no inherent advantages over a constitutional monarchy and that there is no deficiency in the Constitution that the change to a republic would necessarily rectify. He argues that no material benefit could possibly result from Australia's becoming a republic and that change to a republic would not make Australia more democratic or independent. Further, he warns that the changes to the Constitution which would be necessary for Australia to become a republic would be numerous, complex and substantial. He contends that the substitution of a President for a Governor-General would be a radical change to the substance of the Constitution and not a change of something inessential. Particular problems could arise in relation to the powers of the President (especially the reserve powers), to the nature of the presidential office (and the position of the Governors of the States) and to the States themselves. Sir Harry Gibbs also states that, as a matter of law, it may be strongly argued that no fundamental change to the constitutional arrangements could be made unless the Parliament, or people, of every State supported it. Sir Harry considers that other constitutional deficiencies and other important constitutional proposals should be addressed free of the emotion which the republican debate generates.

Writing from the perspective that the 'inevitable' republic is foreseeable Professor George Winterton considers that Australia will soon become in constitutional form what it is in substance, namely, an independent nation with its own Head of State. Professor Winterton contends that Australia is ninety-five percent republican already—a 'crowned republic'. A republic has been defined as a State based on popular sovereignty, in which all public power is exercised by the people or by persons and institutions chosen by them directly or indirectly. He notes that the Australian constitutional system is founded upon popular sovereignty since our Constitution was approved by electors and can be amended only by popular referendum. Further, Parliament is elected by the people, and the judiciary is chosen by the Executive Government who are popularly-elected representatives —thus these public institutions are also 'republican'. He points out that the only office in which the people of Australia have no say is that of Head of State: an hereditary monarch. Professor Winterton examines the constitutional implications of becoming a republic in three broad categories. First, consideration is given to the type of republican government which could be adopted, and the constitutional changes necessary to achieve this. Particular focus is placed on the powers of the Head of State and the method of selection. Secondly, consideration is given to the impact of abolishing the monarchy. The author rejects the view that the monarchy is so fundamental that its removal would undermine the whole of our constitutional system. He further rejects suggestions that the 'minimalist' republican position is not feasible. Finally, the author considers the impact that a republic would have on future constitutional reform and he predicts that such constitutional development would be inspired by the advent of a republic and that it may even strengthen the relative positions of the States in the Federation.

Donald Horne presents a 'conservative' case for Australia becoming a republic; conservative in the sense of having a cautious approach to change and of being sceptical about change, but also allowing for the possibility that change may be the better of two risks. He puts forward several reasons for Australia becoming a republic, including: the need for a strong civic belief system; the need for the presidency to appeal to a sense of citizenship rising above party politics; the need for a clear statement on the mutual checks between President, Prime Minister and Parliament; and the need for a stronger sense of peculiarly Australian policy-making, which passes beyond the dangers of nationalism to the benefits of civic awareness. Donald Horne offers a challenge to all Australians to be part 'of one of those great unfolding events in which people discuss their future among themselves ... until one of the miracles of a democratic society occurs in which they have found a new way of seeing themselves, a new consensus'.

The long history of the idea of the 'inevitable' republic in Australian political culture—an idea nearly two centuries old, has been researched by historian Mark McKenna. He argues that a misplaced faith in historical determinism has sustained the belief in the inevitability of an Australian republic. He concludes that the concept of the 'inevitable' republic is now an impediment to the declaration of that republic, and instead there should be an assertion only of why Australia should be a republic and only one date in time—2001.

Incisive comment on the politics of the republican 'push' is provided by Tony Abbott. He questions why it is inevitable that Australia follow India, Pakistan, South Africa, Fiji and Ireland when republicanism has had such ambiguous results in those countries. He finds the most distressing aspect of the republican debate is its chief protagonists' sneering at our heritage. He fears that 'pushing' for a republic will bring no tangible benefits and could even provoke attempts to end the Australian Federation. The author, who is the Executive Director of Australians for Constitutional Monarchy, considers that republicanism is an issue only because some Australians have become confused about the reality of our independence.

In the context of the issues leading to 2001, Professor Kenneth Wiltshire deals with the question of a republic and argues that the gains to be achieved by Australia becoming a republic would be more in the nature of symbolism than in relation to the substance of governance. However, he considers that even if this means only an increase in the knowledge of citizens as to how they are governed and greater accountability in the political system, it would still be beneficial.

By way of comparative material, papers have been included on both monarchies and republics. Gareth Grainger contends that monarchy is a form of government which is undergoing a resurgence around the world. The reason for this is that a monarchy provides a practical method of ensuring constitutional stability and continuity, whilst at the same time representing an element of dignity and mystery which appeals to the people. Gareth Grainger finds that the monarchy is a fundamental part of the life of Asia in the Pacific region. This he sees as evidenced by the recent Cambodian election in favour of a monarchy, and the enduring role of the Japanese Imperial House. Grainger's study of the history of Norway since 1905, when a foreign Prince was adopted as King of an independent Norway, shows that even a strongly egalitarian people with no tradition of a resident monarch can introduce their own monarch and have their national life enhanced. Is there a lesson here for those who see Australia's problem as being a national system of constitutional monarchy where the Crown is shared with that of another nation? Gareth Grainger considers the system of constitutional monarchy which Australia presently enjoys as having the advantages of incorporating features of the monarchy and features of a republic that appeal to most elements of the community. He advocates that the choices to be presented to the Australian people at a referendum must include an option for some form of localised monarchy.

Alun Preece highlights historic British constitutional developments and practice and suggests that the Australian Constitution is essentially a 'snapshot' of British constitutional practice of the 1890s, the only significant departures being those necessary to accommodate our federal system, and the fact that ours is a written constitution having superior force to ordinary law. This had no counterpart in British constitutional practice.

The Constitutions of two significant republics have been examined: those of the United States and the Federal Republic of Germany. Keith Cline gives an overview of the American constitutional system of government which provided a significant model when the Founding Fathers were considering a constitution for Australia. Of particular interest is the outline of presidential power as a basis for comparison with proposed republican suggestions for Australia.

Isolde Turwitt–Fieber discusses Germany's transformation from a monarchy to a republic. Strong monarchical trends remained in the Weimar Constitution of 1919. However, in the Basic Law of 1949 of the Federal Republic of Germany, greater emphasis was placed on principles of republican, democratic and social government. The writer suggests that the political cohesion on which modern countries are founded does not depend on their being a republic or monarchy but on adherence to principles of democratic government. Isolde Turwitt–Fieber observes that in the post-1871 German Empire, monarchies as well as three republics, Hamburg, Bremen and Luebeck co-existed, suggesting that it is not self-evident that federal and state systems must all be republican.

Leading constitutional lawyer, Professor Darrell Lumb, urges that before any constitutional changes are made there should be a dispassionate analysis of our constitutional fundamentals. These fundamentals are representative democracy, federalism, separation of powers and the monarchy. His paper deals with the important question of the amendment of the Constitution under section 128 by the direct vote of the people and the additional requirement of approval in the majority of States. He also refers to the impact of section 15 of the *Australia Acts* (1986) on a section 128 proposal affecting the monarchical structure of the States. Professor Lumb concludes that it would be extremely difficult to accomplish the republican goal in one 'omnibus' referendum Bill, and suggests that there would have to be referenda on several occasions. He further suggests that the High Court would have the power to determine whether a 'successful' referendum, that is one obtaining the requisite majorities under section 128, would be valid. Such a decision of the High Court on the validity of the constitutional amendment could itself be overridden by the same procedure, which is a referendum under section 128.

Gerard Carney focuses on the position of the States in the current republican debate. In a referendum pursuant to section 128 of the Constitution he considers that it would be technically possible for the Commonwealth to become a republic while one State might choose to remain a monarchy. Gerard Carney canvasses two main issues of concern: first the type of republican system of government in the States including whether a Head of State at State level is necessary and, if so, the procedure for appointment and removal, and the powers and functions of such position; secondly, the legal changes necessary to convert from a monarchy to a republic within a State. Consideration is given to the extent to which the monarchy is entrenched in the State Constitutions and whether the Commonwealth has the capacity to impose republicanism on the States.

Some wider issues touching on the question of a republic have also been included in this work. Suri Ratnapala considers that the representative principle and the rule of law, which are the foundations of republican power, cannot be sustained without enforcing the separation of powers doctrine in a meaningful way. The separation of powers doctrine usually involves a separation of legislative, executive and judicial power. He argues that a true republic, in which government is conducted for the public good, cannot be established in Australia without reviving the separation of powers doctrine which serves as a system of political checks and balances to prevent the dominance of any one branch of the government over another.

Another important question associated with the republic debate is whether the Commonwealth Constitution should contain an entrenched or paramount bill of rights. Gabriël Moens argues that the entrenchment of an enforceable bill of rights in the Constitution would transform the role of the judiciary from a judicial one to a quasi-legislative one. Gabriël Moens foresees the consequences of such transformation as possibly including not only the politicisation of the judiciary but also the promotion of 'judicial activism'. He also addresses the issue of whether a bill of rights is an inherently anti-majoritarian force which might subvert the process of decision-making in a democracy.

The status of Aborigines and Torres Strait Islanders in an Australian republic is addressed by Father Frank Brennan SJ. He considers that in the post-*Mabo* era changes to our constitutional framework are required so that Australia's indigenous people may enjoy full benefits of citizenship without discrimination or threat of involuntary assimilation. If a republic were achieved through the minimalist position then, as all references to the Crown would be omitted there would be a need to draft a new preamble, and the status of indigenous people would require specific inclusion in that new preamble. Aboriginal and Torres Strait Islanders would have significant contributions to make as to the desirability of a bill of rights, not only because of their concerns about individual rights which they should enjoy without discrimination, but also because of their assertion of collective rights to self-determination, self-government, and self-management.

The Republic Advisory Committee's Report provides a valuable foundation for considering the type of republic that could be achieved in Australia. A summary of the Report's conclusions and options is included, together with the response from the Australians for Constitutional Monarchy.

At a time in Australia's history when the people will have a say in Australia's constitutional future, it is hoped that the papers in this book, which address the issues on both sides of the debate, will assist the reader in reaching an informed decision. It is a feature of our democratic system that these issues can be debated in an open manner. Whether Australia should be a republic or a monarchy is the people's choice.

M.A. Stephenson

The Australian Constitution and Australian Constitutional Monarchy

The Right Honourable Sir Harry Gibbs*

The preamble to the *Commonwealth of Australia Act*, which was passed in 1900 to constitute the Commonwealth of Australia, declares that the people of the States 'have agreed to unite in one indissoluble Federal Commonwealth under the Crown of the United Kingdom of Great Britain and Ireland, and under the Constitution hereby established'. As those words suggest, a fundamental characteristic of the Commonwealth is that it is a constitutional monarchy. A study of the Constitution itself confirms that this is so. References to the Queen, and to the Governor-General, as the Queen's representative, pervade the Constitution. The provisions of the Constitution (to which I shall later refer in more detail) on their face enable the Governor-General to control the exercise of all Commonwealth legislative and executive power, as well as to command the military forces of the Commonwealth. The substitution of a President, who would not be the Queen's representative, for a Governor-General who represents the Queen, would not be a change of something inessential —it would be a radical change, a change of substance.

When a change of such importance is suggested, it becomes obviously necessary, to enable one to decide whether to support or oppose the change, to consider what advantages would result from the change, and on the other hand what difficulties or dangers the change would create.

One thing that is clear is that no material benefit could possibly result from the fact that Australia became a republic. In one sense the

---

*Formerly Chief Justice of the High Court of Australia.

Australian Constitution is already republican. That is the case if the word 'republic' is understood in its dictionary meaning, 'a state in which the supreme power rests in the people and their elected representatives or officers'[1] or if we accept the definition given by Thomas Paine in 1791 that 'Republican Government is no other than government established and conducted for the interest of the public, as well individually as collectively'.[2] In Australia the supreme power does rest in the people and their elected representatives subject, of course, to the constraints imposed by the Constitution itself, and that power is intended to be exercised in the interests of the public, and not in the interests of the Monarch or of any particular class. However, that does not mean that if the Queen ceased to be Australia's Head of State, and the Governor-General and Governors, as her representatives, ceased to have their present powers and functions, the change would be only a matter of form.

Australia would not, by becoming a republic, become more democratic or independent. Although the words of the Constitution may suggest that the Queen or her representative has an effective power of sovereignty, it is, as has been said 'a vulgar error to think of a constitution merely as the scrap of paper on which rules and rights are inscribed'.[3] The words of the written Constitution are like the tip of a constitutional iceberg; many constitutional principles, of equal importance, depend on decisions of the courts, or on conventions which have developed in practice and which do not depend on any statutory provisions or judicial decisions. No lawyer who knows anything of the working of the Constitution will doubt that Australia is now completely independent in every aspect of its affairs, foreign as well as domestic—or at least was until quite recently when the Government agreed, by undertaking certain international obligations, to subordinate Australia in some respects to some of the organs of the United Nations.[4] However, if we became a republic we would not be relieved of that subordination. Although our Queen is also Queen of the United Kingdom, no one can now sensibly dispute that we are completely independent of Great Britain, although opinions may differ on the question when that independence became complete.

Further, it should be observed that as a form of government a republic has not necessarily any advantages over a constitutional monarchy. On the contrary, most constitutional monarchies are free societies which respect basic human rights, whereas many republics are not. Australia is one of the oldest democracies in the world; only two republics, the United States of America and Switzerland, have continuously enjoyed free and democratic government since the Australian Commonwealth was constituted in 1901. One reason why constitutional monarchies appear to be exceptional in the degree of unity and stability which they enjoy may be that the monarchy is a centre of national loyalty above politics; as a distinguished English lawyer has said 'one can be a loyal subject of the Crown while regarding the Prime Minister and his Party as a national disaster'.[5] Sometimes, as in Spain, conversion from a republic to a constitutional monarchy has brought freedom and stability with it. On the other hand, when some great dominions such as India, Pakistan and Sri Lanka became republics after having been constitutional monarchies, they experienced periods of totalitarian rule. Of course, one hopes that the different economic and social conditions in Australia mean that the same thing would not occur here. The point, however, is that a change from a constitutional monarchy to a republic is not necessarily beneficial.

Other arguments that have been advanced in support of the view that Australia would derive tangible benefits from becoming a republic have proved, on examination, to be entirely bogus. No one can be expected to believe that Australians would become more patriotic, or would develop a greater sense of national identity and a stronger national will, or would better conduct their trading and diplomatic relations, particularly with Asian countries, or would find a solution to the many grave problems that confront the nation, simply by installing a President as our Head of State. The only argument in favour of a republic that has any possible claim to validity is that our ties with Great Britain have become so much weaker that it is no longer appropriate that the British Monarch should also be our Head of State, and that the Head of State of Australia should be an Australian chosen on democratic and not on hereditary principles. That argument is understandable, but it is an argument based only on sentiment or symbolism. To substitute an Australian Head of State for the Queen would not make our system of government any more effective and would not bring any social or economic benefit in its train. Against an argument based essentially on symbolism must be weighed the disadvantages that would follow from the suggested change.

The constitutional amendments necessary to effect the change to a republic must inevitably be numerous and complex. It is always difficult, if not impossible, to predict the ultimate consequences of constitutional change. There are, however, two respects in which it is obvious that particular problems will arise. The first of these is in respect of the powers which should be conferred on a President if Australia became a republic.

By the express words of the Constitution, the Governor-General, as the representative of the Queen, is invested with sweeping powers. The Queen is technically a part of the Federal Parliament,[6] and no proposed law, which has been passed by the House of Representatives and the Senate, has the force of law unless the Governor-General assents to it.[7] The Governor-General may decide when the Parliament shall sit and may prorogue the Parliament and dissolve the House of Representatives.[8] A general election of the members of the House of Representatives will be held only if the Governor-General issues the appropriate writs.[9] In the event of a disagreement between the Houses, the Governor-General may, in the circumstances set out in the Constitution, dissolve the Senate and the House of Representatives simultaneously.[10] The executive power of the Commonwealth (which extends to the execution and maintenance of the Constitution and the laws of the Commonwealth) is exercisable by the Governor-General as the Queen's representative.[11] The members of the Federal Executive Council are chosen by the Governor-General and hold office during his or her pleasure.[12] The Governor-General may appoint the Ministers of State and they also hold office at his or her pleasure.[13] The Governor-General is Commander-in-Chief of the naval and military forces of the Commonwealth.[14]

Unless these powers were controlled by constitutional principles, it is apparent that the Governor-General could, if he or she wished, dismiss one government and appoint another, close down the Parliament or, if it sat, refuse assent to the laws which it sought to pass and could enforce, or decline to enforce, as he or she thought fit, the laws of the Commonwealth. The Governor-General could make his or her will effective if the need arose by calling out the troops. The powers in form are those of a dictator.

The Governors of the States have similar powers in relation to the laws, the Parliaments and the Executive Governments of the States, although not of course in relation to the armed forces.

Some powers are also conferred by the Constitution on the Queen herself. They include power to appoint or dismiss the Governor-General and control his or her powers and functions[15] and to assent, or withhold assent, to laws reserved, and to disallow any law within one year from the Governor-General's assent.[16]

The Governor-General, and the Governors of the States, usually exercise their powers on the advice of their Ministers. Similarly, if the Queen is called on to exercise the powers invested in her by the Constitution, she does so on the advice of her Australian Ministers. In fact, nowadays, the only power which the Queen does exercise is to appoint the Governor-General on the advice of the Prime Minister or to appoint a State Governor on the advice of the Premier of a State. Similarly, of course, she might, on receipt of the appropriate Australian advice, dismiss a Governor-General or Governor. It appears that on one occasion a citizen presented a petition asking the Queen to exercise her power to disallow an Act of the Commonwealth Parliament but that she was advised by the Prime Minister of Australia not to do so and accepted that advice.[17]

The reason why the discretionary powers of the Queen and her representatives are almost always exercised on ministerial advice is that their exercise is governed by constitutional conventions. Those conventions are rules of political practice, which are regarded as binding by those to whom they apply, but which are not laws and are not enforceable by the courts or by Parliament.[18] The conventions developed over the centuries in England and later in Australia. They are political in inception, and have been said to depend on a consistent course of political recognition.[19] They have enabled the monarchy to adapt itself to the needs of a modern democracy, because, as has been said, 'Ministerial responsibility is the safeguard of the Monarchy. Without it, the Throne could not stand for long, amid the gusts of political conflict and the storm of political passion'.[20] According to the conventions the discretionary powers of the Crown should in general be exercised on ministerial advice, but, there are occasions when the conventions allow the Monarch in England and, in Australia the Governor-General or a Governor, to exercise some of these powers on his or her own account and without the advice, or contrary to the advice, of the ministry. The powers which the Governor-General or Governor may exercise on his or her own account are known as the reserve powers. The purpose of the conventions in allowing the reserve powers to be exercised is to secure the ultimate supremacy of the electorate as the true political sovereign of the State[21] or, in other words, to ensure that the legal framework of the Constitution will be operated in accordance with prevailing constitutional values or principles.[22]

There are a number of instances in which it is clear that the conventions allow the Governor-General or a State Governor to exercise the powers at his or her own discretion, and without, or contrary to, ministerial advice. Thus the Governor-General or Governor may:

(1) Appoint the Prime Minister or Premier following an election or on the death or resignation of the person holding that office, although according to the conventions only a person who may be expected to command the support of a majority in the Lower House of Parliament may be appointed;
(2) Dismiss a Prime Minister or Premier who has lost the confidence of the Lower House of Parliament and who refuses to resign or advise a dissolution of the House, and, in consequence, in some circumstances, bring about a dissolution of the House;
(3) Refuse to accept the advice of the Prime Minister or Premier to dissolve the House of Representatives or Legislative Assembly;
(4) Dismiss a Prime Minister or Premier who is attempting to govern without supply.

There are other cases in which the reserve powers have been exercised. Although some conventions are reasonably precise, others are conflicting or controversial.[23] For example, there has been a conflict of opinion as to whether a government may be dismissed if it is acting illegally, and if so what conditions should exist before the dismissal may be made effective. In Australia, Sir Philip Game exercised his reserve power by dismissing Mr Jack Lang on this ground. The dismissal of Mr Whitlam by Sir John Kerr was also controversial, although if the stage had been reached that Mr Whitlam was attempting to govern without supply a dismissal would clearly have been justifiable. Political crises which call for the exercise of the reserve powers sometimes raise problems never previously encountered and, as has been said, Monarchs and Governors-General 'have to act as umpires in a game where unexpected situations may arise which are not fully covered by any generally accepted book of rules'.[24] A work published in 1991 has reviewed the cases in which the reserve powers have been exercised in a number of countries, and has concluded that the frequency with which constitutional heads in the Westminster form of government have been called on to play a significant role is a good deal greater than is ordinarily understood.[25] In Australia, the reserve powers have been exercised by the Governor-General or a Governor on at least eight occasions since Federation, and have been invoked as recently as 1987 in Queensland and 1989 in Tasmania. According to Dr Evatt 'situations may arise in which the exercise of reserve power will be the only method of giving to the electorate an opportunity of preventing some permanent and far-reaching constitutional change'.[26] He gives, as an example, an attempt by a party which has a majority in Parliament to pass a law extending the life of the Parliament without first obtaining the approval of the electorate. A former Premier of South Australia, Mr Don Dunstan, said:

> In the Westminster system it is quite essential as a protection to the populace that there be a head of state independent of legislature, judiciary and executive. Without such an office one of the essential checks in the Constitution would be missing. The chief function of the head of state is to ensure that the executive acts only in accordance with the power and within the limits defined by the Constitution and by statute.[27]

The reserve powers can serve the purpose of ensuring that the principles of representative and responsible government are observed, and that the laws and conventions of the Constitution are not contravened, only if the powers are exercised with complete impartiality. The conventions require that the Crown and its representatives should be above politics, and in times of political crisis should act as a sort of dispassionate umpire. In practice, the tradition of political impartiality, which developed round the monarchy, has been continued by all Governors-General in Australia, and, at least since Federation, by all State Governors, although I shall later mention one departure from convention made by a political appointee who was acting as Administrator of a State in the absence of a Governor.

These conventions, which require that the reserve powers be exercised impartially and in a way that is free from political influence, apply only in relation to the Crown and its representatives. They have no necessary application under a republican constitution to the Head of State, who could not be expected to be above politics. One of the controversial questions that would need to be answered if the Constitution were to be made republican in form would be how the President should be chosen. Various methods of selection have been suggested. They include appointment by the Prime Minister, appointment by Parliament possibly by a two-thirds majority, appointment by an electoral college and election by the public. Whichever method is chosen it cannot be doubted that the choice would be a political one. Even if, at first, to make the transition more acceptable, someone who commanded national respect was appointed to the office, it is certain that eventually it would become politicised as it has been in every republic in the world. The framers of the United States Constitution devised a method which, they hoped, would ensure that the most worthy and eminent citizen would be chosen as President; the choice is made by members of an electoral college comprised of representatives of all the States. Nowadays, the electoral college decides on strictly party lines, and the world knows who the next President will be before the college has even met. In Australia, where political considerations have intruded into institutions which in the original Westminster model were intended to be apolitical, it would be too much to hope that the President would be chosen for other than political reasons. Of course, even Governors-General have been chosen for political reasons but as I have already indicated, those appointed have always observed the conventions that govern the exercise of their powers. In the absence of express constitutional provision, it could not be assumed that the powers of the President of a republic would be exercised in accordance with the conventions that have developed in relation to a monarchy.

If a President was able to exercise the powers presently vested in the Governor-General but was free from the conventions which control the manner of their exercise, he or she would be able to act as a dictator. On the other hand, if a President was deprived of any reserve powers an important safeguard designed to ensure the proper working of the Constitution would be lost. These difficulties would not arise if our Constitution was remodelled on American lines, but a conversion of that kind would raise difficulties of its own. Those difficulties need not be discussed, since it is not proposed to establish a presidency with executive powers of the American type.

The Republic Advisory Committee has suggested a number of ways in which it might be possible to equate presidential power with the power presently exercised by the Governor-General. The first suggestion is that it might be provided in the Constitution that the exercise of powers by the President should continue to be governed by the existing constitutional conventions which relate to the exercise of powers by the Governor-General, but that this provision should not have the effect of converting constitutional conventions into rules of law or of preventing the further development of those conventions. The second suggestion is that the conventions might be formulated either by Parliament or by a Constitutional Convention and that the statement of the practices, once formulated, could be updated or amended as practice changed and to meet new or emerging situations. If this was done the Constitution could provide that in the exercise of the reserve powers the Head of State should take the agreed practices into account, although the Constitution would not include a statement of those practices. The third suggestion was that the Constitution should be amended to provide that the Head of State would be governed by the conventions formerly applying to the Governor-General but that it should be further provided that Parliament might amend those conventions, possibly by a two-thirds majority in both Houses. This constitutional provision should expressly declare that the conventions were to remain non-justiciable. The fourth suggestion was that the conventions should be codified, either wholly or in part, although it was not intended that the exercise of the reserve powers would necessarily be reviewable in the courts.

All of these suggestions are open to some objection. If the conventions were enforceable by the courts, the delay and uncertainty that might result from litigation could paralyse the government in an emergency. If the conventions were non-justiciable, they would be observed only if the President was willing to act with political impartiality and it could not be safely assumed that a person filling a political office would be prepared to put aside all considerations of party politics. The formulation or codification of rules of practice that are at present uncertain and undeveloped would present considerable difficulties and would necessarily give rise to controversy. One can only speculate which of the existing conventions would be allowed to survive in their present form. It is likely that there would be an attempt to deprive the President of the power to dismiss a government which had a majority in the House of Representatives but which had been denied supply by the Senate. To codify or formulate the conventions would inhibit their development and make it less easy for them to adapt to circumstances presently unforeseen. To allow the House of Representatives to define or amend them would be to subject the President to the will of the government which commanded a majority in the House. There is no easy solution to the question what powers, if any, should be exercisable by a Head of State if the Constitution became a republican one.

It is suggested by some supporters of the republican movement that the change to a presidential system would have no substantial effect on the working of the Constitution. In fact, however, during the last half-century there has been a gradual increase in the power of the Executive and a corresponding decline in the effectiveness of Parliament. There has been a considerable increase in the politicisation of the public service. Politicians of all parties have shown that they are no respecters of convention when power is at stake. The danger of the change to a presidential system is that the power of the Executive may be further increased and the power of the Parliament further diminished.

It is true that an unsuitable person appointed to vice-regal office might be prepared to act unconstitutionally for political reasons. I am aware of only one abuse of power by any vice-regal representative in Australia since Federation and that was by a person who was acting in the office. In Queensland in 1920 an Administrator, who was acting at a time when the retiring Governor had left Queensland and his successor had not yet arrived, was a person who at the time of his appointment had been active in party politics. The Government of which he had been a member had been trying for some years unsuccessfully to abolish the Legislative Council and a referendum seeking to achieve that result had been defeated. However, the Administrator, at the request of the Government, made enough nominations to the Legislative Council of persons prepared to vote for its abolition to enable the Council to be abolished. That was a breach of a convention that requires that substantial changes to the Constitution should not be made unless the electors have signified their approval to the change.[28] However, although it is conceivable that similar abuses could be committed by a representative of the Crown, they are more likely to be committed by a President who would be avowedly political than by a Governor-General or Governor who by long tradition was expected to act in an impartial way. It has rightly been said that 'it is vital that the office [of Governor-General or Governor] should be filled by a fair minded person whose decisions will command public respect'.[29] High statesmanship may be required, and, if governments have any sense of responsibility, that is more likely to be found in representatives of the Crown than in political Presidents.

A second major question of difficulty that would arise in deciding how Australia should become a republic relates to the position of the Queen as Head of each Australian State. The Republic Advisory Committee suggested that one approach would be for the Commonwealth to agree that any State which wished to retain the Monarch as its Head of State could do so.[30] That course would be quite impracticable. For one thing the symbolic purpose of the change to a republic would be lost if the Commonwealth was republican only in part. If, however, one or more States wished to retain the Monarchy, and the Commonwealth wished to propose a constitutional amendment that would attempt to force a State to abandon the Monarchy against its will, that would, in the words of the Republic Advisory Committee, 'raise issues of State rights that went well beyond the question of monarchy or republic'.[31] The *Australia Act* 1986[32] recognises and entrenches the position of the

Governor of a State as the representative of the Queen and the question what procedure would be necessary to alter that position is replete with controversy. The *Australia Act* may be amended by an Act of the Commonwealth Parliament passed at the request or with the concurrence of the Parliaments of all the States. It may also be amended by an Act of the Commonwealth Parliament if the necessary power is conferred on the Parliament by a referendum passed in the future. However, it is a controversial question whether a referendum giving the Commonwealth Parliament power to affect the position of State Governors would need the approval of a majority of the electors in all States, and not merely in a majority of States. That depends on whether the words 'in relation thereto' in section 128 of the Constitution mean 'in relation to any State' or 'in relation to the matters previously mentioned'. The question is a controversial one and can be answered only by the High Court.

There is another, more fundamental question. The people of the colonies agreed to unite in a Commonwealth under the Crown. It may be argued that this agreement was given effect by the *Constitution Act* 1900, and not by the Constitution, so that to bring about a union on a new republican basis it would be necessary to amend the *Constitution Act* and not merely the Constitution. The question how the *Constitution Act* may be amended is one of particular difficulty. As a matter of political principle, a fundamental change of constitutional arrangements should not be forced on the people of the States against their will. In other words, a change of that kind should be supported by the people, or possibly the Parliament of every State. It may be strongly argued that as a matter of law also no change of this kind could be made unless the Parliament or people of every State supported it. Put very briefly, there is a strong argument that the Commonwealth was created by Covering Clauses 3 and 4 of the *Constitution Act*, and that no amendment to that Act could be made under section 128 of the Constitution or by any law made by the Parliament under power given by any such amendment. I shall not discuss those arguments further, for Professor Lumb's paper will deal with the question how changes to the Constitution could be achieved.

If each State did agree that the Queen should no longer be its Head of State, the question would then arise who should take her place. It has been suggested that the States might allow the President of the Commonwealth to be the Head of State of each State or that there might be a combined Head of State of all States. Either of those courses is likely to have the effect of eroding the strength and powers of the States. In India, for example, where State Governors are appointed by the central Government, they have often exercised their powers to give effect to the political purposes of the party which appointed them. Under a republic, it would seem necessary for each State to devise a means of appointing its own presidential style Head of State.

If Australia is to be converted to a republic, it will be necessary first to decide some important questions of policy. Some of the constitutional amendments that would have to be made would be merely mechanical, but others would involve controversial questions concerning the nature of the presidential office, the extent of the President's powers and the position of the Governors of the States and of the States themselves. None of these questions may be insoluble, but it would be unwise to make light of the difficulties to which they would give rise. The movement to make Australia a republic seems to have been launched without much consideration of the sort of republic that was desired—the concern was with the symbolism, rather than the substance, of the change.

Inevitably, once the provisions of the Constitution are thrown into the melting pot for the purpose of making it republican in character, pressures will be exerted to make the change go further, or, in other words, as has been said, the movement towards a republic will be used as a 'battering ram in the demand for new political rights for Australia, embodied in a new Constitution'.[33] Already there are indications that an attempt will be made to diminish the powers of the States and the Senate, and to provide for the recognition of the Aboriginal people.

The Constitution is in no way deficient because it is monarchical, but it has other deficiencies. One critical question that should be addressed is that which concerns the relationship between the Commonwealth and the States, which is quite out of balance. That question can, and should, be considered free from the emotion which the republican debate generates. The consideration of that question will not be assisted by the suggestions that the position of a State Governor may be affected contrary to the will of both the Parliament and the people of a State, and that a change to the fundamental nature of the Constitution may be forced on the people of the States against their wishes. Such suggestions offend against the very basis of the federal compact.

Notes

1. *Shorter Oxford English Dictionary* (3rd ed., Oxford: Clarendon Press, 1973), 'republic'.
2. T. Paine, *Rights of Man* (London: Dent, 1906), 174.
3. K. Minogue, *The Constitutional Mania* (London: Centre for Policy Studies, 1993), 9.
4. See, for example, in 'Human Rights Committee Appointment', Optional Protocol to *International Covenant on Civil and Political Rights* (1992) 66 *Australian Law Journal* 783: see also Australia's substantially unqualified acceptance of the jurisdiction of the International Court of Justice in 'Australia and the International Court of Justice' (1993) 67 *Australian Law Journal* 301.
5. R.F.V. Heuston, *Essays in Constitutional Law* (London: Stevens, 1961), 77.
6. *Constitution*, s.1.
7. *Constitution*, s.58.
8. *Constitution*, ss.5, 28.
9. *Constitution*, s.32.
10. *Constitution*, s.57.
11. *Constitution*, s.61.
12. *Constitution*, s.62.
13. *Constitution*, s.64.
14. *Constitution*, s.68.
15. *Constitution*, s.2.
16. *Constitution*, ss.59, 60.
17. See Sir Garfield Barwick, *The Monarch in an Independent Australia* (Sir Robert Menzies Lecture Trust, 1982), 16.
18. O. Hood Phillips and P. Jackson, *Constitutional and Administrative Law* (7th ed., London: Sweet and Maxwell, 1987), 113; *Reference re Amendment of the Constitution of Canada* (1981) 125 D.L.R. (3d.) 1.
19. *Reference re Amendment of the Constitution of Canada*, supra note 18, 22.
20. Per Lord Esher, cited Heuston, supra note 5, 63.
21. E.C.S. Wade and A.W. Bradley, *Constitutional Law* (7th ed., London: Longmans, 1965), 78.
22. *Reference re Amendment of the Constitution of Canada*, supra note 18, 9.
23. G. Marshall, *Constitutional Conventions* (Oxford: Clarendon Press, 1984), 4–5.
24. D.A. Butler and D. Low, *Sovereigns and Surrogates* (London: Macmillan, 1991), 1.
25. *Id.* 324.

26. H.V. Evatt, *The King and His Dominion Governors* (London: Oxford University Press, 1936), 197.
27. Cited Barwick, *supra* note 17, 8.
28. Dr Evatt's disagreement with Professor Keith's trenchant criticism of the Administrator's action is difficult to reconcile with his view that great constitutional changes should be submitted to the people for approval: see Evatt, *supra* note 26, 141–145, 199.
29. Butler and Low, *supra* note 24, 324.
30. The Report of the Republic Advisory Committee, *An Australian Republic: The Options* (Canberra: A.G.P.S., 2 vols., 1993), vol. 1, 123–124.
31. *Id.* 128.
32. Act No. 142 of 1985 (Cth); 1986 34 Eliz C2 (UK).
33. G. Winterton, *Monarchy to Republic* (Melbourne: Oxford University Press, 1986), 25–26, quoting Professor Donald Horne.

The Constitutional Implications of a Republic

*George Winterton**

Although long considered 'inevitable', the advent of an Australian republic is at last foreseeable. For the first time in our history, the day appears close when Australia will discard the last formal vestiges of its colonial origins and become, in constitutional form, as it already is in substance, an independent nation with its own Head of State. Australia is, of course, already as completely independent in foreign and domestic policy as any other nation but, as long as it borrows the Head of State of another country, over whose succession to office it has no control, it will not be constitutionally free-standing. As John Hirst has noted, we do not have a 'self-sufficient' Constitution: 'If for any reason there ceased to be a monarch of Britain, our Constitution would seize up'.[1] Australian republicans simply believe that, like other nations, Australia should have its own Head of State whose legitimacy and authority are derived from the consent of the Australian people, not hereditary entitlement.

The change to a republic would be more symbolic than substantive, so its greatest impact is likely to be psychological, enhancing Australians' sense of national independence and self-assurance. This can hardly be detrimental to Australia's welfare, economically and culturally. The precise impact of a republic is, of course, difficult to predict accurately, and experience suggests that the advent of a republic will have unforeseen consequences, hopefully beneficial. However, for that matter, the same can be said of our current system, the continued evolution of which is certainly not wholly predictable.

---

*Professor of Law, University of New South Wales.

The *constitutional* implications of a republic are clearer than its political and cultural consequences, and will obviously largely depend upon the specific amendments made to the Constitution in the course of converting Australia into a republic. The constitutional implications of a republic fall into three broad categories:
- the type of republican government adopted and the details of its constitutional structure;
- the impact of such changes on our present constitutional foundations and ethos; and
- more speculatively, future constitutional reform likely to be inspired by the advent of a republic.

Each of these will be examined in turn.

1. Republican Government

A republic is a state based upon popular sovereignty, in which all public power is exercised by the people or by persons and institutions chosen by them, directly or indirectly.[2]

Since our Constitution was approved by the electors before enactment at Westminster[3] and can be amended only through a popular referendum, Australia's constitutional system is clearly already founded politically upon popular sovereignty.[4] The Constitution originally derived its legal authority from enactment by the United Kingdom Parliament as a statute applying to Australia by paramount force. The general demise of the doctrine of paramount force[5] and the United Kingdom Parliament's renunciation of legislative power over Australia[6] should not, logically, have affected the legal source of the Constitution's authority.[7] However, there is little point in distinguishing between the legal and political sources of constitutional legitimacy, and some commentators have therefore concluded that the consent of the Australian people provides the *legal* foundation for the authority of the Australian Constitution.[8]

Indeed, our Constitution embodies popular sovereignty to a much greater degree than the United States Constitution, which purports to be created by 'We, the People',[9] but was actually ratified only by their representatives in State ratifying Conventions. Unlike ours, it was not directly approved by the electors at referenda. Thus, the Australian people exercised their sovereignty much more directly than their American counterparts in adopting our Constitution before its enactment at Westminster, and we continue to do so. Our constitutional amendments are directly voted on by the electors; America's are not.

All our governmental institutions but one are likewise already 'republican' because they are either directly elected by the people, as Parliament is, or else, like the judiciary, are chosen by popularly-elected representatives. The one office in which the people have no say is that at the very apex of the constitutional system, for our Head of State derives her position by hereditary right under British law, not from the consent of the Australian people. Hence, we are ninety-five percent republican already; a 'crowned republic' as we have aptly been characterized.[10] All that is required to make Australia completely republican from a constitutional point of view is for the monarchy to be abolished. All other institutions of government and all other fundamental constitutional doctrines—federalism, responsible government, and the separation of powers—could remain completely intact and untouched. Whether or not that step should be taken is not in issue here. Rather, it shall be assumed that such a change will be made and its constitutional consequences will be considered.

The first and most fundamental question facing Australians is whether the republic should retain our present parliamentary executive (responsible government or 'Westminster') system, or adopt some other governmental model, most likely one embodying a greater separation of the legislative and executive branches, like the American system.

The legislature's independence from the executive is probably the American system's most appealing feature and contrasts with executive dominance of the legislature, or at least its Lower House, which is a great failing of Westminster systems. But the legislature's highly-prized independence has a negative aspect which is responsible for that system's greatest defect, and is one reason why Americans sometimes look longingly at Westminster: deadlock and stalemate, especially over the enactment of legislation. President Clinton is presently demonstrating once again, just as President Carter did more than a decade ago, that legislative deadlock is not avoided by ensuring that the same party controls the White House and both Houses of Congress. The result is that the President is often unable to implement the policies on which he was elected.

But whatever the virtues in abstract of the American system, and however attractive it might look if we were starting from scratch, the critical point is that we are *not* starting from scratch, and Australia now has more than a century and a half of experience in operating the present system and adapting it to changing needs. Introducing a completely different form of government into our dissimilar political culture, with its strong party system and absence of a constitutional bill of rights, could prove extremely disruptive. Moreover, experience elsewhere suggests that a foreign model imported into an alien political and cultural environment would operate very differently from the way it did in its country of origin. One has only to recall that the American presidential system was supposedly transplanted into most of Latin America and the Philippines. Australia could well end up with some hybrid mutant combining the worst features of both systems, and that should be avoided at all costs.[11] Moreover, public opinion polls indicate that Australians prefer their present system of responsible government over an American-style executive by a ratio of about seventy-five percent to twenty-five percent.[12] The current system is certainly not perfect and could well do with reform (much of it requiring parliamentary backbone rather than constitutional change), but its abandonment in favour of an alien governmental system is both unwarranted and dangerous.

Our present *de facto* Head of State, the Governor-General, performs three types of function: ceremonial functions, such as opening Parliament, receiving foreign ambassadors, and conferring honours; exercising 'ordinary' governmental powers on the advice of ministers, such as assenting to legislation and enacting regulations through the Federal Executive Council; and, most importantly, acting as 'ultimate constitutional guardian' through exercising, or more accurately holding in reserve, the few powers which confer an independent discretion to act without or contrary to ministerial advice. These are the so-called 'reserve powers': to appoint and dismiss the Prime Minister, and to refuse to dissolve Parliament. If the monarchy was abolished and the present system of responsible government retained, what would happen to these powers and functions of the Governor-General?

The advent of a republic raises many issues which have recently been addressed in the report of the Republic Advisory Committee.[13] It is obviously not possible to discuss the full range of options here, so attention is focused only on some of the most important.

First, do we need a new Head of State at all? Some of the more radical—and parsimonious—republicans suggest that we could well dispense with the office entirely, as has largely been done in the Australian Capital Territory. It is true that the ceremonial functions usually performed by a Head of State could be performed by someone primarily exercising other functions. Apart from its incompatibility with the separation of powers, the Chief Justice of the High Court is far too busy to act as Head of State, especially in view of the travel involved, so the most likely substitute Head of State would be the Prime Minister and perhaps the Speaker of the House and President of the Senate. But it would hardly be feasible for them to travel around the Commonwealth (a much larger area than the Australian Capital Territory) while Parliament was sitting—admittedly a rather rare event! Would it be wise to augment the Prime Minister's already excessive power by adding to it the aura and prestige which inhere in the Head of State role?

The 'ordinary' governmental functions now performed by vice-regal representatives on ministerial advice could, of course, be fulfilled by the ministers themselves if the office of Head of State were dispensed with on other grounds, but many commentators, including vice-regal representatives and chief ministers, see value in the occasional exercise by those representatives of the right to caution governments against unlawful or inappropriate action, whether addressed directly to a minister or through vice-regal oversight of the proceedings of the Executive Council.[14] So there clearly is some value in retaining a separate Head of State to fulfil ceremonial and governmental functions. How grand that office should be is obviously a political, rather than a constitutional, matter.

Secondly, should the Head of State retain any power to act without, or contrary to, ministerial advice—in other words 'reserve powers'? It is sometimes thought that a system of responsible government could not operate without reserve powers. Thus Professor Peter Hogg, a leading Canadian authority, has asserted that 'a system of responsible government cannot work without a formal head of state who is possessed of certain reserve powers'.[15] However, this is not strictly correct because a study of the governmental systems of other nations demonstrates that a system of responsible government can operate successfully without reserve powers vested in the Head of State, either by dispensing with the need for such powers by laying down detailed rules to cover virtually all contingencies now governed by the reserve powers, or by vesting such powers in some other person or institution. Selection of the Prime Minister could, for example, be left to the Lower House of Parliament, as is effectively the case in Ireland, Germany and Japan, and the parliamentary term could be fixed, as it is in four Australian States,[16] with dissolution otherwise being left to the decision of Parliament, with the Lower House either voting directly to dissolve itself,[17] or effectively so resolving by passing a 'simple' (not a 'constructive') resolution of no-confidence in the government.[18]

However, while the risk of abuse of presidential power may be diminished, elimination of presidential reserve powers reduces the flexibility of the governmental machinery, making it difficult to adapt to unforeseen crises. Indeed, the reserve powers have received something of a fillip in Australia in recent years, where events in Queensland in November 1987 and in Tasmania in June 1989 demonstrated that the mere *threat* of their exercise restrained improper behaviour by a headstrong chief minister.[19]

Moreover, public opinion polls suggest that people favour presidential power, probably to check the powers of the government. Thus recent polls show only a small minority favouring a 'largely ceremonial' President: eleven percent according to an October 1993 poll.[20] However, the terms employed in the poll, such as 'ceremonial' and 'largely ceremonial' are inherently vague, so the poll results must be viewed with considerable caution.

If the Australian Head of State is to retain reserve powers, how should they be defined? The present Constitution simply vests the powers to appoint and dismiss the Prime Minister and dissolve Parliament in the Governor-General in general terms and relies upon conventions to regulate their exercise. However, the latter were not mentioned in the Constitution, partly because the principal draftsman, Edmund Barton, feared ridicule in London if the instrument did not confine itself to the 'law' (as contrasted with the conventions) of the Constitution.[21] It was able to omit reference to the conventions because it operated in the context of the British monarchical system, in which powers legally vested in the Monarch are governed by well-recognised conventions which have developed at least since the advent of responsible government one hundred and fifty years ago.

Subject to specific constitutional provisions, the same conventions govern the exercise of the reserve powers throughout the Queen's dominions. Although largely unwritten and nowhere authoritatively codified, there is broad consensus regarding the core of such conventions, although the boundaries are often indistinct. Thus, for example, no-one doubts that a government in which the Lower House of Parliament has expressed lack of confidence cannot simply ignore such resolution and carry on regardless. It must either resign or seek a dissolution of Parliament, but opinion is divided upon whether, and in what circumstances, a dissolution requested on such occasions could be refused.

If the Governor-General's powers were inherited by a republican Head of State, since the link with the monarchy would be severed, the present conventions governing the exercise of the reserve powers might not subsist. They might if they were regarded more generally as conventions of Australian government (although they are not uniquely Australian, but are, of course, shared with Britain, Canada, New Zealand and others), but if they were seen as conventions of the *monarchy*, abolition of the monarchy might well extinguish them as well.[22] So a republican constitution cannot simply continue the present constitutional position of conferring powers on the Head of State in general terms, relying on the constitutional conventions to govern their exercise.

If a republican Head of State were to have reserve powers, several courses of action would be open:

- First, the Constitution could leave intact the present provisions conferring reserve powers on the Governor-General (sections 5, 57 and 64) and expressly provide that the conventions formerly governing the exercise of these powers should continue, notwithstanding abolition of the monarchy, preferably stating that their status as non-justiciable conventions should remain unchanged, allowing their continued evolution.[23]
- In addition, Parliament might be authorized to regulate these powers. Parliament may already have the power to do so by a simple majority in each House.[24] But because of the quasi-constitutional nature of such rules, it would be appropriate to provide that legislation governing the exercise of these powers should be passed by a super-majority, say a two-thirds majority in each House, in order to ensure bi-partisan support.
- The Constitution could partially codify the reserve powers and convert them into law, for example by prescribing detailed rules on matters on which there is general consensus (such as the appointment as Prime Minister of the person most likely to command the support of the House of Representatives), while leaving more controversial matters to be governed by the general provision continuing the present conventions and, perhaps, Parliament's power to regulate them (if that be considered appropriate).

  Converting the conventions into law need not render them justiciable, since the Constitution could expressly provide that some or all of such rules should not be justiciable.[25] It would be appropriate for provisions conferring a discretion upon the Head of State to be non-justiciable, while mandatory provisions might well be enforced by the courts.[26]
- Finally, the current constitutional provisions could be replaced by detailed rules seeking to govern all contingencies, although one

must question the wisdom of seeking to provide for unforeseeable crises in a Constitution as difficult to amend as ours. Moreover, the inevitable disagreement over some reserve power conventions, such as what should happen if the Senate blocks Supply, could easily side-track the entire republican debate if its resolution were attempted as part of the move to a republic.

The method of selecting the Head of State is closely related to the question of the powers vested in the office. Recent public opinion polls reveal very strong public support (about eighty percent) for popular election in preference to election by Parliament or appointment by the government.[27] This presumably reflects a widespread popular desire to take the choice of Head of State out of the hands of politicians and let the people exercise it themselves, making it one of the features of a republic for which people express considerable enthusiasm. This is understandable, but the practicalities of popular election suggest that the public has not really thought the matter through, for there are also strong indications that many people would prefer a non-politician as Head of State. Yet popular election would almost guarantee the election of a politician. How many private citizens enjoy both wide public recognition and the financial resources to support a national election campaign? Do we want a succession of millionaire entrepreneurs as President?

So unless careful provision was made to keep political parties out of presidential election campaigns (which would be difficult to enforce), and perhaps for the public funding of campaigns by nominees selected by a reputable and impartial presidential nominating commission, political candidates would be likely to dominate presidential elections and inevitably effectively convert them into a referendum on the performance of the government, as has occurred in Ireland.[28] Moreover, even if the election is confined to largely apolitical candidates, a considerable proportion of the electorate is likely to have voted for unsuccessful candidates, making the President's role as a symbol and focus for national unity more difficult.

Popular election admittedly appears to operate satisfactorily in Ireland and Austria but it is well to remember that even the highly regarded current President of Ireland, Mary Robinson, was formerly a politician. However, the greatest danger in popular election is that the Head of State will appear to have a popular mandate (or at least think he or she has), especially if the election campaign was fought on some sort of 'platform', leading to competition and friction with the government. Even if presidential powers were narrowly confined, which would be highly desirable if popular election were chosen, a popularly-elected President could cause the government considerable discomfort through critical speeches, unless even the President's capacity to speak without government approval were carefully curtailed, as it is in Ireland.[29] Of course, some may regard critical commentary from the sidelines as an irritant it would be beneficial for governments to be obliged to endure. But there is no reason to suppose that one elected official would be possessed of greater wisdom than an entire government of elected members supported by the resources of the public service. Moreover, the notion of 'dual mandates' within the government could be exploited by political groups and foreign governments and corporations. No-one could consider the recent French 'cohabitation' between a Socialist President and Conservative Governments as ideal.

Whether the Head of State is confined to a largely ceremonial role, acting as a focus of national cohesion, or possesses wider powers, the office will be successful only if it is seen as apolitical. So the office should be filled on a non-partisan basis, preferably by election by a super-majority, say two-thirds, in both Houses of Parliament, which would require the agreement of both major parties. While it is, of course, true that some methods of choosing a republican Head of State could endanger its political neutrality, the assertion of some monarchists, that a republican Head of State will *inevitably* be politically partial,[30] is simply unwarranted.

Some commentators maintain that the present balance between the political executive and the Head of State could not be maintained under a republic. The Convenor of Australians for Constitutional Monarchy, Lloyd Waddy Q.C., for example, has remarked that 'any change means giving *more or less* power to the executive (and Prime Minister) and *either* change is wholly undesirable'.[31] In other words, the present system represents perfection incarnate!

However, even under the present system, the balance of power and influence between the government and the Head of State is not static and fluctuates depending upon the political situation (for example, whether Parliament is 'hung' or the government enjoys a secure majority) and the personalities involved. But is the present balance so perfect that *improvement* is impossible?

The exact political balance between the government and a republican Head of State will obviously depend upon the President's powers and method of selection and removal, making it impossible to predict before any of these issues have been settled. Several factors are likely to enhance the President's independence and status as compared with the Governor-General's, which may tend to increase the probability of exercises of the reserve powers. But their effect is uncertain, and some have countervailing implications.

First, the President will be the actual Head of State, probably elected by a representative body, perhaps by a 'super-majority', which is likely to exceed the support enjoyed by the government. These factors are bound to give the President greater status and self-assurance than that enjoyed by the Governor-General, who is merely a surrogate, not actual Head of State.[32] This would be even more likely if the Head of State were popularly elected, making it the only nationally elected public office.

A second factor is that, unlike the Governor-General, the President would feel no constraint derived from concern not to injure the monarchy. Yet Sir John Kerr demonstrated in 1975 that this factor could actually *encourage* the exercise of a reserve power, for he failed to warn Mr Whitlam of his possible dismissal partly out of concern not to involve the Queen, which would have occurred had Mr Whitlam advised her to remove the Governor-General.[33]

Finally, although political realities would make the removal of a Governor-General during a crisis extremely unlikely, the President's constitutionally guaranteed tenure would make it *impossible* for a Prime Minister to remove the President to forestall the possible exercise of a reserve power. Yet, if the President is eligible for re-election, concern not to alienate the government might well constrain presidential independence. For this reason, some commentators have argued that a President should not be eligible for re-election.

2. The Constitutional and Political Impact of Abolishing the Monarchy

There can be little doubt that abolition of the monarchy is constitutionally achievable, and that a new Head of State could be substituted. But some commentators have suggested that the constitutional position is more complex, and that the so-called 'minimalist' republican position outlined above is not feasible, although it surely must be conceded that many republics in the Commonwealth—most recently Mauritius—have successfully taken that course.

The argument essentially appears to be that the monarchy is so fundamental to our constitutional system that its removal would undermine it, necessitating the substitution of a completely new system. Professor D.P. O'Connell was one of the earliest to express this view, in 1977: 'The Australian constitutional structure is like a house of cards: Remove one element of the fabric and the whole is apt to collapse'.[34] He found it difficult to envisage removal of the monarchy without, as he put it, 'an overall dismantling of the system of Australian government, including the Federal system'.[35] The monarchy, he argued, 'is the keystone of the system. Remove it and the system must collapse, at least in the absence of a renovation of the overall constitutional arrangements to be achieved at a constitutional convention'.[36]

O'Connell was a staunch monarchist, but a similar argument has been made by the republican Dr Colin Howard, who sees the Crown's role and the constitutional conventions governing its powers as so fundamental to our system that, as he put it, 'Such matters are not safely or sensibly dealt with by fiddling with the text of a monarchical constitution to eliminate the monarchy as a matter of form and then calling the resulting mess a republic'.[37]

These authors' own words are quoted in order not to misrepresent their views because, with respect, there is little substance in them. The conventions governing the exercise of the Governor-General's powers are undoubtedly vital, but there is no reason why they could not be inherited by a republic, especially if the Constitution expressly stipulates that they should continue to govern the exercise of power by the Head of State or embodies them in express provisions, thereby converting them into law.[38]

In a submission to the Republic Advisory Committee, Professor Peter Boyce propounded views akin to O'Connell's, albeit more moderate, offering this explanation:

> [D]espite the obvious uninvolvement of the monarch in Australia's day to day political management, and despite the very limited exercise of discretionary powers by the Queen's Australian representatives, the Crown still constitutes a very real constraint on the behaviour of our elected political executive. ...[T]he Crown as a constitutional entity is considerably more than the person of the head of state or her resident representative. ... [I]t is ... an institution which contains enormous intrinsic authority - both constitutional and moral. After all, the fundamental authority of Parliament *does not derive from the people*.... Rather, *it derives from the undemocratic, unelective Crown*. The Crown is in fact the centrepiece or lynchpin of our entire constitutional edifice, and to suggest that the balance of forces in our political system would remain essentially unaltered by a mere change of title for the head of state, and a repudiation of all reference to the Crown in our constitution, would be foolish.[39]

This passage is quoted at length because it puts the position with great clarity but, with the utmost respect, what it describes is not Australia, or even Britain post-1689 for that matter. 'Parliament does not derive its authority from the people, but from the Crown?'[40] Surely Charles I lost his head for maintaining that (among other things)! It is surely inconsistent with the view of many monarchists that we are essentially already a republic, a 'crowned republic', and indeed contradicts the opinion of John Adams (among others) that, even before the *Reform Act* of 1832, Britain was in substance a republic.[41] As Bagehot put it in 1867, Britain was a 'disguised republic';[42] a republic had 'insinuated itself beneath the folds of a Monarchy'.[43]

In truth, as noted earlier, our system is not based, like Britain's, on the sovereignty of Parliament—technically 'the Crown in Parliament'—but on popular sovereignty. As Chief Justice Mason acknowledged last year, 'ultimate sovereignty reside[s] in the *Australian people*'.[44]

Those who assert the Crown's pivotal role in our constitutional system see it as a vital source of constitutional morality, as appears from the quoted remarks of Professor Boyce. Thus he views a republic as 'a recipe for creeping concentration of power' in the Prime Minister,[45] whereas many commentators fear a growth in the Head of State's powers under a republic. O'Connell, too, warned of the dangers of dictatorship,[46] and similarly dire consequences have been threatened by Lord Hailsham[47] and Sir Harry Gibbs.[48] The English commentator, Ronald Butt, recently wrote: 'Not the least of the advantages of constitutional monarchy is that it is an inducement to politicians to behave better than they otherwise might to avoid risk of embarrassing the Queen'.[49] While this may be true of Britain, it does not apply to Australia, where the Queen is a remote figure and the activities of 'her' governments are certainly not attributed to her. Australian political history surely makes one sceptical as to the Crown's ability to promote political morality, and one wonders how much of that morality was in evidence before the Fitzgerald and W.A. Inc. Royal Commissions.

Indeed, O'Connell reveals the true source of such inflated notions of the Crown's constitutional importance. Having emphasized the need for institutional continuity, he remarked that 'the principle of continuity is nourished by myth and enshrined in mystery, and the inherited monarchy of Australia has worked well mainly because of this'.[50] So in the end we come back to Bagehot's mystery and magic.[51] What we ultimately see is sentiment masquerading as constitutionalism.

Some monarchists have also sought to entrench the monarchy through the 'federal compact', arguing that continuation of the monarchy is one of its fundamental terms, so that abolition of the monarchy without the consent of all parties to the compact (that is, the people or Parliaments of all the States) would constitute a fundamental breach of that compact, supposedly severing the federation. This contention was argued by Sir Harry Gibbs in an opinion issued in November 1993 in response to the report of the Republic Advisory Committee and endorsed by the Legal Committee of Australians for Constitutional Monarchy:

> The peoples of the Australian colonies agreed to unite under the Crown. It was *the basis of the union* that Australia should be a constitutional monarchy. The Crown was *the tie that bound* the peoples of the various colonies in the union. If that bond is severed, a new basis of union must be found, or in other words, *there must be a new agreement to unite.*[52]

With respect, there is no justification for the notion that the existence of the monarchy is a fundamental term of federation or the 'federal compact'. It was the *Commonwealth of Australia Constitution Act* 1900 (UK) which bound the people of the various colonies together, not the Crown; Sir Harry Gibbs' exaggerated view of the Crown's importance resembles that of Professor Boyce, noted above.[53] Indeed, it is arguable that the Commonwealth and the States did not share the same Crown from 1953 to 1986, and perhaps even from 1931 to 1986,[54] so did the 'federal compact' dissolve without anyone noticing it in 1931?

The preamble to the *Commonwealth of Australia Constitution Act* 1900 (UK) recites that the people of the various colonies had agreed to unite in 'one indissoluble Federal Commonwealth under the Crown of the United Kingdom of Great Britain and Ireland' (which, technically, no longer exists[55] and, in any event, no longer reigns over Australia, whose monarch has long been the 'Queen of Australia'). But the preamble is not a prescriptive part of the statute, and it is legally and politically significant that the prescriptive provision, covering clause 3 (section 3 of the *Commonwealth of Australia Constitution Act*) merely authorizes the Queen to declare that the people of the various colonies 'shall be united in a Federal Commonwealth under the name of the Commonwealth of Australia'. No further reference is made to the Crown. The monarchy was indeed an important feature in the Constitution but, like all other elements thereof, it was inherently subject to alteration pursuant to section 128. Moreover, it was not one of the matters especially entrenched in what was originally the final paragraph of that section.[56]

In other words, the existence of the monarchy was merely an ordinary provision of the federal compact, inherently subject to alteration pursuant to section 128, not a fundamental term.

3. Republican Constitutionalism

Finally, it is interesting to speculate briefly on what effect the advent of a republic might have on the subsequent development of Australian constitutionalism. The achievement of a republic would represent the success of a major constitutional reform and institutional embodiment of popular sovereignty, and would also ensure the greater relevance to Australia of the political theory of republicanism. Each of these could have significant constitutional implications.

The success of a major constitutional reform could encourage further reforms, including many presently on the agenda, such as a bill of rights, constitutional recognition of Aboriginal rights, and reform of federal financial relations. The constitutional recognition of popular sovereignty might ease the way for a bill of rights and citizen-initiated referenda, although this might seem ironic to those familiar with the liberalism versus republicanism debate in the United States,[57] and the distinction between republicanism and democracy,[58] which has led some to query whether such referenda are compatible with the United States Constitution's guarantee of State republican government.[59]

Finally, we would be likely to see a diminution in the influence of British notions of parliamentary sovereignty and 'elective dictatorship', and greater familiarity with American and republican theories of balanced government and divided power.[60] American constitutionalism is inherently more *federal* than ours, imbued as ours is with British centralism and parliamentary sovereignty. Consequently, despite the warnings of monarchists like O'Connell[61] and Gibbs,[62] the power and influence of the States may well *increase* under a republic, not diminish. In view of Paul Keating's reputation as a centralist, his championing of the republican cause may prove to be the greatest irony of all!

This paper was presented at The University of Queensland T.C. Beirne School of Law Annual Symposium 1993. An earlier version of this paper was presented as the Ronald Wilson Lecture in Perth on 16 September 1993.

Notes

1. J. Hirst, 'The Time Has Come to Manage on Our Own', *Weekend Australian*, 9–10 October 1993, 34. The Head of State of a British Republic would presumably become 'Queen' pursuant to the *Commonwealth of Australia Constitution Act* 1900 (UK) s.2. Opinion is divided on the question whether the Commonwealth Parliament could alter the succession to the throne: see G. Winterton, 'The Evolution of a Separate Australian Crown' (1993) 19 *Monash University Law Review* 1, 2, including note 8; *R. v. Scott* (1993) 114 A.C.T.R. 20, 28–9.
2. See, for example, *The Macquarie Dictionary* (Sydney: Macquarie Library, 1981), 1467–8.
3. It was approved by referenda in all States and effectively twice by electors in N.S.W., Victoria, South Australia and Tasmania: see J. Quick and R.R. Garran, *The Annotated Constitution of the Australian Commonwealth* (Sydney: Angus & Robertson, 1901), 206–13, 222–6, 249–50.
4. See *Australian Capital Television Pty. Ltd. v. Commonwealth* (1992) 177 C.L.R. 106, 138 per Mason C.J., citing G.J. Lindell, 'Why Is Australia's Constitution Binding?—The Reasons in 1900 and Now, and the Effect of Independence' (1986) 16 *Federal Law Review* 29, 49; G. Sawer, 'Government and Law', in J.D.B. Miller (ed.), *Australians and British: Social and Political Connections* (Sydney: Methuen, 1987), 45, 71, 75. Deane J. sees the authority of the Constitution as derived from 'the compact between the Australian people': *Breavington v. Godleman* (1988) 169 C.L.R. 41, 123. But see G.J. Craven, 'A Few Fragments of State Constitutional Law' (1990) 20 *University of Western Australia Law Review* 353, 360-1.
5. Pursuant to the *Statute of Westminster* 1931 (UK) s.2 and the *Australia Act* 1986 (UK) s.3.
6. *Australia Act* 1986 (UK) s.1.
7. A point noted by Dawson J. in *Australian Capital Television Pty. Ltd. v. Commonwealth* (1992) 177 C.L.R. 106, 181; and M. Moshinsky, 'Re-Enacting the Constitution in an Australian Act' (1989) 18 *Federal Law Review* 134, 136, 144.

8. See L. Zines, 'Commentary', in H.V. Evatt, *The Royal Prerogative* (Sydney: Law Book Company, 1987), C9–C10; L. Zines, *Constitutional Change in the Commonwealth* (Cambridge: Cambridge University Press, 1991), 27.
9. With due respect, the presence of such words in the Australian Constitution would not 'entirely belie the manner of its adoption', as Dawson J. suggested: *supra* note 7.
10. See, e.g., M. Kirby, 'A Defence of the Constitutional Monarchy' (1993) 37(9) *Quadrant* 30, 35.
11. See G. Winterton, *Monarchy to Republic: Australian Republican Government* (Melbourne: Oxford University Press, 1986), 101–2.
12. *Time* (Australia), 26 April 1993, 8 reported a preference of 73% to 22%, and *Time* (Australia), 3 January 1994, 7 a preference of 72% to 21%. For earlier figures, see G. Winterton, 'Presidential Power in Republican Australia' (1993) 28 *Australian Journal of Political Science* 40, 41–2.
13. The Report of the Republic Advisory Committee, *An Australian Republic: The Options* (Canberra: A.G.P.S., 2 vols., 1993).
14. See the views of Sir Paul Hasluck, Sir John Kerr and Sir Zelman Cowen, cited in Winterton, *supra* note 11, 161 note 25; Sir Walter Campbell, 'The Role of a State Governor' (1988 Endowed Lecture of the Royal Australian Institute of Public Administration, Queensland Division), 4–7; R.E. McGarvie, 'Governorship in Australia Today' (unpublished Address to Senior Executive Chapter Luncheon of the Australian Institute of Management, Melbourne, 8 September 1993), 12-6. For the working of the Federal Executive Council, see Republic Advisory Committee Report, *supra* note 13, vol. 2, Appendix 5.
15. P.W. Hogg, *Constitutional Law of Canada* (3d ed., Toronto: Carswell, 1992), 253. Accord Sir Harry Gibbs, 'Republic: Difficult and Dangerous', *Canberra Times*, 28 June 1993, 11.
16. Victoria, South Australia, New South Wales and Tasmania.
17. See, e.g., the Austrian Constitution, art. 29(2). Accord C. Saunders, 'A Republican Model: Would More be Better Than Less?', in J. Beaumont (ed.), *Where To Now? Australia's Identity in the Nineties* (Sydney: Federation Press, 1993), 86, 93.
18. *Cf.* the German Basic Law, art. 68.
19. See G. Winterton, 'The Constitutional Position of Australian State Governors', in H.P. Lee and G. Winterton (eds.), *Australian Constitutional Perspectives* (Sydney: Law Book Company, 1992), 274, 303, 304 ff.; Sir Harry Gibbs, 'The Australian Constitution and Australia's Constitutional Monarchy' (unpublished paper presented at Australians For Constitutional Monarchy Seminar, Sydney, 4 June 1993), 14–16.

20. The figures are: AGB McNair poll, *Bulletin*, 19 October 1993, 13: largely ceremonial 11%, similar to Governor-General 42%, greater power 37%, don't know 10%. For earlier polls, see Newspoll, *Australian*, 19 July 1993, 2; AGB McNair poll, *Bulletin*, 11 May 1993, 14.
21. See Winterton, *supra* note 11, 3.
22. As Sir Harry Gibbs has stressed: Gibbs, *supra* note 15; Sir Harry Gibbs, 'Remove the Queen, and the Whole Structure Could Fall', *Australian*, 7 June 1993, 11.
23. See, e.g., G. Winterton, 'A Constitution for an Australian Republic', *Independent Monthly*, March 1992, s.60A.
24. G. Winterton, *Parliament, the Executive and the Governor-General* (Melbourne: Melbourne University Press, 1983), 98–101. But see G.J. Lindell, Book Review [of *id*.] (1983) 6 *University of New South Wales Law Journal* 261, 267–8.
25. See, e.g., the Constitution of India, art. 74(2); the Constitution of Papua New Guinea, s.86(4); K.W. Ryan, *Opinion for Standing Committee "D"* (Australian Constitutional Convention, 1978), paras. 26–33.
26. See Republic Advisory Committee Report, *supra* note 13, vol. 1, 90, 103-5; Constitutional Commission, *Report of the Advisory Committee on Executive Government* (Canberra: A.G.P.S., 1987), 39–43.
27. *Time* (Australia), 3 January 1994, 7 (popular election 76%, parliamentary election 18%, appointment by government 3%); *Bulletin*, 19 October 1993, 13 (popular election 80%, parliamentary election 16%); *Australian*, 19 July 1993, 2 (popular election 79%, parliamentary election 10%, appointment by Prime Minister 2%); *Bulletin*, 11 May 1993, 14 (popular election 83%, parliamentary election 8%); *Time* (Australia), 26 April 1993, 8 (popular election 71%, parliamentary election 21%, appointment by government 4%).
28. J. Duffy, 'Ireland', in Republic Advisory Committee Report, *supra* note 13, vol. 2, 109, paras. 3.21, 3.29, 3.35, 3.42, 3.45.
29. *Id*., 132-33 (paras. 2.60–62); Irish Constitution, art. 13.7.
30. See Sir Harry Gibbs, *supra* notes 15 and 22.
31. L. Waddy, 'Inevitable? Not at All' (1993) 28(5) *Australian Lawyer* 16, 18. Emphasis added.
32. See, for example, Kirby, *supra* note 10, 34.
33. Sir John Kerr, *Matters for Judgment* (Melbourne: Macmillan, 1978), 332.
34. D. O'Connell, 'Monarchy or Republic?', in G. Dutton (ed.), *Republican Australia?* (Melbourne: Sun Books, 1977), 23, 26.
35. *Id*., 23. See also *infra*, text accompanying notes 52–56.
36. O'Connell, *supra* note 34, 23–4.
37. C. Howard, 'Republic Talk Lacks Design', *Australian Financial Review*, 7 April 1993, 13.

38. The Constitution could, theoretically, spell out the conventions and provide that they should retain the status of non-justiciable conventions, but the likely practical effect would be to convert them into non-justiciable rules of law, differing from conventions principally in their inability (or reduced ability) to evolve and adapt to new situations.
39. P.J. Boyce, Submission no. 85, 24 June 1993, 2. Emphasis added.
40. Paraphrase of *ibid*.
41. See Winterton, *supra* note 11, 3, 150 note 18.
42. W. Bagehot, *The English Constitution* (London: Fontana, 1963), 266 note 1.
43. *Id.* 94.
44. Cited *supra* note 4. Emphasis added.
45. Boyce, *supra* note 39, 2.
46. O'Connell, *supra* note 34, 25, 32–33.
47. Quoted in Winterton, *supra* note 11, 143.
48. Gibbs, *supra* note 22.
49. R. Butt, 'Uneasy Lies the Head', *Times Literary Supplement*, 11 June 1993, 24.
50. O'Connell, *supra* note 34, 36.
51. Bagehot, *supra* note 42, 100.
52. Sir Harry Gibbs, *The States and a Republic* (unpublished opinion, undated, released 3 November 1993), 3. Emphasis added. This opinion is noted in S. Kirk, 'Republic Move "Puts Federation at Risk"', *Sydney Morning Herald*, 4 November 1993, 5.
53. *Supra*, text accompanying note 39.
54. The argument being that a separate Australian Crown existed from the enactment of the *Statute of Westminster* 1931 (UK), or at least the *Royal Style and Titles Act* 1953 (Cth), but that the Queen of the United Kingdom remained the Head of State of the Australian States until the enactment of the *Australia Act* 1986 (UK), especially ss.7(5) and 10. The present writer disagrees with the last proposition. See generally Winterton, *supra* note 1.
55. The Royal Style and Title ceased to refer to 'the United Kingdom of Great Britain and Ireland' in 1927: see Proclamation of 13 May 1927, pursuant to the *Royal and Parliamentary Titles Act* 1927 (UK), reprinted in A.B. Keith, *Speeches and Documents on the British Dominions, 1918–1931* (London: Oxford University Press, 1932), 171–72.
56. With respect, Sir Harry Gibbs' argument that removal of the Crown from State governments may require the approval of the electors in *all* States (Gibbs, *supra* note 52, 2; accord unpublished opinion of Australians for Constitutional Monarchy, 8 September 1993) is highly questionable: see, e.g., Quick and Garran, *supra* note 3, 991; E.

Campbell, 'Changing the Constitution—Past and Future' (1989) 17 *Melbourne University Law Review* 1, 1 note 2.
57. For a recent overview of the literature, see J.D. Hoeveler, Jr., 'Original Intent and the Politics of Republicanism' (1992) 75 *Marquette Law Review* 863.
58. See James Madison, *Federalist* Nos. 10 and 14, in J.E. Cooke (ed.), *The Federalist* (Middletown, Conn.: Wesleyan University Press, 1961), 62, 84; G. Maddox, 'Republic or Democracy?' (1993) 28 *Australian Journal of Political Science* 9.
59. See United States Constitution, art. IV, § 4; H.A. Linde, 'When Initiative Lawmaking is Not "Republican Government": The Campaign Against Homosexuality' (1993) 72 *Oregon Law Review* 19; H.A. Linde, 'When is Initiative Lawmaking Not "Republican Government"?' (1989) 17 *Hastings Constitutional Law Quarterly* 159; W.M. Wiecek, *The Guarantee Clause of the U.S. Constitution* (Ithaca: Cornell University Press, 1972), 259–68.
60. This is already occurring: see, e.g., H. Emy, 'In Praise of Federalism: A Personal View' in C. Fletcher (ed.), *Encounters With Federalism* (Canberra: Federalism Research Centre, 1993), 9, 15.
61. O'Connell, *supra* note 34, 23, 32.
62. Gibbs, *supra* note 19, 19, 20 (the earlier comment is reprinted in Gibbs, *supra* note 22).

A Civic Identity—Not A National Identity

*Donald Horne**

> *'How to be a nation without being nationalist
> ... and how to be tolerant without falling apart'*

What I am about to do is to present a conservative case for Australia becoming a republic. I am assuming that this welcome event would come only after discussion had been freed from the point-scoring of party politics and some accommodation had been found in defining the relations between Parliament, Prime Minister and President. My case is based on making a civic definition of Australians. It abandons the idea of Australia as a 'nation'.

The case is not conservative in the sense that there is some sacred body of precept and practice called conservatism that must be maintained forever. In a modern-industrial society that kind of nostalgic stubbornness is always self-defeating. It is self-defeating because there is a kind of conservative principle of relativity: if you stand still when all else has moved you have moved without knowing it. That is why conservatives who, at times of change, don't shift any of their position cease being conservative and become crackpots or reactionaries or, as some of them boast, 'radicals'.

By 'conservative' I mean having a cautious approach to change. It doesn't mean putting one's head in the sand: we live in modern capitalist societies that are, by definition, societies of change. What it means, in the first place, is refusing to believe that change is good for its own sake and it means being sceptical about even

---

* Author and former Professor of Political Science, University of New South Wales.

proposals for change that seem admirable—because they may have results different from those that were intended. It does not mean, however, opposing all change—simply remaining sceptical about change (a sense of irony is useful) but also allowing for the possibility that change may be the better of two risks. The essence of intelligent conservatism is to combine a scepticism about change with a scepticism about not changing—because, if, all around you, there is change and if you wish to defend those sound traditions that can still be viable you may have to adjust position. Intelligent conservatives are not fundamentalists—in fact all zeal, especially doctrinaire zeal, is one of the principal threats to the conservative approach as I have defined it. In the interest of maintaining what still works an intelligent conservative will abandon what has stopped working.

Intelligent conservatives are sceptical of superficial views of society founded only on economic or legal perspectives. They base their views of the present and the future on taking seriously, for better or for worse, the values and beliefs, the habits and symbols of people in the society around them. It is these values and beliefs and habits and symbols that both express a society's potential and define the limits of that potential. As distinguished from utopians, intelligent conservatives accept that you have to work with what you've got. That is why they value the diversity of a society—because this offers opportunities for change through a kind of organic self-renewal that can grow within the society itself and not be imposed on it. A strong society contains within itself many peaceful alternatives.

My argument here is not concerned with the shallow question of whether it is republics or monarchies that have inherent virtue but I will spend a paragraph on this school debating approach. First—affirming the inherent virtue of monarchies does not take into account that, in the ordinary sense of the word, Australia is not a monarchy, but a Governor-Generalate with an absentee monarch and that this can offer a confusing, even debilitating, view of Australia. Second—insofar as claims are made for the inherent virtue of a constitutional monarchy as a way of controlling the excesses of governments—it's the other way around. Constitutions were developed not to restrict Parliaments (which seems to have become the Australian argument) but to restrict monarchs (the Glorious Revolution of 1688, Magna Carta, etc); the result is that most constitutional monarchs have no powers or fewer powers than those of the Governor-General and that becoming a republic might be seen as the natural end of constitutionalising a monarchy. Third —if checks and balances are what is needed we might remember that Australia already has more checks and balances than any constitutional monarchy. Britain, for example, has no checks and balances. The 'Westminster System' (which Australia does not have) is one of unqualified sovereignty for the House of Commons, whereas the sovereignty of our House of Representatives is qualified by State Parliaments, by our Constitution as interpreted by the High Court and by the strong powers of the Senate. In theory, the Monarch might intervene in British politics, but since a British Monarch has a dynasty to risk by intervention, and not merely, as with Sir John Kerr, a reputation, intervention is not very likely—at least not under Elizabeth II who has learned the prudence of reigning. Fourth —the world's two oldest republics (Switzerland and the United States) are both democracies. Fifth—constitutional monarchies are not in themselves a guarantee against tyrannical conduct (Mussolini, for example, to name but him). Sixth—taking the view of conservatism as an attitude to change and not as a body of fixed beliefs, there is no conservative commitment to monarchies as such: their value must be estimated in overall equations of change. In Australia some people can still equate 'conservative' not with an attitude to change, but with maintaining 'British tradition'. That can be a mistake very costly in the development of civic consciousness.

As to constitutions—the true conservative position is to be somewhat sceptical about constitutions, in themselves, whether monarchic or republican, and to look at the political culture of a country along with its constitution—the values and beliefs, the habits and symbols inherent in the actualities of how people see politics, and go about politics. From this perspective there is plenty of good news in Australia. It is a measure of the desperation of some self-perceived Australian conservatives that they should quote the problems of President Yeltsin—or even President Idi Amin—as an example of what can happen in a republic. Because we have had more practice, we have a great deal more going for us than Russia or Uganda.

The suggestion that if we become a republic we might become a dictatorship is demeaning to the democratic robustness of Australian citizens, of the Australian polity and of Australian society. It is demonstrable that we have a remarkable capacity for resilience—showing a capacity both for change and for stability and, increasingly (and surprisingly), an effective capacity for tolerance. These virtues have not been maintained by the link with the British Crown. They have been part of the continuing story of the development of liberal-democratic ways of doing things in Australia. Nor have these virtues been sustained by that politically arcane document, the Commonwealth Constitution. On the contrary. They have been sustained despite the Constitution. The Constitution is primarily a document defining State and Commonwealth powers and naming some of the parts of a framework of government—without actually saying how that framework should work. (Indeed it leaves a few false trails.) There are scarcely any overtly liberal or democratic statements within it and its most democratic statement, that the Constitution can be amended by the people, voting in a referendum, is constantly denied by the Constitution groupies whose cry 'Hands off our Constitution' ignores how the Constitution says, in effect, put your hands on me, and amend me at your will. Since the Constitution, so far as we know, was not the word of God, it becomes the word of the people. That the Constitution was adopted by the people and can be amended only by the people is its only source of legitimacy.

It is with this background statement of respect for Australian potential that I put forward four conservative reasons for Australia, in due course, becoming a republic. I will argue that for three of them, perhaps all four, republicanism (which is not inherently a radical doctrine) is the only way. The reasons are:

- The need for a strong civic belief system, so that we can be aware of those things which, in our diversity, hold us together, as citizens, in some unity.
- The need for the presidency to appeal to a sense of citizenship rising above party politics.
- The need for a clear statement on the mutual checks between President, Prime Minister and Parliament that is not likely to challenge the overall legitimacy of our political system.
- The need for a stronger sense of peculiarly Australian policy-making, based on a sense of Australian distinctiveness that passes beyond the dangers of nationalism to those of civic awareness.

1. The need for a strong civic belief system

On Empire Day, 1933, I stood up in the School of Arts in the Hunter Valley town of Muswellbrook and gave my first public speech. It was on the duties we owed to the British Empire. The speech was quite well-presented. It referred to freedom, honesty, fairness and a number of other noble aspirations, and at the time everything I said was credible—because there was the Empire, out there, and there we were, at Muswellbrook, as members of it. But where can we look to now for an expression of the minimum common values that Australians should hold?

I am not suggesting that somehow we evoke the departed spirits of British imperialism. I just want to recall that it was in being members of the British Empire that Australians found a way of imagining themselves as belonging to something that was bigger than them, that had a number of principles attached to it (freedom, honesty and fairness, for example—even race tolerance, in principle if not in practice) and in which Australians played an active part. I have done this as a reminder that this was not a very efficient start for developing principles of citizenship in a liberal-democratic state. We were British subjects, not Australian citizens. Our passports said so. It was the Empire that, ultimately, we belonged to. Being Australian was a lesser matter.

For conservatives, the legitimacy of the state and the healthiness of the civil society are essential and in Australia that means the legitimacy of a liberal-democratic state and the healthiness of a liberal-democratic society. Yet, even now, we lack a civic belief system that openly enunciates and praises those principles that could express, despite all our differences, a fundamental harmony. (Even civil disobedience, in the Whig interpretation of history, is a kind of respect for the law. Simon de Montfort instituted the Barons' War and John Hampden refused to pay ship money because they wanted better laws.)

There are three extraordinary features of this lack of a public civic belief system. One is that those who are most concerned that, as a multicultural society, Australia has become a 'nation of tribes' are also those most likely to cling to nostalgic remnants of the Empire instead of helping work out a minimum civil contract—a few declared principles of liberal-democratic practice that define an Australian way. The second is that defining an Australian civil contract does not require an imposition from on high (which wouldn't work); what it requires is an articulation of ideas and practices already familiar to most Australians. The third is that, at a time when the nationalism of ethnicity can return to a terrorist pitch we have in Australia, by accident, the opportunity to show the world how to be a nation without being nationalist, and how to be tolerant without falling apart. However to achieve this does mean that relics of sentiment for the Crown must be allowed to complete their historic role of withering away—although there has to be a small, final snip.

What alternatives are there to making a civic definition of ourselves as Australians?

After the Empire departed there was a stopgap arrangement. We were British, but we were British without the Empire. It was a matter of sentiment. Sir Robert Menzies, British to his boot heels, had no illusions (as Malcolm Turnbull has pointed out) that Queen Elizabeth was in some mystic way, Australian. She was also British to her boot heels, and we were to be loyal to her because she was British.

But being British could not finally appear to hold Australians together—because there were all those people being British over there in Britain and, now that the Empire was gone, what did we have to do with them? It was seen, by people who thought about it, as a matter of heritage. But which British heritage? The only answer could be the Australian version of being British. It is true that, until the 1950s, the Europeans who came to Australia were predominantly, although not exclusively, from the British and Irish Isles—but that means that our 'heritage' was not only British but Irish (about one quarter Irish), a fact that was brought out with great poignancy in 1992–93 by those critics of the republican cause who dismissed it as an emanation from 'the bog Irish' (who are an essential part of our heritage). And in any case the fragments of British and Irish (and Scottish, Welsh, Cornish, etc.) society that were deposited here arrived in different proportions and in different social mixes from those prevailing in the then United Kingdom (and, of course, they had many unique experiences once they arrived here). The only useful way out of this is to explore how modern-industrial Australia has a general European inheritance (along with exploring our Aboriginal inheritance and the general influences of the world at large): knowing something of our European inheritance is essential to the understanding of our history, but it is not being adequately handled in either universities or schools.

However, the idea of our being 'British' is a different matter from accepting the significance of our European heritage and it is useless and in fact harmful to us now if we are looking for ways of seeing it as something that might hold us together. If it is to have any effect it must be to pull us apart. The idea of being exclusively 'British' has no modern meaning for Australians. No, that's not true. It would be more accurate to say that its most significant meaning now is as an expression of a fanciful ethnic prejudice ('bog Irish' again)—that can also have a coded racist under-meaning—and as a way of distracting attention from how we might define ourselves by a civic code. To say that our inheritance is European, rather than British, is not only more accurate: it is also more useful to present and future needs. It is not Britain we deal with now, but Europe, and in Europe Britain is second among several.

An apparent alternative to being 'British' is to adopt the mystical concepts of 'the Crown': 'the Crown' as infinitely divisible, so that there is a 'the Crown' for us and a different 'the Crown' for Grenada; 'the Crown' as above politics (which leaves a segment of mainly aged Australians imagining the Crown as a kind of umpire, guaranteeing our freedoms); and in our case (I'm not sure about Grenada) 'the Crown' as embodying a history of growing tolerance, liberty and parliamentary democracy. One thing wrong with these doctrines is that they cannot be taught in schools (an absolute test in looking for a civic definition of an Australian). We can't go back to honouring 'the Crown' at school assemblies. Whether the exponents of the mystic doctrine of 'the Crown' intend this or not, it also implies defining Australian values in terms of a royal person. (How does that enrich Australian society?) What is even more wrong is that if we want to talk about tolerance, liberty and parliamentary democracy, why not do it directly, in Australian terms and in terms of Australian achievement? The mystique of 'the Crown' is a way of avoiding interest in the nature of the state, and of civil society.

In countries where the monarch is a resident and a national of that country and acts with a decent modesty—Denmark, for example, Sweden, Norway, the Netherlands—the monarchy can also be a symbol of local civic spirit. But our Monarch doesn't live here, she is not an Australian and she makes no claim to represent Australia. If she goes to address the European Union, to take one example, she represents the British Government and says what they want her to say. When she is in Australia she can scarcely begin a speech with the words 'We Australians'. (In fact even back home 'the royals' do not speak the language of civic virtue. They are a way of turning minds away from contemplating civic virtue.)

Along with 'Britishness' and the mystic doctrine of 'the Crown' we have more distinctively Australian leftovers from nineteenth century ethnocentric nation-making. There were various cultural stereotypes of being a dinkum Aussie, usually of a redneck variety —caricatures of Australians—the Man from Snowy River, the larrikin, the digger, the lifesaver and so forth; more recently, the Ocker, and, in an absolute degeneration of a myth that until then had some decency about it, Yobbo, son of Ocker. There is nothing useful in these stereotypes and a great deal that can be harmful: their true place now is as mythic stereotypes in the entertainment and advertising business. Associated with them is the Anzac myth, which is infinitely re-workable, so that it can mean different things to different generations, but that, in any re-working, is limited in scope. How can one define Australia in a way that excludes all women and most men? There are also, of course, the dramas of sport, which are nation-defining in any modern society, but in a necessarily limited way; the obsession with 'Nature' and with characteristic landscapes as nation-definers; and a belief that there are certain distinctively Australian ways of going on—an openness of manner, a laconic style, the (again exclusively male) values of mateship, the belief in a fair-go, etc.

All of these have the disadvantage that they are assertions of 'national character'. Even landscapes are assertions of 'national character'. (Is there anyone as truly Australian as a gum tree, or Ayers Rock?) They are inescapable as myth, and can be drawn on in metaphors, but they are related to Australia as a society. Yet 'society' is an enormously complex idea, never fully examinable because of its diversity. We can keep on putting a frame around aspects of a society but there are equally many other frames we could put around other aspects of a society. You can't sum up a society—at least not in these caricature terms, which put up as 'typically Australian' stereotypes that are in fact only minority views, most of them by now crazily unrelated to a 1990s Australia. Anyway the gum tree is not the typical Australian tree.

There was one set of beliefs that did combine caricature views along with basic political habits. That was the long-standing cult of 'national development' (which ended only with the Hawke Government) that was pursued with a religious faith that was concerned with great fears and hopes of geopolitical strategy, dreams of a purer and more civilised existence, ideas of justice, a craving for bigness and a kind of patriotism in which it was the soil of Australia, not its people, that became the real Australia. Along with it went the bush landscapes, the bush yarns, the bush ballads and the cult of mateship, born in the bush, and along with that also the Anzac myth, also seen as a creation of the bush. The combination of national development and national security (Anzac), upheld by the faith in the bush was the civil religion of Australia.

However illusory it was in part, faith in national development was something people could feel they belonged to. Now we have 'the economy'. No one can belong to 'the economy' in its present terms. 'The economy' is something whose latest mysteries are revealed nightly on television—but an 'economy' is a highly abstract and simplistic concept. It is a way of looking at parts of a society's statistics, not at a society.

To return to the idea of 'society'; one of the aspects of a society that can be generalised about are those that make up a polity, the political system of a state (which is called, in this case, the Commonwealth of Australia). We can all, or most of us, imagine ourselves as belonging to a polity—which is a way of determining some of our affairs, and providing minimum rules for our relations with each other and with the state. And it is relatively easy to describe. It is the development of this idea that can help give us a working unity in our diversity. As Australians we must learn to make not an ethnic definition of ourselves or a cultural chauvinist definition of ourselves or a nationalist definition and certainly not a leftover imperialist or racist definition. We should be making a civic definition of ourselves. That is to say, we must imagine that we are Australians because we accept certain civic principles in common. And when we want to explain to school pupils or immigrants, or whoever, what an Australian is we would describe those principles.

What might those civic principles be? When we say we are Australians we could mean we are committed to the land we share, we are committed to the Australian Constitution as amended by the people, we are committed to the rule of law, to the liberal democratic approach in politics and to the principle of tolerance, and that we respect the equal civil rights of Australians.

Just look over those again—respect for the land we share, the Constitution, the rule of law, liberal democratic behaviour, tolerance, equal rights. Perhaps we might also add another, communitarian, belief—the belief that within the communities in which we live each of us should try to be a good citizen.* Many more Australians believe in these civic principles (or would do so if they were spelt out for them) than are ever again likely to believe in 'the Crown'. Is it not possible to imagine a Commonwealth of Australia in which these principles were the basis for a civic patriotism?

In schools students could be taught a civic definition of Australians as members of a polity: they would learn something about rights and responsibilities, about the principles of parliamentary democracy and the meanings of democracy, about respect for the rule of law and for the Constitution as amended by the people, about freedom of expression and action, and about equality of civil rights, about tolerance, and about the negotiation of social, economic and cultural diversity. They would also learn something about the civic history of Australia—how we got where we are—and, in forms that might change in detail from school to school there could be appropriate ceremonies of affirmation of the Australian civic code.

Some of these ideas would seem strange to immigrants. These ideas should be explained to them as the Australian way, so that they can understand what they have contracted into and, if it comes to naturalisation ceremonies, these should be given greater imaginative power. (What kind of stupidity could get into self-perceived conservatives that they should object to the new naturalisation oath that was introduced in 1993, with its commitment of 'loyalty to Australia and its people whose democratic beliefs I share, whose rights and liberties I respect, and whose laws I will uphold and obey'?) All oaths or affirmations of office should contain references to upholding the Constitution and serving the Australian people. Historians who can write readable stuff should be encouraged to produce material at all levels giving some idea of the development of the Australian way. Rhetoricians should be encouraged to widen the concept of 'the fair go' so that

---

* I imagine that my kind of conservative would find merit in individualism as a declaration of human potential and dignity, but not as a loosening of individual selfishness and greed. Concern with youth crime, drugs etc. should look to communitarian values as well as to the police.

it includes new meanings and is given a distinctively Australian feel. Once again, as happened at the beginning of this century, foreigners might come here to write books about Australian democratic achievement.

But now here is the problem: how can you place those ideals as central to our common membership of a democratic state, if also central to the idea of being an Australian is the ideal of loyalty to the distant monarch?

What we have going for us is that most Australians believe in a commitment to the rule of law and to our Constitution, as amended by the people. They accept the ideals of parliamentary democracy and the rights to individual dignity of all Australians. Most Australians, on the other hand, either do not believe in the monarchy or support it simply because they are puzzled or scared by the word 'republic'.

Unless we are to maintain at the centre of our national symbolic system an increasingly trivial nothingness Australians must learn more effective and new ways of talking about Australia, based on a common form of allegiance that is accepted not by a minority of our citizens, but by an overwhelming majority of the Australian people.

2. The need for the presidency to appeal to a sense of citizenship rising above party politics

How to elect the President may be a more difficult question to settle than what the President's powers should be (although the two are related). However this is mainly because too much is expected of the person of the President and not enough of the office of the presidency. Many Australians do not understand, for example, how a United States President may be personally detested, while the office of the presidency is revered. A conservative view would be that we do not declare personal loyalty to a Head of State, but to the institutions that this person represents.

The essential symbolic feature of an Australian republic would be the declarations of belief in our basic civic principles. It is these that rise above party politics to a consideration of those principles that unite us despite party political divisions. These divisions—in some form or other essential to a liberal democracy—operate within certain accepted rules and all of the symbols of the state should express their spirit. Compared to this, the presidency is less important.

As to the presidency ... One of the great cultural resources of Australia has been that in outward manners we have been a rather sceptical kind of people when we think about those in power. Our scepticism can run to a fault, of course. But not as often as the alternative. As a consequence, we have developed a high appreciation of the importance of ordinary people, and an appreciation of our common humanity. Anzac Day, for example, is not necessarily (and never exclusively) a jingoistic militarist day. It can be seen as a day of commemoration of ordinary people in the military ranks. In a sense, Anzac Day is a display of our respect for the great worth that can lie in the potential of ordinariness, and in our implicit feeling that ordinary people deserve a fair go. 'Weary' Dunlop could seem a hero because he also remained an ordinary person.

When this belief in the potential of ordinary decency, of a common humanity and of equality of opportunity rather than in inherited position and prestige becomes a central affirmation in our public life and we clearly state in our Constitution that we are the Commonwealth of Australia not by grace of a monarch living in Britain but by grace of our own democratic strengths and achievements, a President, appropriately chosen, will be a continuing reminder that in symbolic terms it is finally not the leaders of the political parties who are at the centre of the state, nor the President, but the Australian people.

There will be no question of personal loyalty to a President. We won't be expected to serve Presidents. A President will be a modest reminder of the dignity and worth of the Australian people. A politician who stands in the presence of a President will be standing in the presence of the shared democratic traditions of Australia.

3. The need for a clear statement on the mutual checks between President, Prime Minister and Parliament that is not likely to challenge the overall legitimacy of our political system

Nothing has ever more clearly demonstrated the weakness of self-styled conservative thinking in Australia than the almost universal support by 'conservatives' for the action of Sir John Kerr in dismissing the Whitlam Government because, he said, they were not going to get Supply from the Senate. To a conservative of the kind I have in mind what matters most in a Head of State is to preserve the legitimacy of the Constitution. Kerr disturbed that legitimacy not only by acting precipitously (he should at least have waited until a decision was made in the Senate as to whether it would withhold Supply); he also acted on the basis of two hitherto unrevealed doctrines—that the principle of responsible government included responsibility to both Houses of Parliament (which could mean that whenever a government lost a vote in the Senate it should resign) and that it was his constitutional duty to dismiss a government that could not (or so he thought) obtain Supply. Neither of these doctrines is stated in the Constitution, nor were they a feature of any of the 'conventions' surrounding discussion on the Constitution. Given a constitution so general in the powers it gives a Governor-General and so non-specific about their application and given the widespread belief ('convention') that it was the House of Representatives the Government was responsible to, and given that the Whitlam Government was not acting illegally, what Kerr should have done, if he was concerned with maintaining the political order, was nothing. Unless Whitlam did act illegally (in which case Kerr should have at once dismissed him) he should have left it to the politicians to solve their own differences, within the framework of the Constitution—as they do all the time in the United States.

The opinion polls showed at the time that half of those interviewed disagreed with what Kerr did, and half agreed. (That more than half voted against Labor is another matter: they wanted a change of government, even if some of them thought it should not happen this way.) The Constitution should not be left open to arbitrary interpretation in a manner that is bound to weaken its legitimacy. No future Head of State should be caught up, as Kerr was, in constitutional controversy about the use of powers that, if taken literally, are much the same as those of George III.

One can, I believe, overstate the need for changing the Constitution: what is usually more important are the things in which we believe and the ways in which we behave. But there is a central part of our Constitution that is in need of a clearer statement. That is the part that describes how a government becomes a government and what the reciprocal checks are between a Head of State and a Parliament and a Prime Minister.

In the interests of predictability and common understanding we need a constitution that actually describes what happens and that can be taught in schools. The only true basis of respect for a constitution is that the citizens know what it says. These changes could be made now, but on the path to a republic it would be essential to make it quite clear what was to be the constitutional balance between President, Prime Minister and Parliament.

There are three principles. One is that the Constitution should say that the head of government is the Prime Minister and that Prime Ministers remain in that office only by maintaining the confidence of the House of Representatives. Another is that it should say that, normally, the President acts only on the advice of the government. The third is to state the exception to this, which is that it would be the duty of the President to defend the Constitution in two regards—to dismiss a government that had lost the confidence of the House of Representatives and to dismiss a government that continued in conduct that had been determined to be unlawful.

The first of those duties is easy enough to understand. The second has the difficulty: who will do the determining? The answer to that is something we could settle in non-partisan public discussion over a period of several years. The decision to federate and to devise a constitution stating the framework for that federation was a much more severe challenge than this.

4. The need for a stronger sense of peculiarly Australian policy-making, based on a sense of Australian distinctiveness that passes beyond the dangers of nationalism to the benefits of civic awareness

One thing that the republican debate should not be seen as being about is the issue of 'national identity'. There never has been and there never will be a common national identity—if, by that, one means a quick, overall summing-up of all Australia as a society although one can provide useful, overall perspectives on Australia —as a polity, for example, or as an economy, or in a summary of its public culture. Like any other society, Australia is richly diverse, thereby providing the source for many organic renewals. 'National identities' are strategic claims or programs, not descriptions. They are not richly diverse. They are limiting.

However it would seem obvious (but it isn't, even yet) that in policy-making there should be a concern with Australian distinctiveness. How much of the economic improvisations of the 1980s, for example, was based on what was distinctive about the

Australian economy, and how much of it was merely a zealous carrying out of certain abstract rules that were never considered in the light of the economic conditions actually prevailing in Australia?

It should seem obvious—but it isn't—that there are things about Australia that are not quite the same as anywhere else. Determining what those differences are is a matter of driving importance to our Commonwealth. There are things that are distinctive about our economy, and our trading potential, about our geographical placing and our general strategic position, about our particular kind of social and cultural diversity, about our public culture, about our mix of lifestyles and values and our general demographic mix, and about the problems and opportunities of work, education and caring.

In all, or most of these, we have been shedding ourselves of colonial attitudes that long outlasted our membership of the Empire. To take one example: it is only very recently that we have dared imagine that we could export elaborately transformed manufactures. Earlier, in the modest colonial mode, the best we could imagine for our manufacturing industries was that they should provide jobs and replace imports. In the same way we have been slow in recognising new kinds of success—the almost unique success of our multicultural policy, for example.

In this we might well ask: how does remaining a monarchy help in the critically important task of defining our own problems and our own opportunities so that we can develop a distinctively Australian sense of self interest, concentrating attention on the Australia of the 1990s? One of the things that matters most about the republican debate is that it is a way of understanding new Australian potential. We need new stories of success.

What we do not need is empty chauvinist boasting. The kind of conservatism I am thinking about, based on the recognition that accommodating to change is an essential part of a conservative program and that diversity within a society is essential for those changes to occur peacefully, can regard with coolness any kind of nationalist tub-thumping. The 'nation' state, the ethnically defined state, was an invention of the nineteenth century, when all kinds of ethnicities were fabricated to dominate the emerging public cultures of each of these 'nations' as if the state were a clan or a tribe. The only form of tribalism that Australians could credibly engage in was being 'British'. Apart from fragments of 'Britishness' left among the royalists, we have gone beyond that.

We must not invent some monster of our own. We must instead use our luck in this regard, in being demonstrably and declaredly of a multi-ethnic mix and show the world how to be a state without being a 'nation', how to provide a civic definition of ourselves as a commonwealth in a way that provides for some unity in our beliefs as citizens while allowing also for our diversities.

In these processes, we must hope that the right civic leadership emerges from among us. That means that republicans should adopt a civic rather than a nationalist stance and that constitutional monarchists (as distinguished from sentimental royalists) should face up to civic issues with which they might find they are very largely in agreement. Radicals of both right and left may never take an interest in this issue, because it can seem too mild, but conservatives can act properly as conservatives, raising doubts, but not engaging in irrational scare campaigns. We have a chance of being part of one of those great unfolding events in which people discuss their future among themselves, trying out this, trying out that, until one of the miracles of a democratic society occurs in which they have found a new way of seeing themselves, a new consensus.

A History of the Inevitable Republic

*Mark McKenna**

> The independence of the Australian colonies is not a mere abstract idea. It is certainly approaching as is the dawn of tomorrow's sun.
> *The Peoples Advocate*, 17 June 1854.

The history of republicanism in Australia is the history of an imagined destiny. The Australian republic is a two century old dream not realised, the captive bird that waits patiently for the door of the cage to open. The idea of an inevitable republic has been so pervasive in Australian history that we could be forgiven for thinking the republic already existed—as if it were merely a matter of our inexorable movement towards some final republican station. The belief that an Australian republic is inevitable is the *raison d'etre* of the republican debate in the 1990s just as it was in the 1880s and 1850s. Inevitability is the shaky pillar upon which many Australians have rested their case for the declaration of a republic. Declaring the inevitability of an event is obviously one way in which human beings legitimise their beliefs. Proponents of any number of political or religious creeds have employed the concept of inevitability to reassure the faithful of the rightness of their cause. Communism, democracy, anarchy, the second coming, doomsday and election victories have all been seen as inevitable at one time or another.

When we say 'it is inevitable' we express our conviction that there is no response to a particular set of circumstances other than the steady progress of a certain train of events. In the case of the inevitable Australian republic, the set of circumstances to which we respond is largely historical. Australians of all political persuasions have long perceived the eventual destiny of their country as republican. Where they have differed is on the question of the appropriate time for the republic's declaration rather than the reality

---

* Historian, University of New South Wales.

of its coming.[1] Consequently, the current noises about the inevitability of a republic are nothing more than subtle variations on a theme which is two hundred years old.

This paper is an attempt to reveal the long history of Australians' belief in an inevitable republic and to explain the historical conditions of European settlement in Australia which have laid the foundation for that belief. Finally, the paper argues that the notion of inevitability has been, and still remains, one of the greatest hindrances to the declaration of an Australian republic. For contemporary republicans, like their nineteenth century antecedents, protestations of republican inevitability have been too often assumed and too little understood.

Historical Determinism

> The universal republic must come
> Alfred Deakin, *Notebook*, 21 October 1888.[2]

One of the most pervasive beliefs which British migrants carried to Australia in the nineteenth century was the notion of individual, social and economic progress. In a New World environment, this fundamental enlightenment and faith in human progress was held even more fervently, and it permeated all levels of colonial society.

In 1832, Horatio Wills, editor of *The Currency Lad*, Australia's first newspaper devoted specifically to the interests of the native born, articulated the optimistic faith in human advancement which typified the age in which he lived:

> Distinctions are levelled with the dust, man approaches nearer to his fellow man and government must eventually unbend to the wisdom of the age. The intellect of man in the last century has become wonderfully enlightened ... The era is fast approaching when everyone shall receive according to the benefits he may confer upon society. When the sword shall be turned into the pruning hook and every man shall repose under the shade of his own fig tree; an era when the whole world shall rest on the broad and universal wings of republicanism.[3]

Will's conviction that a new and enlightened age was imminent was also shared by the elite of colonial society. Robert Dixon's *Course Of Empire* (1986) methodically documents the 'Enlightenment myths of social and economic progress which dominated the art and literature of colonial society'.[4] Dixon places particular emphasis on the ideas of the Scottish enlightenment: 'To survey the catalogues of Australian libraries of the 1830s is to realise the massive impact of

Scottish thought on colonial culture. Adam Smith's *Inquiry Into The Nature And Cause Of The Wealth Of Nations* appears at least once in every library catalogue'.[5] For Adam Smith, and for many of his contemporaries, the gradual progression of human society to the commercial state was indisputable, so much so that it 'acquired the force of natural law'.[6] In a similar fashion, as Eric Hobsbawn has pointed out, the idea that human societies moved methodically towards more advanced states was also reflected in the concept of 'nation'. From 1830 to 1870 says Hobsbawn, 'it was accepted in theory that social evolution expanded the scale of human social units from family and tribe to country and canton, from the local to the regional, the national and eventually the global. ... Thus in the perspective of liberal ideology the nation (that is, the viable large nation) was the stage of evolution reached in the mid-nineteenth century'.[7] The belief that history marched to pre-ordained laws was also evident in the public understanding of popular histories such as George Bancroft's *History Of The United States* published in 1837. American history was often seen as dividing neatly into three periods. The colonial, the revolutionary and the national or republican.[8] In Europe, the same perception of history was evident in Lamaritine's *Circular To The Diplomatic Agents Of The French Republic Of 1848* —a document frequently quoted by the Australian republican John Dunmore Lang. Lamaritine wrote that 'governments like individuals, have their different ages, the principles which govern them have their successive phases. Monarchical, Aristocratic, Constitutional and Republican governments are the expression of different degrees of maturity in the genius of the people'.[9]

The belief that republicanism was 'the inevitable future of all nations'[10] was also fuelled by the conviction that democracy was inevitable. The evolution of human societies in Europe and America to what Adam Smith had referred as the commercial state, encouraged the view that governments should also evolve to a state commensurate with the smooth functioning of commercial principles. Thomas Paine, for example, insisted that government must be contemporary:

> The older they are the less correspondence they can have with the present state of things. Time and change of circumstances and opinions, have the same progressive effect in rendering modes of government obsolete as they have upon customs and manners.[11]

Equally for Alexis de Tocqueville there was no alternative to the spread of democratic government. After his extensive travels in the

American republic de Tocqueville remarked, 'Can it be believed that the democracy which has overthrown the feudal system and vanquished kings will retreat before tradesmen and capitalists? The gradual development of the principle of equality is a providential fact'.[12] In the Australian colonies, where there was no established aristocracy or clergy, the perception that Australian society was naturally democratic quickly encouraged the belief that republicanism was the only logical form of government for the colonies.

Some of the most widely read authors in Australia in the 1880s and 1890s, such as the Americans Henry George, Edward Bellamy and Laurence Grönlund, also saw history as a predictable movement towards a Utopian socialist state. Edward Bellamy in his futuristic novel *Looking Backward* published in 1888, took up Henry George's call to bring about the coming 'Golden Age—the city of God on Earth'.[13] In the *Cooperative Commonwealth,* Laurence Grönlund spoke of the coming socialist stage not as 'a class movement but a growth of the whole body politic'. 'Socialism', said Grönlund, was 'inevitably the next stage of development'.[14] Much of the republicanism sentiment in late nineteenth century Australia drew inspiration from these writers. As New South Wales republican, Thomas Walker MP, said in 1888 'the good ship of republican thought' was inevitably sailing towards the Australian colonies and there was little that could be done to stop it.[15]

What the above evidence demonstrates is that the bedrock of the belief in the inevitability of an Australian republic was historical determinism. Because it was a widely accepted view in Australia that all societies moved gradually along a linear plane of development from primitive to more advanced states, it was hardly surprising that Australians should perceive their inevitable destiny as republican at a time when there was no identifiable mid-point between colonial dependence and republican independence. Notions of inevitability applied to a range of human activities in nineteenth century Australia and in this light declarations of republican inevitability were very much a part of mainstream political thought. It is not that republican futures were the only vision of Australia's destiny, but it is time to acknowledge that they co-existed and at times intermingled with other more imperial visions of Australia's future.

Perhaps the most interesting characteristic of the language which republicans used to articulate their belief in the inevitability of a republic was its certainty. Australia's republican destiny was frequently elevated beyond the realm of disputation until it acquired the status of an incontrovertible truth. *The People's Advocate* provided a perfect example in 1853:

> For the progress and ultimate triumph of republicanism let no man fear. Republicanism is truth, truth in politics and society with her right divine ... as demonstrable as the truth of geometry.[16]

Thirty years later *The Bulletin* passed a similar comment when it proclaimed that separation would come 'in deference to a law as inexorable as multiplication'.[17] Even politicians who were not identifiably pro-republican asserted that Australians had no choice about the coming republic. Speaking in 1884, one time Premier of Queensland, John Douglas, remarked that: 'The Australian people, even if they may wish to struggle against it, must some day accept their absolute independence not only as a duty but as a necessity'.[18] Charles Harpur, the republican poet of the 1850s, also saw the republic as the 'great Finality of the Future'.[19] For John Dunmore Lang the eventual introduction of republican government in Australia was a 'matter of course a settled point',[20] while his colleague Daniel Deniehy claimed that Australia 'could only develop itself into a republic'.[21] The certainty of republicans was also reflected in their choice of metaphors. The coming republic was often depicted as the sun rising or fruit ripening.[22] This self same certainty concerning the inevitability of a republic is still evident in the contemporary debate. Republicans of the 1990s are just as certain as their compatriots in the nineteenth century that the republic is unstoppable. In February 1992 *The Age* spoke of an 'inevitable historical evolution' towards republicanism in Australia.[23] One month later the *Financial Review* referred to 'the inevitable drift of history' which was leading Australia towards a republic.[24] Writing in *The Australian*, Greg Sheridan warned readers that the process of historical evolution was almost complete and that they 'should face the inevitable—the coming republic'.[25]

Our belief that the wheels of history are pushing Australia steadily towards a republic has been expressed with such certainty that we have been seduced into thinking the republic will come of its own accord.

The Connection

> The day of separation will unquestionably arrive. Could any sane man believe that this country can long remain a dependency of the Empire; a mere perquisite of the British Crown? *The Argus*, 1853.

During the early colonial period Australia was an amorphous collection of isolated British communities. Each colony possessed a distinct relationship with its imperial overlords in London. For much of this time the colonies were governed in a manner similar to the colonies of any Empire. Imperial Governors were posted to outlying possessions of the British Empire where they ruled as autocrats on instructions from the Colonial Office. The relationship between imperial overlords and colonial subordinates necessitated the use of unique forms of political language to accurately describe the novelties of the imperial world.

First and foremost, the imperial relationship included the notion of a 'connection' between coloniser and colony. Long after autocratic rule in the colonies had given way to self-government and federation, this 'connection', which was variously described as a link, thread, tie, chain or apron string, continued to occupy a central place in Australia's political and social culture.

For the last two centuries, the most commonly employed metaphor to describe the 'connection' has been the filial one. It is impossible to overstate the importance of the filial metaphor as it has frequently been the only metaphorical cage used by the British and Australian people to describe their relationship. In 1852, John Dunmore Lang offered a perfect example:

> As every human being who attains maturity of age must pass through the three stages of infancy, youth and manhood, so must every colony: and as the infant must be nourished and cherished, and the youth guided and governed by his parents, so must the colony. But there is a time when the youth is no longer to be *under tutors and governors* ... Now I maintain that there is, in like manner; a time for every colony and especially a group of colonies, to attain their majority, so to speak, and to guide and govern themselves henceforward.[26]

For Lang, the fact that colonies must eventually become sovereign and independent communities was 'an ordinance from God'. In a similar fashion the popular press in nineteenth century Australia frequently personified the colonies as infants undergoing a process of maturation which would end in republican independence.[27] While nineteenth century republicans underestimated the English genius for compromise, the use of the filial metaphor has continued into the late twentieth century despite the fact that Australia is now a fully independent country—at least practically if not symbolically. The charter of the Australian Republican Movement calls on Australia to 'assume its full maturity' and demonstrate that 'we are taking our destiny into our own hands'.[28] At the launch of the Movement in July 1991, chairperson Thomas Keneally spoke of a republic as 'an important growing up process for Australia' which was 'inevitable'.[29] In July 1992, Thomas Keneally addressed the National Press Club in Canberra and repeatedly compared Australia to a 'child leaving home'. His rhetoric was not dissimilar to that used by John Dunmore Lang in 1853.[30]

If Thomas Keneally is right, then Australia has been forced to endure a puberty of one hundred and fifty years. Nonetheless, the persistent repetition of the filial metaphor has done much to ensure that the traditional image of Australia as a colony has not disappeared. In turn, it reminds us that 'the connection' is still to be broken. Thus, we wait for the last thread to tear, for that moment when the laws of history will finally separate us from our colonial past. To bolster this belief, Australians have usually turned to one of the five supporting arguments listed below:

- The historical example of America;
- The perception that Australia is a New World society;
- The rise of a distinct national identity in Australia;
- The gradual emergence of different economic and geo-political interests;
- The passing of time, which will inevitably lead to final separation.

America and The New World

> The day is not far distant when America will have the pleasure of hailing Australia as the latest born and next to herself, the greatest of republics.
> *New York Herald*, 1852[31]

By far the greatest contributor to the nineteenth century belief that the Australian colonies would eventually sever the connection with Great Britain was the historical example of the United States. The image of a prosperous and democratic American republic had always loomed large in the Australian colonial mind. The American *Declaration of Independence* in 1776 proved to be a watershed in colonial relations. Long before Phillip arrived at Sydney Cove in 1788, the possibility that the colonies in the Antipodes would be forced to make war to gain their independence had markedly diminished. The British would never forget the loss of the American colonies and Australian colonists would never tire of reminding them.[32] The American experience demonstrated that aggrieved colonies could reject imperial rule and prosper independently of their former rulers, while American republican government quickly became the paradigmatic vision of colonial development. America's size, British origins and flourishing democracy endeared it to Australians as the society most analogous to their own.[33] More than anything else, America demonstrated that complete independence could be attained only after complete separation from the mother country, an historical precedent with a legacy still identifiable in late twentieth century republicanism in Australia.[34]

Before the colonies were granted self-government in 1856, it was often assumed that Australia would follow in the footsteps of the United States. As John Dunmore Lang observed in 1837:

> It is natural that Australia should look upon the United States with more than ordinary interest. Throughout the whole of her history there are certain broad features bearing no imaginary resemblance to our own. America was once a British dependency, as Australia is now. America receives her language, her manners, her literature and the germ of her laws and political institutions from the British Isles, so also has Australia. America at length outgrew the trammels of national juvenility and asserted her prerogative of matured manhood which she in the end compelled her reluctant parent to acknowledge. It is perfectly consistent with loyalty and with common sense to predict that at some future period —far distant no doubt it is—Australia will pursue a similar course with similar success.[35]

Lang's confidence in the future Australian republic was also encouraged by a British press and colonial office which believed for most of the nineteenth century that the Australian colonies, like America, would separate and become independent communities.[36] Predictions of separation citing the American example were commonplace in both Britain and Australia. Yet the desire of Australian colonists to emulate America did not always extend to complete independence. On many occasions Australians imagined their future republic safe under the watchful eyes of the United States. The protection of England would be exchanged for the protection of the United States. As *The [Launceston] Examiner* suggested in 1851:

> Sooner or later these settlements will become an independent confederation or seek shelter under the wing of the American eagle. America must become the first nation on earth and as the nearest most powerful and most enlightened state—Australia, if not strong enough to stand alone would naturally flee to the United States for protection.[37]

The powerful image of a democratic American republic continued to be felt in Australia well into the late nineteenth century, despite the fact that a degree of self-government had been granted to the Australian colonies in 1856 under the imperial umbrella. As one member of the New South Wales Parliament said in 1888:

> We have only to look to the history of America for the last 100 years to see the future history of Australia. For, as sure as we are now upon the floor of this house there will be a republican government within Australia in the next twenty to thirty years.[38]

Much of the affinity Australians felt for the American republic stemmed from their identification with America as a fellow New World society. Australia, like America, was frequently perceived as the breeding ground for a new and enlightened society which would naturally sever the connection with the Old World which was corrupted by 'monarchy ... well fed female faineants and able bodied male loafers'.[39] Monarchy, according to *The [Brisbane] Boomerang*, was a 'remnant of barbarism'.[40] Republicans believed that Australia's egalitarian character necessitated separation from the class ridden society of Britain. The laws of history dictated that the age of Kings, Lords and aristocratic toadies was about to end. It was *The [Brisbane] Boomerang* again which put it best in 1890:

> The era of self-government—government of the people by the people and for the people ... is beyond doubt. The marvellous success of the American republic, the gradual purification of its institutions and its growing stability amongst the falling thrones of the Old World has proved ... that Kings, Lords and State Churches are excrescences and not necessary to a country's welfare.[41]

It is probably in this area that the residual influence of the American republic is most often felt in the current republican debate. While America's influence was most obvious in the nineteenth century, it was a model which helped to shape Australians' perception of their own society as one which was fundamentally different from the Old World. This perception still drives much of the republican rhetoric in the 1990s. Republicans frequently argue that the connection with England should be severed because Australia needs to be 'born again' and assert its naturally democratic character by rejecting the last vestiges of the Old World.[42] In February 1992, *The West Australian* put the case simply:

We will be better off ... a fully independent forward thinking nation, rather than one that clings to a colonial past and notions of being European.[43]

The Canberra Times said likewise, but just a touch more eloquently, on the same day:

> Australia is a vibrant young multicultural nation of the Pacific rim. It is a community with a fervent belief in the egalitarian ideal. As such, it is incongruous, not to say ludicrous, that it perpetuates the notion through its head of state that some people are superior to others simply by reasons of birth ... That is not the Australian way or perhaps more correctly the Australian aspiration.[44]

So the republic is inevitable. England is old, class ridden and steeped in antiquated traditions. Australia is young, egalitarian and forward looking: a choice between the past and the future, youth and old age, tradition and invention. So it has been for two hundred years.

Natives, Nations and the National Interest

> The inevitable destiny of Australia is separation from Great Britain ... The majority of the Australian born are nationalists and the Australian born are going to shape and control the destiny of the Australian colonies.
>
> *The Australian Star*, 1888[45]

In 1832, when Horatio Wills argued that the rising numbers of native born Australians would carry the 'buoyant spirit of independence' he was one of the first Australians to tie the inevitable increase of the native born to inevitable separation from Britain.[46] Throughout the nineteenth century those who took up *The Bulletin's* cry of 'Australia for the Australians' readily assumed that the inevitable republic would ride on the back of the native born Australian.[47] In July 1888, a letter from Wagga to *The [Newcastle] Radical* explained:

> Just ask any Australian boy or girl what he or she thinks of the institutions of monarchy ... The rising generation of Australia are natural republicans and are only too ready to imbibe radical notions ... No one will ever stop the spread of anti-monarchical sentiment in these colonies.[48]

Although more than sixty-five per cent of the Australian population were native born in 1888, there was little evidence that such Australians were about to break away from Britain.[49] One of the fundamental flaws in the theory that a republic would come with a predominantly native born population was that the native born grew up in a culture which worshipped Britain, imperialism and the

Monarch. Instead of encouraging a republic, this culture tended to foster an inherent duality in Australian nationalism wherein loyalty to Australia and loyalty to Britain co-existed. Underlying republican claims of inevitability has been the assumption that these two loyalties must eventually disconnect, that loyalty to Australia cannot forever include a shared loyalty to England.

The nineteenth century faith in the native born as the flag bearers of the republic gave way in the twentieth century to an emphasis on 'youth' and the multicultural composition of Australian society. Essentially the argument was still demographic, it had simply shifted focus to suit the prevailing ideological fashion. Since the dismissal of Prime Minister Gough Whitlam in November 1975, youth and multiculturalism have been two of the mainstays of republican inevitability. Speaking at a republican rally in Sydney Town Hall in 1976, Franca Arena reminded the audience that an oath of allegiance to the British Queen was no longer appropriate for new immigrants and added: 'Three-quarters of the total population of Australia is now under twenty-five years of age. Young people are just not interested in Kings and Queens'.[50] More recently, the *Sydney Morning Herald* offered much the same reasons to support the inevitability of a republic. 'It is precisely the issue of national identity that makes an Australian republic inevitable. For most young Australians and for most of that growing number of citizens whose heritage is not British, the monarchy is an object of neither affection, awe nor symbolic power.'[51] While it may well be true that Australia's youth are predominantly pro-republican according to the polls, and Australia's multi-ethnic composition is undeniable, republicans have often overlooked the fact that these factors do not necessarily translate into a republican vote in the heated context of a national referendum. Achieving bi-partisan support for a republic for example, would contribute much more to the inevitability of a republic than merely relying on assumptions about the voting behaviour of a future electorate.

Emphasis on youth and multiculturalism are not in themselves arguments for a republic unless they are extended beyond statistical observations of demographic change.[52] One religious journal published in Melbourne in the 1880s was able to argue for a republic by using multiculturalism in a manner which demonstrates that not all late nineteenth century republicans conformed to *The Bulletin* stereotype. It might also offer an example of the real challenge facing republicans in the 1990s.

> We cannot think that Australia can ever be a nation in the old sense of the word. We are of all languages tribes kindreds and creeds here. The conditions are altogether new. The history which has made the European nations can never be ours. Australia as an independent country will never probably be a monarchy ... Its form of government ... will more likely be of a local, home rule or republican character.[53]

The idea that Australia would one day cease to be British to the bootstraps, either by becoming a nation of native born republicans, or by young republicans growing to a majority, or non-Anglo republicans with no emotional ties to Britain, has helped to sustain the myth of inevitability.

Highlighting demographic change has always been one way for republicans to assert that Australian national identity will gradually cease to draw its ethos from Britain. Linked to this has been the idea that Australia's economic and geo-political interests will increasingly diverge from those of Britain. Thus the republic becomes inevitable because of Britain's increasing irrelevance to Australia's national interest. In the late nineteenth century, during the rise of a new age of imperialism in Europe, the perception that Australia's interests were not those of Britain, especially in the areas of foreign policy and defence, helped to encourage the notion that a republic might be inevitable. In 1888, *The [Melbourne] Age* articulated the case for separation by employing the same arguments John Dunmore Lang had used with so little success in the 1850s:[54]

> So far indeed, from receiving any commercial advantages from the English connection it would not be difficult to show that commercially speaking the colonies would be better off without it, for as long as we are involved in the wars of the Empire we shall be exposed to the risks and interruptions of trade which they inevitably bring in their train. Pecuniarily speaking it may be doubted whether separation would not be ultimately the most profitable policy for all parties. The mother country would then be spared the expense of defending the colonies and the colonies would not be put to the trouble of defending themselves.[55]

This dream of an isolationist republic, safe from entanglement in imperial war, was flatly rejected when the colonies federated in 1901, but it was still the first example of Australians imagining an inevitable republic on the basis of specific national interest.[56] It was not until the 1960s that republicans resurrected this argument. Under Donald Horne's editorship, *The Bulletin* ran a series of articles on Australia's relationship with Britain. Here was a detailed explanation of Australia's diverging interests in defence, trade and foreign policy which attempted to prove that Australia's relations with Britain were in 'gentle decline'. Headlines like 'BRITAIN—THE END OF THE AFFAIR' implicitly suggested the inevitability of a republic.[57]

More recently, republicans of the early 1990s have also shown a fondness for emphasising the necessity and inevitability of a republic on the grounds that Australia's national interest is no longer compatible with the British connection. Usually, this has been achieved by drawing attention to Australia's economic and political interests in the Asian region. Alternatively, republicans stress that the Queen is 'foreign', 'distant' or an irrelevant British emissary.[58] Putting any analysis of the merit of these ideas aside their function is clear. By stressing the differences between Australian and British interests, republicans hope to build an image of the present Constitution as incongruous and inappropriate for Australia in the late twentieth century. The republic is therefore inevitable because it is believed that there must be an alignment of Australia's constitutional system with the contemporary reality of national interest and wider public culture. In the words of *The West Australian*:

> It is inevitable that Australia will one day shed its final constitutional links with Britain ... One of the few certainties of the next century is that Australia will have to find its destiny as an active and equal participant in the growth of the Asia Pacific region ... Our security and prosperity will depend on pragmatic trade and political relationships rather than continued links with the Commonwealth.[59]

Then there is Paul Keating speaking at Corowa in July 1993:

> Read in 1993, it [the Constitution] is an uninspired and uninspiring document complex legalistic and virtually impossible to relate to contemporary Australian life ... our Constitution should be one made to reflect our national values and aspirations, evoke pride in our Australian heritage and confidence in our future and help to unite us as a nation.[60]

Finally, writing in *The Australian* after the release of the Republic Advisory Committee's Report in October 1993, historian John Hirst stressed the 'absurdity' of Australia maintaining the Queen of England as its Head of State:

> As the other reasons for keeping the monarch weaken, the contradiction between what the Queen is and what Australia is becomes more glaring. Here is democratic egalitarian Australia maintaining a hereditary head of state. A land which early separated Church and State accepts that its monarch will head the Anglican Church and that she cannot become a Catholic. Is this the best symbol we can get of the Australian nation?[61]

While this is probably the most cogent case for a republic, it is important not to forget that the British connection has seemed incongruent, unnecessary and inevitably doomed for a good many years before the present republican debate—and to little avail.

In 1885 *The Bulletin* believed an Australian republic inevitable and suggested that it was absurd to propose that Australia could remain connected to the Empire. Three years later, in the year of the Centenary, Brisbane's *Courier Mail* remarked that the British connection was becoming 'more and more illogical and indefensible'.[62] The British connection has always seemed illogical, incongruent, absurd, anachronistic and irrelevant as an indefinite proposition, yet it has also proved remarkably adaptable and resilient. Many republicans would not have imagined the degree of self-government achieved in 1856 by the Australian colonies as being possible without separation. Others who looked forward to federation as the occasion for republican independence would have been equally disappointed.[63] As the English observer, J.A. Froude, remarked in the 1880s the English realised very quickly 'that a slack chain is less easily broken than a tight one'.[64]

In March 1992, Greg Sheridan listed the 'grotesqueries' of Australia's constitutional history in a tone of amazement:

> We have an Australian monarch who does not live in Australia and is not seen by anybody else in the world to represent us. We do not have a head of State who can play any part in promoting Australia abroad. We have a monarchical system in which the monarch plays no part. We have a flag, the chief purpose of which is to identify the country, which cannot be distinguished from the flags of half-a-dozen other countries. The governor-general is effectively appointed by the prime minister and enjoys far greater powers in Australia than does the Queen in Britain.[65]

To acknowledge the 'absurdity' of the above is to realise that historically speaking 'incongruity' in Australia's constitutional arrangements has not provoked a welling tide for change. However, there is no doubt that the number of Australians who believe that the British Monarch is not an appropriate Head of State for Australia is now greater than at any other time in our history. The chameleon like performance of the 'connection' may finally have exhausted all its options.

Time: The End of the Inevitable Republic

> This colony must sooner or later become independent.
>
> Maurice Margarott, 1804.[66]

> That the colonies generally and Australia especially, will in the nature of things and in submission to the organic laws of historical development become independent nations is doubted by few in England and least of all by the British government.
>
> *The Argus*, 20 December 1853.[67]

> In 1988 the Australian Federal Republic will be mistress not only of her own continent but of the whole Eastern Archipelago.
>
> *The Spectator*, London 1888.[68]

> The Australian republic will come—perhaps within the decade.
>
> Donald Horne, 1976.[69]

> It is not a question of *if* there will be an Australian republic but when.
>
> Gough Whitlam, 1977.[70]

For two hundred years the passing of time has been the *raison d'etre* of the inevitable Australian republic. We have never doubted that the day will finally come when we will sever the last gossamer thread that binds Australia to Britain. Either we will assert our independence or the British Monarchy will totter off into oblivion.

What will be demonstrated in the final part of this paper is that the idea of an inevitable republic has been the Achilles heel of republicanism in Australia. In a very real sense, the river of inevitability has run its course. Proclaiming the inevitability of a republic has ceased to be of any utility. Metaphors which speak of Australia maturing, ripening, rising or flowering are no longer enough to sustain the republican debate. It is suggested that those who support the declaration of an Australian republic would do best to dispense with the notion of inevitability and concentrate on demonstrating why Australia needs to become a republic.

Historically speaking, inevitability has been one of the primary reasons for the postponement of an Australian republic. What many republicans have failed to realise is that the inevitable republic has not only been the cry of republicans but also of anti-republicans. By agreeing that the republic is inevitable but insisting that the time is not yet ripe, anti-republicans have been able to successfully delay the declaration of an Australian republic. John Dunmore Lang touched on this point as early as 1850 when he delivered his 'Coming Event' lectures in Sydney:

> It is universally admitted that there must ultimately be a time for the separation of a colony or group of colonies from the parent state. "But

nobody surely" it will be added, "can be mad enough to suppose that the time has come yet! Wait a while longer by all means, it is only a question of time." This question of time is just the point upon which the whole case turns.[71]

Lang was well aware that the concept of inevitability naturally lent itself to metaphors of maturation which could be eternally delayed. For Australians who have supported the maintenance of the British connection the time for a republic has always been in the distant future. The *Sydney Morning Herald* articulated this argument as early as 1833:

> This country will at some distant day be independent. It is decreed by the nature of things that she shall cut the apron strings. But what man in his senses would hold language of independence and open defiance at this moment ... ?[72]

In 1853, when the New South Wales Legislative Council was debating William Wentworth's controversial Constitution Bill, many of the councillors avoided discussion on the issue of a republic by claiming that a republic was a question for 'a future age'. Even the champion of the bunyip aristocracy, William Wentworth, told the House that 'in the long run Australia would become a republic'.[73] Similar statements can be found in the years before Federation. When Australia celebrated the Centenary of Settlement in 1888, talk of a republic was often deemed to be 'premature'.[74] The effectiveness of this approach has not been lost on anti-republicans in the 1990s. Writing in *The Bulletin* in late 1992, David McNicoll offered a perfect example of blue blood strategy in the republican debate:

> Anyone with any common sense knows that eventually Australia will become a republic. What I and many others object to is the effort by Horne and others to pressure cook it to their requirements ... It is sad to read of the hard times overtaking the automobile division of Rolls Royce ... There is a magic about the Roller which no other car maker was ever able to match.[75]

In one way McNicoll's Rolls Royce republicanism is extremely shrewd. It allows anti-republicans the luxury of appearing to be sympathetic to a republican perpetuity, while at the same time keeping the republic at bay. Thus, inevitability is one of the building blocks of the republic '*sine die*' (without naming a day). One of the greatest mistakes of republicans, throughout Australian history has been their reliance on historical determinism. By relying on the laws of historical development to usher in the republic, republicans have left themselves vulnerable to counter arguments that the wheels of history have not yet completed their inevitable journey. In this way inevitability has often been used to push republicanism off the political agenda. To use a Joycean image, this has meant that the Australian republic has always been in waiting—an event for the 'not so far distant day'.[76]

Another significant effect of Australians' belief in the inevitability of a republic has been the fostering of a complacent and often uninspiring republican language. Talk of an inevitable republic has saturated the historical debate to such an extent that much republican rhetoric is lacking in any sense of urgency. It has been too often assumed that the republic will eventuate simply by osmosis—as if republicans in Australia merely had to sit like 'Norm' and wait for the republic to appear. In turn, this has encouraged a lack of involvement on the part of the Australian people. It is difficult to see a sense of struggle in something which is inevitably going to happen. There have been no martyrs for an inevitable cause. Consequently, every time republicans have relied on the concept of inevitability to legitimise their support for a republic they have provided Australians with one more reason not to participate in the republican debate. Declaring the inevitability of a republic is an invitation to see political change as a spectator sport.

As far back as 1851, John Dunmore Lang was forced to reassure the colonists of New South Wales that he did not wish the move to a republic to be brought too suddenly or by a '*coup de main*'.[77] Like many present day republicans, Lang went to extreme lengths to show that the republic would come 'without a single cry on the part of the parent or the slightest struggle on the part of the child'.[78] Yet it is precisely this sense of struggle which is conducive to political success. Our affection for Britain has always prevented us from pressing the point, and unfortunately, we have always had the inevitability of it all to fall back on when things seemed to be getting too difficult.

When Malcolm Turnbull addressed the National Press Club after the release of the Republic Advisory Committee's Report on 5 October 1993, he acknowledged the difficulties that any republican proposals would have in achieving success at a referendum. Yet unwittingly, he did so in a manner not dissimilar to many republicans before him. 'No one would argue that Australia would not be a republic by 2101. If it is to occur by 2001 its supporters will have to fight hard.'[79] Turnbull acknowledged the difficulty of achieving a republic by 2001 and wisely stressed the need for active participation.

What was mystifying, however, was the fall back on the inevitability card, the very delusion that has sustained a lack of urgency and encouraged a false sense of posthumous fulfilment amongst republicans for one hundred and fifty years—1888, 1901, 1988, 2001 and now 2101. Surely the republic will be inevitable by 3001! So far as the current debate is concerned it has simply ceased to matter whether Australia will be a republic one hundred or two thousand years hence. The mere mention of a republic in the context of distant futures tends to discourage the emergence of the very fight which Malcolm Turnbull desires.

In 1851, *The [Launceston] Examiner* had some useful advice for republicans in the 1990s:

> It is right and proper to contemplate what seems to be inevitable though many who now resolve the subject in their minds will mingle in the dust before the question is brought to a practical issue.[80]

If the current crop of republicans does not wish to have mingled in the dust by the time the Australian Republic is declared, it is essential that the inevitable republic be put to rest. There is nothing more to be gained by saying, 'It is inevitable'. Instead, there should be only assertions of why Australia should be a republic and only one date in mind—2001.

Notes

1. See especially E. Sylvester, 'The NSW Constitution Bill' the speeches of the Legislative Council (York Street, Sydney: Thomas Daniel, 1853).
2. Alfred Deakin, Private Papers, Australian National Library, Series 3—Notebooks and General Manuscripts Box 12.
3. *The Currency Lad* (5 January 1832).
4. R. Dixon, *The Course of Empire* (Melbourne: Oxford University Press, 1986), 5.
5. *Id.* 2.
6. *Id.* 1.
7. E. Hobsbawn, *Nations and Nationalism Since 1780* (Cambridge: Cambridge University Press, 1990), 33, 39.
8. See *The Empire* (20 December 1853) for comments regarding Prescott's essay on Bancroft's history.
9. Quoted by J.D. Lang, *Freedom And Independence For The Golden Lands Of Australia* (Sydney: F. Cunninghame, 1857), 22.
10. The phase is Victor Hugo's, *id.* 318. Democracy and republicanism were often seen as synonymous in the first half of the 19th century.

11. T. Paine, *Common Sense* (Harmondsworth: Penguin, 1986), 49.
12. A. de Tocqueville, *Democracy In America* (London: Longman, Green, Longman & Roberts, 1862), 7.
13. E. Bellamy, *Looking Backward* (Harmondsworth: Penguin, 1987). See the Introduction by Cecila Tichi, 18.
14. L. Grönlund, *The Co-operative Commonwealth* (London: Swam, Sonnenschein, Le Bas and Lowrey, 1886), 105.
15. See Walker's speech in the NSW Legislative Assembly on 21 November 1888, NSW *Parliamentary Debates*, (First Session 1888-1889) Government Printer 1889, 583.
16. *The Peoples Advocate* (19 November 1853).
17. *The Bulletin* (18 August 1883). Also quoted in H. Hall, *Australia And England* (London: Longmans Green & Co., 1934), 90.
18. Quoted in Hall, *supra* note 17, 90.
19. M. Ackland (ed.), *Charles Harpus Selected Poetry And Prose* (Melbourne: Penguin, 1986), 26.
20. J.D. Lang quoted in K. Elford, 'J.D. Lang, Prophet Without Honour' (1968) 54 (2) *Journal Of The Royal Historical Society*, 164.
21. See D. Deniehy's lecture reported in *The Peoples Advocate* (18 March 1854), 4–5.
22. For 'the sun rising' see *The Peoples Advocate* (17 June 1854); *The Bulletin* (15 February 1890) 6; and several quotes at the beginning of Anonymous, *A Plea For Separation* (Sydney: G. Robertson, 1888). For fruit falling from the tree, see *The Argus* (30 December 1853) 4; *The Bulletin* (editorial, 9 August 1884).
23. *The Age* (editorial, 26 February 1992).
24. The *Financial Review* (editorial, 6 March 1992).
25. *The Australian* (14 March 1992) 18. See also M. Steketee's article in the *Sydney Morning Herald* (18 April 1992): 'Australia's rush of republicanism has an air of certainty—more a case of when, rather than if'. In addition, see also the *Financial Review* (editorial headline, 23 March 1992): 'The relentless march of republicanism'. The *Financial Review* (6 March 1992), spoke of 'irresistible transition to fully fledged nationhood'. The *Sydney Morning Herald* (editorial 26 January 1994) 10 pronounced that Australia's national identity 'will now find expression in an Australian republic'. The best mid-nineteenth century example of this certainty is *The Argus* (30 December 1853) 4.
26. Lang, *supra* note 9, 22.
27. There are many examples of this particular metaphor but I will list only a few. See, for example, *The Radical* (7 May 1887) 50; Queensland *Parliamentary Debates* (8 August 1889) 1055; J.D. Lang, *The Coming Event* (Sydney: D.L. Welch, 1850); NSW *Parliamentary Debates*, vol. 43, (2nd ed. 1889) 462; *The Republican* (4 July 1887) 2; see also B. Mansfield, 'The Background To Radical Republicanism In NSW In

The 1880s' (1953) 5 (20) *Historical Studies* 344. Finally, see *Sydney Morning Herald* (26 January 1994) 10 'Australia quite simply has outgrown the monarchy as a child outgrows its old clothes'.
28. Charter of the Australian Republican Movement, (July 1991).
29. *The Sun Herald* (7 July 1991).
30. *The Australian* (16 July 1992) 5. Also see the last paragraph of Keneally's letter to *The Manly Daily* (10 September 1991). Compare Keneally's July 1992 statements at the National Press Club to Lang's *Freedom And Independence For The Golden Lands Of Australia*, supra note 9, 26.
31. The *New York Herald*, quoted in N. Noel McLachlan, *Waiting For The Revolution* (Harmondsworth: Penguin, 1989), 81.
32. The best example of the use of the American experience is Robert Lowe's speech at an anti-transportation meeting at Circular Quay on 11 June 1849. See *The Peoples Advocate* (16 June 1849) 4.
33. See N. McLachlan, 'A Future America' (1977) 17 *Historical Studies*, 361-383.
34. The platform of the Australian Republican Movement (1991) insists, for example, that Australia cannot be fully independent until the monarchical connection is severed.
35. Elford, *supra* note 20, 164.
36. See Hall, *supra* note 17, 72. Also see *The Argus* (31 March 1853); and F.W. Egglestone, *Cambridge History Of The Empire*, vol.7 Part 1 Chapter 17, (Cambridge University Press, 1988), 521.
37. *The Launceston Examiner* (11 March 1850) 156. Also see note 80.
38. NSW *Parliamentary Debates*, Legislative Assembly, First Series Session 1888-1889, vol.35, (21 November 1888) 589 (Mr Lyne).
39. *The Bulletin* (21 November 1885) 5.
40. *The Boomerang* (2 June 1888).
41. *The Boomerang* (25 January 1890) 6.
42. See J. Davidson, 'Countdown To The Republic' (April 1992) *Modern Times* 13.
43. *The West Australian* (22 February 1992).
44. *The Canberra Times* (22 February 1992).
45. *The Australian Star* (12 November 1888) 4.
46. *The Currency Lad* (8 September 1832).
47. *The Bulletin's* call 'Australia for the Australians' was first enunciated by G. Meudell in *The Melbourne Review* (1882) 315-324. Deniehy used it also. See *Goulburn Herald* 'The Forthcoming Elections' (20 October 1855).
48. *The Radical* (4 August 1888). Also see NSW *Parliamentary Debates* (May 1890, vol.44) 431.
49. J. Jupp, *The Australian People* (Sydney: Angus & Robertson, 1988), 70.

50. *Adelaide Advertiser* (20 September 1976) 4.
51. The *Sydney Morning Herald* (26 January 1994) 10.
52. See for example Hawke *The Sun Herald* (5 April 1992), and 'Youth Poll' in *Newcastle Herald* (13 September 1993). See also A. Wynn, 'The Republicans Are Coming', in G. Dutton, *Republican Australia* (Melbourne: Sun, 1977), 173.
53. *Our Good Words* (August 1888) 16 (a religious and social magazine, edited by the Reverend Charles Strong, Melbourne) Victorian State Library.
54. See Lang, *supra* note 9, 134–141.
55. See *a Plea For Separation*, *supra* note 22, introductory quotes.
56. Immigration was also a cause—especially Chinese immigration.
57. *The Bulletin* (8 April 1967) 22.
58. See *The West Australian* (22 February 1992). T. Keneally, unpublished speech to the National Press Club, 15 July 1992. See also A. Grassby, *The Australian Republic* (Sydney: Pluto Press, 1993), 263. Prime Minister P. Keating, H.V. Evatt Lecture—'New Visions For Australia' (28 April 1993) some of which is quoted in the *Sydney Morning Herald*, (29 April 1993).
59. The *West Australian* (22 Febrary 1993).
60. Unpublished speech by Paul Keating at the Corowa Shire Council Centenary Dinner, (31 July 1993, Corowa RSL Club).
61. J. Hirst, 'The Time Has Come To Manage On Our Own' *The Australian* (9 October 1993) 30, 34.
62. *The Bulletin* (28 November 1885) 1. See also *A Plea For Separation*, *supra* note 22, (Introductory pages) and J. Purves quoted in Hall, *supra* note 17, 6.
63. See examples in B. Wise, *The Making Of The Commonwealth* (London: Longmans, S. Green & Co., 1913), 45. Also G. Searle, *The Rush To Be Rich* (Melbourne: Melbourne University Press, 1971), 221–222.
64. J. Froude, *Oceana Or England And Her Colonies* (London: Longmans Green & Co., 1886), 227.
65. Sheridan, 'Our Inevitable Republic' *The Australian* (14 March 1992) 18.
66. *The Argus* (20 December 1853).
67. N. McLachlan, *Waiting For The Revolution* (Harmondsworth: Penguin, 1989), 43.
68. Quotes in the *Freeman's Journal* (17 March 1888).
69. Quotes in the *Adelaide Advertiser* (20 September 1976) 4.
70. Quotes in G. Dutton, *Republican Australia* (Melbourne: Sun, 1977) 7.
71. Quoted in A. Gilchrist (ed.), J.D. Lang, *Chiefly Autobiographical* (Melbourne: Jedgarm, 1951), 474.
72. The *Sydney Morning Herald* (March 1833).

73. Sylvester, *supra* note 1, 218. Wentworth believed the republic inevitable if elected Upper Houses were introduced in Australia.
74. See for example, *The Freeman's Journal* (30 June 1888), or J.L. Purves in *The [Adelaide] Advertiser* (11 April 1888).
75. *The Bulletin* (27 October 1992, 'Republicans are Pedalling Too Fast').
76. J. Joyce, *Ulysses* (Harmondsworth: Penguin, 1982), 163.
77. *The Empire* (13 February 1851) 20.
78. Lang, *supra* note 27.
79. M. Turnbull, unpublished speech to the National Press Club, Canberra on the occasion of the release of the Republic Advisory Committee's Report (5 October 1993).
80. *Launceston Examiner* (11 March 1850) 155. Also see 3 February 1853, 21 June 1851 and 27 March 1852.

'Mañana'—The Politics of Becoming a Republic

T. Abbott[*]

For an 'inevitable' event, the Australian republic has been a long time coming. There have been so many false dawns: from John Dunmore Lang and Daniel Deniehy in the middle of the last century, through the Bulletin nationalists and Labor radicals of the Federation era, Donald Horne's forecast of the imminent republic in 1964, the Dismissal republicans and the Bi-centenary republicans. Is Thomas Keneally more Australian than Henry Lawson; is Malcolm Turnbull a better advocate than William Lane? If not, why should today's 'tippex republicans' succeed where all their predecessors have failed?

Even the feeling that a republic is 'inevitable' is at least one hundred years old. A republic is 'inevitable' in much the same way that rich people 'inevitably' mix with other rich people; that businessmen 'inevitably' vote Liberal; and that politicians 'inevitably' fabricate. But why is it 'inevitable' that Australia follows India, Pakistan, South Africa, Fiji and Ireland in becoming a republic when republicanism has such ambiguous results? And if a republic is 'inevitable' why are republicans so anxious to force the pace? Surely nothing is inevitable in a democracy unless that is what the people actually decide.

The dynamics of politics, the logistical difficulty of change and, above all, the psychology of the issue mean that a republic will remain 'inevitable' but always unrealised. At times a distant dream, at times just around the corner; in the absence of some great redefining event such as a new Gallipoli, a republic will always be tomorrow's issue.

---

[*] Executive Director, Australians for Constitutional Monarchy.

Republicanism's Empty Heart

The argument for becoming a republic, that 'we will become a grown-up nation' has not changed for one hundred and fifty years. The resistance to that argument—that we are more or less pleased with our existing identity and proud of our Australian achievement—has always frustrated the republican plan.

Republicanism is one manifestation of the great Australian insecurity. From Donald Horne's exultation in things 'un-Australian',[1] through Thomas Keneally who concedes a time 'when it was every writer's sacred duty to be alienated by Australia—to be a European soul descended into this terrible place', to Paul Keating with his desire to put a 'knife into the heart of Menzies' creation',[2] leading republicans have subscribed to the 'black arm-band' view of Australian history: that our story comprises a litany of genocide and exploitation that ended with Whitlam's election in 1972—only to start again with his dismissal in 1975.

The story of the Australian Aborigines notwithstanding, Australia lacks an elaborated history from time immemorial. Unlike the Americans, we have never fought a colonial oppressor nor expiated in bloodshed a great evil such as slavery. For some Australians, it has been hard to feel proud of a country without an heroic dimension; and ever since Henry Lawson linked the fight against Royalty with 'blood on the wattle',[3] some Australians have equated republicanism with national redemption—as if Australia has ever needed to be redeemed.

There are exceptions, of course. But when womens' activist, Ann Sherry, declared that the first President should be a woman and that the republican movement was 'the tip of the iceberg of a widespread value shift' covering *Mabo*, anti-vilification law, equality before the law and social issues including the perception of women, a republic seemed transmuted into the Holy Grail of the '60s generation.[4]

The fundamental difficulty with the republican case is that it constitutes a none-too-subtle smear on Australia's history. If Australia can only be 'complete' as a republic, all the achievements of non-republican Australia are debased—the stories of the Gold Rush, Gallipoli, and the Cattle Kings become less relevant, in the way events B.C. are ancient history compared to events A.D.

Not surprisingly, few Australians warm to this idea of 'republic as culmination'. But what other reason is there to become a republic when it won't take a dollar off the debt, nor one person off the dole nor reconcile black and white Australia.

A serious, credible country, like a serious credible person, needs a clear and compelling reason for drastic change. People don't marry or divorce lightly. People don't change jobs, friends or clubs without a wrench. If becoming a republic would achieve any extra freedom, end any oppression, or remedy any injustice it should be considered urgently. Otherwise, it seems like trading in one's spouse for a better image.

It might be objected that this is just carping without a single positive argument for preserving the established Constitution. On the contrary, support for the existing Constitution stems from the highest ideals of honour, loyalty, respect and love.

It is not necessary to hearken to some 'golden age' to appreciate continuity and to resist frivolous change. As Barry Humphries recalls after meeting Percy Grainger in war-time Melbourne: 'I, a mere Melbourne schoolboy, had now shaken hands with the creator of The Magic Flute; for had not Percy shaken hands with Greig who had shaken hands with Liszt who had shaken hands with Beethoven who had shaken hands with Haydn, who had clasped the hands of Mozart?'[5] This is not the spirit of unyielding conservatism—rather it is humility in the face of greatness and acknowledgment that we owe almost everything to someone else.

Australia has but two hundred and five years of constitutional history yet the monarchy is a living link to one thousand years of political culture. Our Constitution arises from the interplay of great minds and great events. Our entire national life is the merest segment of our real history so how can an *ad hoc* committee—such as that chaired by Malcolm Turnbull—however brilliant, approach it without reverence and awe?

Anyone shaped by Australia owes a debt to the institutions which helped make the country and which helped form the person. No-one should be glad when something magnificent is destroyed and the most distressing aspect of the republican debate is its chief protagonists' sneering at our heritage.

At present, in the wake of the Turnbull Report,[6] republicans argue the need for a long education process so that more and more Australians understand our Constitution and the various options for change. This assumes that these matters are to be decided in the same manner as choosing one accounting system over another. However, even the choice of a car is never made on such a bloodless basis. The fact that the chief republicans now want seven years of 'education' leading, perhaps, to a referendum at the close of the decade either reveals their total misunderstanding of human nature or hides a crass political calculation that endless debate will bore voters into submission.

The passion to 'debate' these issues is not a sign of political strength nor cultural maturity. There must be a presumption in favour of our national institutions and symbols. Of course, that presumption can erode. But if so, the question must be resolved quickly because a credible country cannot long proceed undecided about itself. People in authority who are not prepared to change the system must support it. To denounce our system, and then to delay resolution into the political never-never, is to engage in a constitutional tease and to practise constitutional vandalism rather than reform.

Becoming a republic evokes fundamental questions about our very national being and arouses the sort of passions which make people enlist in the army or the Church. Yet nothing is forcing the asking of these questions nor stirring up these unpredictable passions. The Queen has not asked for a vote of confidence nor has her contract expired. The Prime Minister's demand that a decision is made by the centenary of Federation is as unnecessary and inappropriate as a youth's insistence on deciding whether to be a doctor or a politician by the age of eighteen.

It should be clear, therefore, that becoming a republic is not quite a managerial issue like reducing the national debt; neither is it a moral question like reconciliation with Aborigines. Hence, it cannot be resolved by the usual tools of politics—pragmatic reason and moral indignation—which help explain why the politics of this issue are so murky.

Why the Liberals will Never Back the Present Prime Minister's Republic

Most political issues can be resolved by legislation alone. So the constitutional question is unique. Unlike industry policy, *Mabo*, industrial relations and so on, it is singularly dependent upon the opinion of ordinary voters who alone can change the Constitution. The people, voting at a referendum, not the Government's forcing legislation through Parliament, will decide whether or not Australia remains a constitutional monarchy. Only people can determine whether the republic succeeds or remains just a gleam in the Prime Ministerial eye.

Contrary to myth, support for the monarchy has not steadily eroded over time. Polls showed remarkably persistent support for the monarchy at over sixty per cent while republican support languished at under thirty per cent from the 1940s through to 1991.[7] Moreover, the work of Murray Goot explodes the myth that increasing ethnic diversity means a swift end to the Australian monarchy.[8]

Declining support for the monarchy is, in fact, a very recent phenomenon. On Morgan's figures support for the monarchy dipped from fifty-six per cent in July 1991, to forty-nine per cent in March 1992 and to just thirty-eight per cent in April 1993.[9] This sudden collapse can be explained partly by the misbehaviour of the junior royals but mostly by sustained, and virtually uncontradicted, attacks on the monarchy from July 1991 when the Australian Labor Party committed itself to a republic till April 1993 when the Prime Minister announced the formation of a Republic Advisory Committee.

However, recent polling shows that republican momentum stalled at almost the same time that influential political and community leaders began to campaign in support of the Australian Constitution. The influential Newspoll (1993) showed support for a republic steady at forty-six per cent between April and July but falling to just thirty-nine per cent in September while opposition to change rose from thirty-five to thirty-six per cent to forty-four per cent in the same period.[10]

The November Newspoll (1993) showed that the release of the Turnbull Report[11] did not help the republican cause. Despite wall-to-wall publicity, the numbers remained forty-four to thirty-nine against a republic.[12] This does not prove that a republic is doomed any more than previous polls proved the imminent demise of the monarchy; simply that what accelerates in response to political support can also diminish in response to public criticism. While consistent majorities in favour of a republic ensure that the Prime Minister's promised referendum will go ahead, not even substantial majorities in favour of the republican idea guarantee that any particular form of republican constitution will emerge.

The Prime Minister's worst nightmare is a popularly elected President to act as a rival focus of loyalty and power,[13] yet overwhelming majorities say that, if Australia is to become a republic, a President must be popularly elected.[14] So a referendum for an elected President will be opposed not only by monarchists, but also by republicans worried about the potential for governmental deadlock. A referendum for an appointed President will unite monarchists with republicans concerned about an elective dictatorship. None of this seems to have occurred to leading republicans who, at the first opinion poll encouragement, declared that they were pushing on a 'door lightly locked'. Even as seasoned a politician as Mr Keating seems to have assumed, after two years of virtual silence from the Liberal Party, that a republic would be achieved unopposed.

In fact, since the Prime Minister first put constitutional change on the agenda, both Paul Keating and John Hewson have grappled with a debate which is out of their control and increasingly has become the focus of dissatisfaction with each one's leadership. Paul Keating's contribution to the republican movement has been both impulsive and headstrong. John Hewson's uncertain defence of the constitutional monarchy has suggested a thin, if strengthening, commitment to the 'faith, flag and family' concerns which are the heart of conservative politics. Where Mr Keating's approach has been too party-political to inspire the middle ground, Dr Hewson's has been too non-political to enthuse his own side. A republic has become almost an obsession for Mr Keating but Dr Hewson still finds it hard to become indignant about the assault on our history, culture and traditions.

There is little doubt that the Prime Minister's role in the republican debate has exasperated senior Labor colleagues. Ex-Senator John Button's call for politicians to take time-out[15] may be just the tip of an iceberg of Labor discontent. It is highly significant that, speaking to a Senate Estimates Committee in late 1993, Senator Gareth Evans failed to endorse the Prime Ministerial timetable of a republic by 2001.[16] At least one well-placed Canberra journalist has reported that Cabinet insiders want to delay the republican movement.[17]

Although republicans allege that the issue will eventually split the Liberal Party, so far the most serious dissent has been on the Labor side. The Four Corners programme, in which both Mr Keating's predecessors as Labor Leaders took lethal potshots at his republic, highlights serious division inside Labor's ranks.[18] Moreover, the November Newspoll (1993) showed more monarchist Labor voters than republican Liberal voters.

When the two thousand five hundred delegates at the New South Wales Labor Conference voted for a republic without dissent, they did not indicate unity so much as a Stalinist approach to party democracy. Although few Labor figures are yet prepared to endorse constitutional monarchy, ex-Prime Minister Bob Hawke's repeated call to defer republicanism until after the present reign and consistent declaration that Australia has more important issues to consider amounts to a virtual declaration of war on his successor's plans.[19]

While most Labor frontbenchers are sentimental republicans, most are also quite comfortable with our existing Constitution. Like Mr

Hawke, most resolve the paradox by putting it off. They are 'mañana republicans'—'inevitable' means 'one day....'. They can tolerate almost any party policy and practice, like the socialisation objective and the union bloc vote, provided it does not require action now or cause problems today.

Perhaps Mr Keating has done himself greatest damage, inside a party which remembers the Split, rubbishing Australia's British heritage and casually telling an Irish journalist that, for him, Catholicism means republicanism.[20] Labor's greatest hero, John Curtin, referred to Britain as the 'motherland'[21] and Mr Hawke declared in Britain, just four years ago, that 'our shared language and culture, the strong bonds of history and of kinship, our familiar institutions of political, economic, legal and academic life' mean that Australians 'can never arrive as strangers'.[22]

Meanwhile, the Labor Left derides the 'minimalist' republic as a monarchy-without-the-Crown and worries about Paul Keating's Bonapartist tendencies. Unless support for republicanism increases, Prime Minister Keating will face pressure to bury the issue by referring it to the Constitutional Centenary Foundation: pressure not just from the Democrats who initiated this move but from Labor insiders who are looking for a way out of the republican issue.

While Paul Keating's 'republic or bust' drive is putting him at odds with his own side, John Hewson has struggled to adapt himself to the Party of Menzies. The first plank of the foundation platform of the Liberal Party was support for the constitutional monarchy and pamphlets now given to prospective members, listing the Party's deepest convictions, declare 'we believe in a constitutional monarchy' immediately above 'we believe in a just and humane society'.

This didn't stop Dr Hewson claiming in April 1993 that the 'hard-line monarchist position' was 'out of touch' and allowing himself to be portrayed in the media as a 'closet republican'.[23] His change of heart has followed pressure from leadership rivals and acknowledges overwhelming Party sentiment.

In June 1993, when republican momentum looked unstoppable, more than fifty per cent of Federal Liberal MPs nevertheless told the *Sydney Morning Herald* they supported the existing Constitution. Even though Dr Hewson had flagged change and New South Wales Liberal leaders, Fahey and Greiner, had both declared that a republic was 'inevitable', only three Liberal MPs were prepared to back a republic even off-the-record.[24] A survey of Liberal Branch Presidents and Secretaries showed that only seven per cent in South Australia, four per cent in Queensland and eight per cent in Western Australia wanted a republic. Party conferences everywhere except the Australian Capital Territory have expressed confidence in our existing Constitution including the Crown.

Even before the 1993 election, both John Howard and Bronwyn Bishop were outspoken defenders of the constitutional monarchy. Post election, Peter Costello's first major post-election speech was a rebuke to Liberal republicans. Peter Reith declared the strategy which Dr Hewson eventually adopted: to express confidence in our Constitution while putting the onus on Mr Keating to make a persuasive case for change. At the Queensland and Victorian Liberal conferences, Dr Hewson signalled his current stance: expressing pride in our existing Constitution and attacking the Keating republic. Although Dr Hewson's commitment to the Constitution may be the product of political necessity as much as deep conviction, the Liberals cannot be accused of 'knee-jerk' monarchism and, by showing an open mind, the Liberals may have helped swing uncommitted voters behind the Constitution.

Although former New South Wales Premier, Nick Greiner, is an active republican and senior New South Wales Liberal, Peter Collins, has been critical of his Federal colleagues for opposing a republic, Liberal 'divisions' are more apparent than real, and any Liberal receptiveness to the republican idea springs not from unhappiness with the constitutional monarchy but from a desire not to take political risks.

Just as the Liberal Party ultimately opposed all four 1988 referenda questions, the political dynamics almost guarantee Liberal opposition to any republican proposal while Labor remains in government. Even republican Liberals are likely to find technical reasons to oppose a republic. Hence, republican Liberals are most likely to lapse into silence—in much the same way that Labor supporters of a consumption tax were struck dumb once the goods and services tax became Liberal policy. Liberal republicans will be reluctant to support any Labor-sponsored republic for much the same reasons that Labor never supports Liberal union legislation (such as the Greiner industrial law) notwithstanding its actual merit. Liberals who could contemplate 'mercy-killing' the monarchy would never allow it to be butchered in cold blood.

Leading republican, Professor George Winterton, conceded as much when he told a University of New South Wales seminar that the Liberals held a virtual veto over the republic. Professor Winterton also conceded that 'snowballing legal complexities' could derail the whole process.[25] Leading republicans concede that the change is symbolic. Only a 'republic or bust' attitude would pursue symbolic change regardless of social cost. Leading republicans also concede that there is no point even considering a referendum until a clear majority favours change. Yet constitutional reality makes this a highly unlikely prospect.

Unscrambling the Constitutional Egg

As it stands, our Constitution gives vast power to the Governor-General who summons and prorogues Parliament, appoints ministers to serve at his or her pleasure, commands the armed forces and signs Bills into law. We enjoy Cabinet Government only because of unwritten conventions that the Governor-General (or Crown) acts only on ministerial advice. Take the Crown out of the Constitution, however, and the conventions go too.

Until recently, leading republicans had asserted that change was as easy as substituting 'President' for 'Governor-General' in our existing Constitution.[26] The Turnbull Report, however, revealed the complexity of change conceding that 'tippex republicanism' posed the real risk of autocracy and recommended that the Head of State's powers be in some way codified.[27] However, writing down the existing powers changes them from convention to law and makes them more likely to be used. A government which could not get its budget through the Senate could hardly refuse an election if the Constitution stated that the Head of State could dismiss a government unable to secure supply.

However, any codification of the Head of State's powers is haunted by the ghosts of 1975. On the one hand, the Australian Labor Party is unlikely to concede that Sir John Kerr was correct by entrenching the power to dismiss a government with a House of Representatives' majority. Yet on the other, the Coalition is unlikely to support any diminution of the existing reserve powers. Hence, even if both sides could agree on the republican principle, they are likely to remain deadlocked on republican practice. Of course, great events and powerful need can break political logjams. This is why the republicans' admission that change is essentially symbolic is so damaging to their cause.[28]

Then there is the problem of the States. Australia is a monarchy in six States as well as one Federal Commonwealth. The alleged silliness of an absentee monarch is nothing compared with the prospect of becoming a 'monarlic' or 'repubarchy'—a Federal republic containing one or two State monarchies. To become a credible republic, either all States must agree to change or unwilling States must be coerced by the Federal Government. The necessity to carry every State means that passing a republican referendum is even harder than passing other referenda. Alternatively, some legal device must be found under which the States can be forced to change their Constitutions.

On one reading, the words of section 128 of the Constitution prevent any alteration of State Constitutions without majority support in those States. Although the Turnbull Report claimed that this did not stand up as a legal argument, it admitted that *as a political suggestion*, the idea, that coercing the States amounted to a breach of the Federal compact, 'may have some force'.[29] So pushing for a republic will bring no tangible benefits and could even provoke attempts to end the Australian Federation—and this is just what the republicans concede!

Why is Republicanism an Issue?

It will be bitterly opposed by one side of politics and will divide the other. It involves the greatest leap into the political, legal and constitutional dark in Australia's history. The resultant dislocation will make the logistics of implementing a goods and services tax look easy. What is remarkable is not why Australia is still a constitutional monarchy but why republicanism is even entertained as a serious option.

Under the present system, our Head of State is an international figure of vast distinction; as well-known as the Pope; as well respected as Mother Theresa; the friend of Churchill, Menzies and Eisenhower; an heroic survivor from an age of giants; a symbol of continuity and stability in difficult times; a figure of romance amidst the grey humdrum; an embodiment of history in an age that lives only for today. The choice between a constitutional monarchy and a political presidency is the choice between a Mercedes Benz and a Leyland P76. It is only an issue because some Australians have become confused about the reality of our independence.

The fact that a republic has been a staple of political discourse over the past eighteen months is entirely due to Prime Minister Paul Keating's remarkable political skills. Neither surging poll support for republicanism during the Whitlam Government nor Whitlam's post-1975 conversion to republicanism nor the Australian Labor Party's endorsement of republicanism in 1981 turned it into a front page fixture. It has been Australia's biggest political issue solely because of Prime Ministerial sponsorship.

Until the Prime Minister indicates that it is no longer on his agenda, it will remain a 'hot' political story despite its inherent implausibility. Prime Minister Paul Keating almost achieved the impossible previously; in 1985 he came close to introducing a consumption tax. His ability to survive political scandals demonstrates a Houdini quality. Mr Keating has the ability to almost hypnotise vast swathes of Australia's elite so if anyone could make Australia a republic, he could. Yet the histrionics and browbeating which impress or intimidate Canberra insiders also alienate the electorate. Paul Keating is the most feared and respected Prime Minister in recent history. Without him the republican cause would get nowhere, yet with him it is doomed to fail.

Notes

1. *Good Weekend*, the *Sydney Morning Herald*, 22 May, 1993: 'Donald Horne wrote in 1958, "To a boy from the suburbs, (AD) Hope seemed to represent the finest flowering of European civilisation: he was un-Australian"'.
2. Paul Keating on the television programme '*60 Minutes*', quoted in the *Australian Financial Review*, 22 March, 1993.
3. H. Lawson, 'Freedom on the Wallaby' in H. Lawson, *A Camp-Fire Yarn* (Sydney: Lansdowne, 1984), 146.
4. A. Sherry, quoted in *The Age*, 12 November, 1993.
5. B. Humphries, *An Autobiography* (Harmondsworth: Penguin, 1992), 90.
6. The Report of the Republic Advisory Committee, *An Australian Republic: The Options* (Canberra: A.G.P.S., 2 vols., 1993).
7. M. Goot, 'Contingent Inevitability' in G. Winterton (ed.), *We, the People: Australian Republican Government* (to be published by Allen and Unwin, 1994).
8. *Ibid.*
9. Morgan Poll, Finding No 2395, in *Time Australia*, 26 April, 1993.
10. Newspoll, quoted in *The Australian*, 29 September, 1993.
11. See Republic Advisory Committee Report, *supra* note 7.
12. Newspoll, quoted in *The Australian*, 18 November, 1993.
13. See Laurie Oakes, *The Bulletin*, 10 August, 1993.
14. See, for instance, AGB McNair poll, the *Bulletin*, 11 May, 1993 showing that 83 per cent want the people to elect the President in any Australian Republic.
15. John Button, in the *Sydney Morning Herald*, 3 November, 1993.

16. Estimates Committees, *Hansard*, 8 November, 252.
17. Fia Cumming, in *The Sunday Telegraph*, 24 October, 1993.
18. The television programme *Four Corners*, 13 September, 1993.
19. Bob Hawke, Address at Oxford University, in *The Australian*, 28 October, 1993.
20. See the *Canberra Times*, 17 September, 1993.
21. Quoted by David Day, *The Australian*, 15–16 February, 1993.
22. Bob Hawke, Address at Mansion House, 22 June, 1989.
23. Quoted in *The Australian*, 30 April, 1993.
24. See the *Sydney Morning Herald*, 5 June, 1993.
25. See the *Sydney Morning Herald*, 8 September, 1993.
26. See, for instance, Malcolm Turnbull, 'The Queen is British' (1993) 28 *Australian Lawyer* 16, 18: 'It is quite a simple matter to amend the Constitution so as to constitute a President as Head of State rather than the Queen (represented by the Governor-General). All that is required is to delete references to the Queen and the Governor-General, replace them with references to a President and then state how the President is to be appointed.'
27. See Republic Advisory Committee Report, *supra* note 7, vol.1, 116.
28. See, for instance, Nick Greiner in *The Australian*, August 25, 1993: 'By 2010, Australia will of course be a republic. I do not believe this will have a great deal of impact on either quality of Government or material standard of living although it certainly won't hurt either ... .'
29. See Republic Advisory Committee Report, *supra* note 7, vol. 1, 130.

The Republic and the Issues of 2001

*Kenneth Wiltshire**

> Some years ago a few ardent but irresponsible advocates of Australian federation indulged in predictions that the time would inevitably come when Australia would separate from the mother country and become an independent Republic. Those ill-considered utterances caused, at the time, strong expressions of disapproval throughout the colonies, which effectually prevented the repetition of such suggestions, as being beyond the arena of serious contemplation and debate. Throughout the political campaign which preceded the election of the Federal Convention, not a solitary public writer or speaker seriously discussed the possibility, much less the probability, of separation.
>
> Quick and Garran[1]

Discussion of a republic had no place in the moves of the 1890s towards independence and the creation of the Australian federation. It had begun around the middle of last century and reached a peak in the late 1880s but tapered off quite dramatically, remaining at a relatively low level for the bulk of the twentieth century. If opinion polls are to be believed, in 1993 about fifty per cent of Australians favoured a republic although they differ on the form of republic they would prefer. Since the first monarchy-republic poll in 1953, support for a republic has more than trebled; between the late 1960s and the late 1980s support for the monarchy remained relatively stable at around sixty per cent with support for the republic varying somewhat more over the same period, usually between about twenty-five and thirty per cent.[2]

---

* J.D. Story Professor of Public Administration, University of Queensland and Board Member, Constitutional Centenary Foundation.

Against this background it can be asked what role a republic would play in the future governance of this nation. Such a comprehensive question cannot be approached in its entirety here, but one way of considering the issue is to identify some of the key forces currently shaping Australia's political system together with some of the major sources of tension which are begging for resolution, and postulate whether a republic has a place in either scenario.

Political Forces

Perhaps the major political force impacting on this nation in the approach to the next century will be the phenomenon of globalisation, particularly of the economy. Every day decisions made in Washington, New York, Tokyo, Brussels, London and many other capitals affect Australia instantly. With the continued reduction of protective barriers, the economy will become even more exposed to international decision-making especially, as seems likely, the world will divide into several trading blocs as part of overall endeavours to reduce international barriers to trade. Add to these factors the revolution in international transport and communication, the arrival of the global village in telecommunications, rapid identification of health and ecological impacts across the globe, the substantial potential identified by OECD (Organisation for Economic Co-operation and Development) and UNESCO (United Nations Educational Scientific and Cultural Organisation) of 'learning without frontiers' using the latest technology, and the escalation in international human professional networks in the vast majority of disciplines, and it becomes clear that very few nations, and least of all Australia, will be able to afford the luxury of formulating domestic policy in isolation. We know this already from experience of the past quarter century.

The most tangible manifestation is that Australia is signatory to over one hundred and thirty international conventions or agreements, be they multilateral and associated with the International Labour Organisation, the United Nations, United Nations Educational Scientific and Cultural Organisation, World Health Organisation, Food and Agriculture Organisation, General Agreement on Tariffs and Trade, or bilateral economic, social or cultural agreements. We are citizens of the world and will become more so in the future. We are already familiar with the tensions which globalisation can cause in our political system, particularly the strain created as this centrifugal force impacts on the federal system. Debates over the use of the external affairs power are a constant reminder. Many countries including the new European Community are grappling with the issue which is often seen as a supra-national invasion of national sovereignty.[3] Of course, the implementation of international treaties and conventions ultimately requires domestic legislation/law-making. Moreover, 'The conduct of external affairs is essentially an executive function';[4] and although it falls to the Commonwealth Parliament ultimately to ratify the actions of the Commonwealth Government in law-making relating to treaties, that has become something of a formality given the rigidity of party discipline in the Parliament. It seems that Australia can be taken to war, to trade, to environmental protection, or to the guarantee of human rights by a Prime Minister and Cabinet with minimum involvement of the Commonwealth Parliament.

Some, but not many, international treaties make provision for signatories from federal countries acknowledging their political difficulty in imposing international agreements on state or provincial governments. However, it is this federal-state tension that lies at the heart of dispute in Australia over the use of the external affairs power. As Zines observes regarding the Tasmanian Dams case:

> Applying the approach ... of giving the subject a broad interpretation and ignoring the consequences for state power, it seems clear that to give legislative effect to a treaty obligation might reasonably be characterised as a law with respect to external affairs.[5]

Of course, Commonwealth legislation and action have addressed this matter in various ways. State Governments are usually fully consulted before international treaties are signed, they are often asked to send representatives to the meetings of international bodies where ratification is to be discussed, they have avenues of appeal to the High Court, and they are sometimes able to pursue compensation for the adverse effects of application of international instruments to their activities. Australia also has something of a reputation (not always approved in international quarters), of experiencing a considerable delay between signing of international treaties/conventions and ratifying them and their protocols, and this is due in some part to concern over State Government reaction. Of course, the state governments do not, as in Germany and

Canada, have more clearly defined powers in the foreign policy process under the Australian Constitution, although they do engage in a range of activities abroad.[6] The latest initiative to address the matter of State Government involvement in external affairs comes in the form of the COAG (Council of Australian Governments) arising from the New Federalism of the Hawke Government which has one of its stipulated roles, 'consultation on other major issues by agreement such as (1) international treaties which affect the states and territories and which have not been resolved through the agreed processes'.[7] This is, of course, another executive solution but it at least formalises a channel of consultation for the State Governments.

For the future it can confidently be predicted that the scope of activity arising from international affairs impacting on Australia's system of government will expand exponentially. Yet our political institutions remain ill-equipped to cope with the interface between foreign policy and domestic policy. Quick and Garran's prophecy ironically is still relevant—that external affairs 'may hereafter prove to be a great constitutional battleground'.[8]

Somewhat related to the globalisation trends are two other aspects of Australian life which will inevitably also feature strongly in the next century—economic union and the promotion of human rights. Although the international dimension is only one facet of these areas it is clear that Australia cannot accommodate its growing internationalisation without addressing the need for, or creation of, a more efficient internal market and the guarantee of the rights of citizens, especially minorities. Survival in the political world of the twenty-first century will require action in both arenas.

In relation to economic union there have been significant initiatives in the 1980s under the rubric of micro-economic reform directed towards this end. They include mutual recognition of the European model, national and uniform standards for various industries, new national policy bodies for several industries including railways, electricity, non-bank financial institutions, and road transport; and vocational education and training. New intergovernmental agreements have been added to the welter of other agreements (over one hundred and fifty operating under the aegis of forty-one ministerial councils) which characterise Australia's administrative federalism, most notably the new environmental agreement which includes a uniform approach to environmental impact assessment; a national approach to data collection; elimination of duplication of assessment procedures; a national greenhouse steering committee; closer co-operation on world heritage matters; and a national approach to the protection of rare, vulnerable and endangered species encompassing a co-ordinated approach to the international convention on biodiversity. There has also been set in place, though a little tardy to begin, national performance monitoring of government trading enterprises, beginning with State and Territory enterprises in energy, rail, water, major ports and urban public transport; and with national government enterprises in telecommunications, postal services, shipping, airports, and pipelines. National accounting standards are also to be developed, including standards for asset valuation. Other matters affecting government trading enterprises to be addressed include borrowing arrangements, taxation arrangements and competition policy.

These developments are important because Australia's export performance is significantly influenced by the cost imposts for our export industry arising out of a fragmented internal market and especially the impact of government charges which are, in turn, affected by the efficiency of government enterprises and government regulatory regimes. The federal system with its perceived lack of policy harmonisation, absence of uniformity, fragmentation, overlap and duplication, has long been seen as one of the key impediments to the micro-economic reform necessary to achieve macro-economic efficiency, especially as regards the provision of infrastructure and government facilitation of investment and industrialisation.

Economic union, and more specifically interstate trade, was probably the key obstacle of the 1890s to the creation of the Australian Federation—the 'lion in the path' as it was described. There has indeed been more litigation over section 92 than any other clause of the Australian Constitution. We do not yet have a true common market—we will need to pursue that objective as rigorously as our founders did but this time for international as well as national reasons.

In relation to human rights the situation is very clear. Australia is a multicultural society and, given demographic trends, is destined to become more so in the future. Experience in other countries reveals the need for the system of governance to ensure that rights are well protected in such a situation, particularly the rights of cultural minorities. The past two decades in Australia have witnessed growing concern as to whether our pattern of protection of rights, hinging on the common law, the role of

Parliament, and the courts as appeal mechanisms, is adequate in this regard. Some prefer a constitutionally entrenched bill of rights, others urge faster action in the form of Commonwealth or State or joint legislation, as in the case of the *Mabo* debate and its current resolution. The country most often cited in comparison with Australia in this regard is Canada because of its federal model operating also in a Westminster system with a multicultural population. The Canadian experience includes a constitutionally entrenched charter of rights and freedoms (though with some potential for opting out by provinces) where the courts have now built up a substantial load of case law and changed the approach to protection of rights significantly,[9] as well as resorting to international instruments of human rights. For the indigenous population the approach has extended even further to include treaties, models of self-government on a municipal pattern, tripartite agreements (federal/provincial/native band), fishing and trapping rights, designated Premiers' conferences, and, in the case of the Inuit, a proposed new province Nunavit, to give a real form of self-government. It is interesting to note that Canada began its journey towards greater entrenchment of rights by way of federal legislation and similar legislation in some of the provinces. While Canadian precedent cannot be regarded as an infallible guide to Australia's future path, it would be surprising if the broad directions for this country do not prove to be similar in the medium to long-term. The Canadian system of governance was obliged to change quite significantly.

Political Tensions

Apart from the international and domestic trends impinging on Australia, a few of the main ones having been identified, there is also a litany of domestic running sores in our political system which can only become more aggravated with time. Space does not permit an exhaustive treatment; the main ones are well known. They include the role of the Queen's representatives, both National and State, particularly in relation to the reserve powers, and the issue of whether these should be codified, and clearer procedures for their implementation adopted. There is the issue of the power over Upper Houses to defer or block supply, especially given the heightened prominence of the minority parties currently holding the balance of power in many Australian Upper Houses, especially the Senate, and the unprecedented enforced fragmentation of the

1993 federal budget to make the process more reminiscent of the American budgetary contretemps between Congress and President. There is a raft of issues which might be encapsulated under the heading of Parliament Executive relationships including questions of the genuine independence of Parliament, its powers of seeking information, allocating resources, censuring the Executive, demanding the presence of cabinet ministers, and so on.

Significant uncertainty reigns in Australia in relation to the separation of powers, quite apart from the matters already mentioned. It is recognised that the founders did not have a clear notion from which they operated. Sawer goes so far as to say:

> There is no evidence that the Federal Fathers in general had the slightest desire to imitate the French theory of the separation of powers, which was based on a misinterpretation of English practice, nor the American theory which was based on a misinterpretation of the French.[10]

Nonetheless, Australia has endeavoured to maintain some semblance of a formal separation of powers despite the complications produced by a Westminster derived system of responsible government where the pivotal characters in our daily life, cabinet ministers, are at the same time members of both the legislature and the Executive. Here lies the source of our dilemma because it is the breakdown of Westminster principles in practice which has made the notion of any separation of powers seem so absurd. The signs are unmistakable and they flash more distressingly every day: the rigidity of party adherence on the floor of Parliament; the breakdown of ministerial responsibility together with the subservience of individual ministerial responsibility to collective ministerial responsibility;[11] the control of the fiscal and human resources of both the Parliament and courts by the Executive; the substitution for the notion of a permanent neutral public service with modern notions of less permanent 'responsive' bureaucracies whereby elected governments should, it is said, be entitled to public servants who are responsive to their wishes (a short step from a political bureaucracy); presidentialisation of politics through large-scale offices of Prime Minister or Premier accompanied by ascendant departments, monopolisation of policy flow, domination of the media, and even the architectural design of Parliaments and use of office space to entrench such presidentialisation; increased power for the executives at both National and State level through the myriad pathways of executive federalism; and the very determination by the Executive of Parliament's time, its duration of sittings and its debating procedures.

The response to some of these elements in Australia has been to create a welter of para-parliamentary and para-judicial avenues to attempt to address the rising power of the Executive. They include a new administrative law, freedom of information legislation, appeals tribunals, new crime and criminal justice authorities, etc., and in this regard Australia clearly leads the world. But they merely fill in cracks in the separation of powers, create more bureaucracies, cause confusion for the aggrieved citizen, and a loss of confidence in the system; they do nothing to resolve the fundamental problem of the declining importance of Parliament in our system of government.

If one wanted to add to the list, the area of Federal-State relations would be fertile ground, especially financial relations. As a result of the uniform taxation arrangement, High Court interpretations of excise duties and the willingness of State and Territory governments to acquiesce in the income tax situation, the Commonwealth Government effectively drives most policy areas through the fiscal powers it has accumulated and which are growing. The resulting vertical imbalance produces a distortion of political accountability long observed, especially since the Second World War, but never rectified. This centralisation has accelerated in the 1980s; it will not cease in the 1990s. By and large, the States and Territories and local governments have little room of their own for policy manoeuvring, particularly given the ongoing use of conditional funding under section 96 of the Constitution, now representing more than half of State receipts from the Commonwealth. Their position has not of course been helped by many of their poor fiscal accountability performances but the fact remains that, had they possessed more autonomy, political pressures may well have forced them to behave more responsibly. It is an area in desperate need of clarification—the Constitution and its division of powers are largely redundant.

Herein lies the problem—in relation to both the separation of powers and the division of powers in our system of responsible government and federalism borrowed from the United Kingdom and United States, the practice of governance no longer fits the formal description. Thus we are every day deluding ourselves as to how democratic accountability is being played out by those we elect. It can only get worse in coming years unless the framework and its logic are revised either to adapt to current practice or practice is forced to adapt to the letter of our constitutional system and its conventions. Otherwise we shall go on having a 'washminster' system of government where those in power can continue to hide behind the obfuscation that this blurring produces.

A Republic

Taking these brief comments as some indication of the likely directions to be taken by Australia, is there any advantage in moving to a republican form of government? For example, would a globally oriented, multicultural nation with its own internal customs, union and free market be better served if ties with the monarchy were cut? The role of the Queen's representative in Australia's external affairs was somewhat blurred in the earlier days of the nation when legal ties to the British Commonwealth and Britain itself were stronger but virtually all commentators are now agreed that Australia has complete independence in the conduct of its external affairs. In the words of Dawson J.:

> Of course, it is true that in an international sense Australia has achieved nationhood and this has resulted in the Crown represented by the governor-general exercising certain prerogative powers previously exercised by the Imperial Crown. ... The governor-general can now exercise the prerogative of declaring war and making peace. ... The governor-general can now ratify treaties on behalf of Australia whereas previously the Imperial Crown acted on its behalf with respect to such matters.[12]

These roles for a Governor-General in the area of foreign affairs are very similar to those of Presidents of republics including republics with parliamentary systems and non-executive Heads of State.[13] Possessing a Governor-General rather than a President would seem to offer little in the way of technical impediments to Australia's continuous globalisation. Other factors may provide more impediments such as the federal system: as Wheare prophesied federalism and a spirited foreign policy go ill together.[14] Again it is assuredly the federal system which has been and continues to be one of the main obstacles to the creation of a true Australian internal market.

The matter of the protection of rights is more problematical. From a legal perspective there would be no problem in introducing additional means for the protection of rights including a bill of rights, into a constitutional monarchy. Indeed, it has been successfully accomplished elsewhere. The arguments are more about the symbolism and whether a multicultural society can accept the granting or withdrawal of citizenship, legislating for human rights, signing international treaties relating to human rights, pronouncing on treasonable or alien acts and the granting of pardons by a government whose titular head is formally appointed by the sovereign of another country. These concerns have surfaced from time to time and no doubt they are vital to those affected, even though they are more related to perceptions of reality than reality itself. Still, in politics, perceptions are often more potent than reality, although many other countries in similar situations have not had any great degree of difficulty, for example, New Zealand, Canada, Jamaica. It is true that most of the multicultural countries in the British Commonwealth are republics but there is no evidence of cause and effect on this issue. At any event, over seventy per cent of the member countries of the British Commonwealth are republics.

As to the problems of the future which the Australian system of government will have to face, very few of them directly relate to the issue of republic versus monarchy. There is no reason to suppose that the reform of Parliament, role of Upper Houses, a more efficient federal system, clearer accountability, less politicisation of the public service, etc., would necessarily be better addressed under a republican form of government. It might be that the issues surrounding the separation of powers may be more clearly resolved and it would certainly afford the opportunity to clarify, indeed codify, the reserve/prerogative powers of the Head of State. Of course, a shift to a republic would definitely have an impact on these issues as spelt out in the Report of the Republic Advisory Committee.[15] They do not claim any advantages in areas other than those relating immediately to the Head of State and the powers that would go with the office, the sources of advice to the office and the method of appointment to, and dismissal from, the office, all of them worthy issues in their own right but not ones on which the functioning of the rest of our system of government is hanging in expectation at the moment or in the foreseeable future.

It does remain true that a shift to a republic and the consequent constitutional changes required would afford the chance to tidy up many aspects relating to accountability in our political system, a task that would be slightly more messy to achieve whilst retaining a constitutional monarchy.

In short, one is forced to the conclusion that runs through most of the literature and debate on republicanism, that any gains for the foreseeable future in Australia would be more in the nature of symbolism than in relation to the substance of governance. This may of course be no bad thing, especially if it increased the knowledge of citizens as to how they are governed, and especially if it engendered a better standard and code of behaviour in our politicians and leaders. It would be nice to think that the credibility of our political system and the faith of the Australian populace in its democracy were restored by 2000 when we go on show to the world at the Olympics and the year after when we celebrate our independence and Federation.

Notes

1. J. Quick and R.R. Garran, *The Annotated Constitution of the Australian Commonwealth* (Sydney, 1901: Reprint 1976, Legal Books), 95.
2. J. Western and B. Holmes, *The State and the Flag: An Examination of Attitudes to and Opinions of the Present Constitutional System of Government in Australia* (Brisbane: Social Research Consultancy Unit, University of Queensland, 1992).
3. L. Zines, *Constitutional Change in the Commonwealth* (Cambridge: University Press, 1991), 101.
4. M. Coper, *Encounters with the Australian Constitution* (North Ryde: C.C.H., 1987), 9.
5. Zines, *supra* note 3, 93.
6. P. Boyce, 'International Relations of Federal States: Responsibility and Control' in M. Wood, C. Williams and C. Sharman (eds.), *Governing Federations* (Sydney: Hale and Iremonger, 1989), 189–190.
7. K. Wiltshire, 'Australia's New Federalism: Recipes for Marble Cakes' (1992) 22(3) *Publius* 165, 175.
8. Quick and Garran, *supra* note 1, 631.
9. P. Russell, *Canadians and the Charter* (Toronto: University of Toronto Press, 1989).
10. G. Sawer, *Australian Federalism in the Courts* (Melbourne: Melbourne University Press, 1967), 152.
11. P. Finn, *Law and Government in Colonial Australia* (Melbourne: Oxford University Press, 1987).

12. D. Dawson, 'Commonwealth Prerogatives' in C. Saunders, *et al.* (eds.), *Current Constitutional Problems in Australia* (Canberra: Centre for Research on Federal Financial Relations, 1982), 66.
13. Constitutional Centenary Foundation, *Heads of State: A Comparative Perspective* (Carlton: Constitutional Centenary Foundation, 1993), 6–7.
14. K. Wheare, *Federal Government* (4th ed., London: Oxford University Press, 1963).
15. The Report of the Republic Advisory Committee, *An Australian Republic: The Options* (Canberra: A.G.P.S., 2 vols., 1993).

Monarchy: Mystery and Practicality

Gareth Grainger[*]

1. The Institution of Monarchy—Dignity, Continuity and Practical Purpose

Monarchy is a form of government experiencing renewed vigour and relevance in these last decades of the twentieth century. In Europe, Spain since 1975 has made the transition from Fascist dictatorship to open democracy under a resuscitated Bourbon dynasty headed by King Juan Carlos I. In Africa, the Ugandan Government in mid 1993 reinstated the position of Kabaka of Buganda. In Asia, the Cambodian people have recently voted for the restoration of the Norodom dynasty to the ancient Khmer throne. In a number of Eastern European countries, notably Serbia, Bulgaria, and Romania, the heads of the former reigning Houses have emerged as significant potential solutions for restoring stability and continuity in the wake of collapsing Communist dictatorship. The portentous pronouncement in *The Age* newspaper editorial on 16 October 1993 that monarchy is not an appropriate institution for the twenty-first century flies in the face of its resurgent success.

No analysis of the present Head of State debate in Australia can afford to dismiss the real prospect that Australia's highly effective system of constitutional monarchy may withstand the test of a referendum and that Australia may recommit itself to its present form of government. If this does occur then the present debate will not have been wasted. What has already resulted is a far greater awareness of our Australian Constitution, and an identification of those areas where some improvement or strengthening of the Australian Head of State system can occur. There is much which, if we choose, could be done to upgrade the position of

---

[*] Visiting Associate Professor of Law, Bond University.

Governor-General: to address the mode of selection of candidates; to provide for the position to be able to obtain constitutional advice from the High Court; to document the most obvious of the reserve powers; and to increase the national and international recognition of the Governor-General. The choice is ours to do all this and to do it without referendum or divisive debate. This will address many of the concerns voiced by the more rational republican arguments. What is unlikely to be changed by a referendum in the foreseeable future, and what should not be changed if Australia genuinely wants to preserve the benefits of its present successful Constitution, is the need for a monarch to be at the pinnacle of the system. When other countries are adopting systems of constitutional monarchy we would be well-advised to consider why they are doing so. The answer in its simplest form is that no other form of government so clearly provides both a practical method of ensuring constitutional stability and continuity in the life of a nation, whilst also addressing the mystical needs which religion and psychology suggest are essential to the inner being of humanity.

It has become almost axiomatic to define what we now call constitutional monarchy by reference to Walter Bagehot's text *The English Constitution*. He stated that 'the sovereign has, under a constitutional monarchy such as ours, three rights—the right to be consulted, the right to encourage, the right to warn'.[1] In Australia these rights are exercised on the Queen's behalf by the Governor-General at the Commonwealth level and by the Governors at the State level. In doing so they are guided by the standards set by Queen Elizabeth II who 'has been the outstanding contemporary exponent of the appropriate way for the powers and functions of a constitutional Head of State to be exercised under the Westminster system which operates here'.[2] Yet Bagehot's words describe only a small part of what the Monarch does, and do little to identify why constitutional monarchy has been so successful in nations as diverse as the United Kingdom, Norway, Spain, Thailand, Jordan and Japan with a resident monarch; and in post-colonial independence by such countries as Australia, New Zealand and Canada with an absent monarch and a resident Governor-General.

Since the British-derived monarchy is generally acknowledged to have been the most successful of the twentieth century we must consider what its own practitioners have considered to be its key elements. King George V, when Duke of York, received lessons on the law and practice of the Constitution in 1894. He summarised those lessons and appears to have pursued throughout his reign the principles embodied in his summary. What is contained in his notes from 1894 seems to have shaped the conduct of his son, King George VI, and his granddaughter, Queen Elizabeth II:

Monarchy
1. The value of the Crown in its *dignified capacity*
   (a) It makes government *intelligible* to the masses.
   (b) It makes government *interesting* to the masses.
   (c) It *strengthens* government with the *religious* tradition connected with the Crown.
   (d) The *social* value of the Crown.
   (e) The *moral* value of the Crown.
   (f) The existence of the Crown serves to *disguise* change and therefore to deprive it of the evil consequences of revolution.
2. The value of the Crown in its *business* capacity. The Crown is no longer an 'Estate of the Realm' or itself the executive, but the Queen nevertheless retains an immense unexhausted *influence* which goes some way to compensate for the formal *powers* which have been lost; this influence can be exercised in various ways:
   (a) In the *formation* of Ministries; especially in choosing between the Statesmen who have a claim to lead a party.
   (b) During the *continuance* of Ministries. The Crown possesses *first* the right to be consulted, *second* the right to encourage and *third* the right to warn. And these rights may lead to a very important influence on the course of politics, especially as under a system of party government, the Monarch alone possesses a *continuous political experience*.
   (c) At the *break up* of a Ministry.

Thus, though it would be possible to construct a system of political machinery in which there was no Monarchy, yet in a State where a Monarchy of the English type already exists it offers a splendid career to an able Monarch; he or she is independent of parties and therefore impartial, his or her position ensures that advice given would be received with respect; and he or she is the only statesperson in the country whose political experience is continuous.[3]

We are accustomed to discussing the role of the Crown in its business capacity. It provides a safe haven for essential reserve powers which are difficult to document exhaustively; it provides an uncontroversial method of ensuring that a Head of State holds office in a manner removed from the political fray; and it ensures that the Head of State has training and expertise in the task of overseeing those who are charged by the people with the responsibility of actual government.

What stands out in George V's summary is the analysis of the value of the Crown in its dignified capacity. The success of the Crown in its business capacity is in no small part dependent on the antecedent dignity of the Crown. That dignity derives from the antiquity of the institution of monarchy; from the continuity it represents in the life of the family of the nation; from the semi-sacred and quasi-religious overtones with which it is invested; from its elevation above divisive partisan politics; from its moral integrity; and from its comprehensibility to people as the symbolic focus of the nation. In Australia the advocates of a republic have almost entirely neglected this element of the Head of State role. Removing this dignified element which is integral to the Crown would be to rob our Head of State system of an entire dimension. The institution of the Governor-General has been successful because it is invested with the dignity of the Crown. An Australian President would be a completely different creature, with few of these dignified attributes of the Crown. The difficulty of keeping the presidential selection out of the party political process and the impossibility of documenting all of the reserve powers which reside by convention with the Monarch are two problems which would arise in trying to convert the business side of our present Head of State system from a constitutional monarchy to a republican form. The loss of the dignity of the Crown would, however, be far less easily replaced in an Australian republic. We, as a people, would be diminished in the process.

As the debate proceeds about whether Australia should replace its present successfully functioning form of constitutional monarchy with an as yet undefined republican model, one argument which has regularly been propounded is that Australia must do this in order to relate better with our Asian and Pacific neighbours. Whilst the notion that any nation should adjust its form of constitutional government to suit its own perceptions of what its neighbours might think is a novel one not followed by any other country in the world, it is at least worth exploring the way in which the concept of monarchy has been handled elsewhere in the Asia-Pacific region. In October 1993 Norodom Sihanouk was installed as King of the resuscitated Kingdom of Cambodia. He owes his throne in no small part to the work of Senator Gareth

Evans and the efforts of Australia's Labor Government over the last five years in achieving a peaceful resolution to the conflict in that ancient land. Perhaps the Cambodians who elected a monarchist majority in the recent United Nations sponsored general elections did not know Cambodia was part of Asia when they made their choice to restore a system of government which embodies so much of their history. Perhaps, of course, they did not care so long as they secured an end to the instability which thirty-five years of republican misgovernment had given them. I leave the latest essay in Cambodia's monarchy to future writers and wish instead to look at the most significant trading partner Australia has in this region, Japan.

2. The Monarchy in Japan—Growing With a Nation and Evolving as a Symbol

Emperor Akihito is the one hundred and twenty-fifth Tenno, or Emperor, of Japan. From a modest residence within the tranquil wooded enclosure of the Tokyo Imperial Palace compound he reigns over the most successful trading nation in the late twentieth century world. He represents the evidence of continuity of Japanese life from its earliest origins to the present time. His legendary ancestress Amaterasu, the Sun Goddess, founded a dynasty which drew together the strands of a pre-existing Polynesian-type population with the inflow of people from Korea and Northern Asia. The Emperor Jimmu is the first Monarch to emerge in any way clearly from the clouds of legend and appears to have founded a principality called Yamato on a fertile plain around the present Osaka and Kyoto approximately two thousand years ago. Jimmu can have been little more than a tribal chief but he laid down certain essential precepts which have been continuously cherished by the Imperial Family down to the present day—the veneration of the Sun Goddess from whom he descended; the cultivation of rice and its offering as a ritual sacrifice; and a devotion to cleanliness represented by ritual bathing. All of these precepts became incorporated in the evolution of Shinto, the native religion of the Japanese people.

The Yamato princes were successful in expanding their power and maintaining the continuity of their dynasty at the same time as they struggled against hostile surrounding forces. Emperor Nintoku in the fifth century appears to have been the first Japanese Monarch to entrust day to day administrative power to members of

the nobility, an important precedent for the future of the Japanese imperial dynasty. Three roles, however, remained with the Monarch:
1. to lead the Japanese people, as head of the nation's family, in worshipping the spiritual pantheon headed by his ancestress, Amaterasu, and in this role to be the principal intermediary between the people and their gods;
2. to declare war and to make peace;
3. to oversee the developing clans and families which made up the emerging Japanese society.

A feature of Japanese politics at this time was the way in which, when direct succession to the throne failed, the political rulers invariably sought a descendant of Jimmu's line to become Monarch. No attempt was ever made to replace the imperial dynasty even when it exercised minimal political or administrative power. This was tested to the fullest with the introduction of Buddhism into Japan in the sixth century. Elements of the Imperial Court took different sides in the debate over whether the introduced creed should be adopted. Emperor Yomei 'believed in the laws of Buddhism [while at the same time] believing in Shinto' and allowed the introduced creed to co-exist with the ancient worship of the Imperial ancestors. One of the attractions of Buddhism was a more colourful ritual than that of Shinto, which was almost Calvinistic in its classical severity and simplicity. The struggle culminated in the assassination of Emperor Sushun in 592 A.D. by a minion of the Buddhist high priest. Sushun was succeeded by Japan's first reigning Empress, Suiko, who was allowed even less political authority than had been enjoyed by her recent male predecessors, other than that of heading the nation-family and acting as high priestess of traditional Shinto worship. Real power was enjoyed by her cousin, Prince Shotoku, who in 604 A.D. gave Japan its first Constitution—the Jushichi Kempo or 'Seventeen Article Constitution'. Drawing on Chinese sources it reflected a mixture of the teachings of Buddhism and Confucianism with the aim of embodying principles for an orderly society. The Constitution therefore set out a strict relationship between the Emperor and his or her subjects, who were divided into ranks which dispensed with the old class structure. The new system allowed the Monarch to choose courtiers and officers of State, and award rank on merit rather than strictly hereditary principles, a reflection of the Chinese form of bureaucratic government. The new Constitution thus permitted outsiders to permeate the formerly closed world of Japanese power. This Constitution stipulated that 'the Members and functionaries should make decorous behaviour their leading principle, for the leading principle of the government of the people consists in decorous behaviour'.[4] Also drawing on contact with the Imperial Court of China which was developing at this time, the title of the Japanese Monarch was changed from O Kimi, 'Great King', to Tenno, 'Son of Heaven', which has remained the title principally used for the Japanese Monarch to this day.

In the struggle for power that surrounded the Imperial office following the death of Prince Shotoku in 621 A.D. and Empress Suiko in 628 A.D., administrative power passed into the hands of Nakatomi Kamatari in 645 A.D., founding the Fujiwara dynasty which was to dominate the Imperial Court intermittently until the ritual suicide in 1945 of Nakatomi's lineal descendant, Prince Konoye, last wartime Prime Minister of Japan and grandfather of the present Japanese Prime Minister, Hosokawa. There commenced a period of vigorous improvement in public administration known as the Taika or 'Great Change' reforms.[5] This reform included the nationalisation of land ownership, placing all rice-growing land under the control and disposition of the Crown; systematisation of the taxation system; the complete reorganisation of the provincial boundaries; and the codification of civil and criminal law statutes known as the Ritsu-ryo, or 'penal and civil' codes. The culmination of these reforms was the laying out of a new Imperial capital. Whilst Nakatomi Kamatari's period as Prime Minister strengthened the shift of political power from the Imperial House, the role of the Emperor as sole intermediary with the traditional gods was strengthened, and thus the very process of stable reform under a series of able administrators made use of the ongoing prestige of the Imperial House. One of the methods by which the Fujiwara clan ensured their ongoing support with the Emperor was gradually to secure the privilege of providing the Emperor with his principal wife, and to ensure that it was her son who succeeded to the throne. Emperor Hirohito's mother, Empress Sadako, was the last Fujiwara Empress of Japan and died in 1951, thirteen centuries after her ancestor Nakatomi Kamatari came to power.

In 793 A.D. the Imperial capital was relocated to Kyoto and the Japanese monarchy entered into the golden period of the Heian era. Here fine arts and courtly life reached their peak and the passage of political power from Emperor to ministers was completed. From 1160 to 1598 several families, including the

Taira, Minamoto, Ashikaga and Hosokawa, imposed a form of military government, or bakafu, on Japan, often under the title of Shogun or 'Generalissimo'. The Emperor remained in Kyoto, enduring serious financial deprivations, but always continuing to be the supreme intermediary with the gods and the symbol of the Japanese State.

In 1603 A.D. Tokugawa Ieyasu, of the Minamoto clan, emerged as the unrivalled political leader of Japan, ruling as Shogun from the military headquarters at Edo, the present day Tokyo. The loss of political power of the Emperor was complete, but the Tokugawa Shoguns were usually punctilious in maintaining the dignity and splendour of the Imperial Court at Kyoto. This splendour consisted of a palace complex of approximately twenty-seven hectares and the Emperor rarely travelled outside of this area during his reign except to fulfil religious functions at such key shrines as that at Ise. One Western historian, Herschel Webb, described the effective operating area of the Emperor's existence as being 'about the size of the deck of a large modern aircraft carrier'.[6] Succession to the throne was not automatic but was confined to the Imperial House. Accordingly interregnums of at least a week took place between reigns while a decision was made within the Imperial Court as to the succession. Thereafter, elaborate accession and enthronement rites would follow, and the purified Emperor would be able to preside at the various annual religious ceremonies. Whilst contact between this cloistered Emperor and his subjects was almost non-existent, virtually every home in the country incorporated a tokonoma, or bed recess, reserved for the Emperor.

In 1615 the Tokugawa Shogun promulgated the 'Laws Pertaining to the Nobility' in which it was stipulated that 'the Emperor should devote himself, first and foremost, to study and learning'.[7] All key political functions were relocated to Edo. The Imperial estates were administered by a Shogunal deputy, robbing the Emperor of any capacity to assert independence. In spite of this process of disempowerment, the Emperor maintained strong moral authority which was periodically asserted to demand that the Shogun act to eliminate some outstanding wrong in the land. This occurred most notably in the process of restricting contact with European powers. On the other hand, the Shogun could attribute natural disasters to want of virtue in the Emperor and demand his abdication, as occurred with Emperor Gosai. That the Emperor was not forgotten by the nation was indicated with the writings of the eighteenth century moral philosopher Ansai Yamazaki who sought to combine Confucian and Shinto teachings in asserting that the Emperor was the supreme figure in the Japanese State and that everyone, including the Shogun, depended on him for favour. Proponents of this concept were executed or exiled by the Shogunal government but the seeds of the idea were sown and slowly germinated amidst the signs of decay in the Tokugawa government.

In 1846 Emperor Komei succeeded to the Chrysanthemum Throne at a time of growing tension in Japan. Even the confinement of European contact to the Dutch trading post of Nagasaki was insufficient to prevent knowledge of Western learning from creeping through the country. Prolonged peace led to a decline in military discipline and an increase in expectation of improved living standards. New ideologies developed such as the National Learning Movement, producing demands for reinstatement of the Emperor as the genuine ruler of Japan. Emperor Komei himself requested only that the Tokugawa Shogun in Edo should restore tranquillity throughout the land and particularly that the Shogun should resist the increasing threat from the outside world.

In 1853 Commodore Perry arrived on a U.S. warship at Edo to demand access to Japan for U.S. traders. The letter he bore from U.S. President Fillmore was simply addressed to 'His Imperial Majesty' since the Americans were unclear what the respective roles of the Emperor in Kyoto and the Shogun in Edo actually were. The Shogun informed the Emperor Komei immediately of the nature of Perry's message, and the Emperor instructed the Shogun to protect the sacred soil of Japan from outside intrusion. The Shogun then summoned the principal daimyo, or provincial rulers, to consult them on the best course of action to take in achieving this objective. This attempt at consultation in the face of a major national crisis totally undermined the already weakened Tokugawa rule. Ironically, Perry's actions had led to the demand for reinstatement of the Emperor as the real ruler in order to turn back the foreign threat. The Shogun would not comply with Emperor Komei's demands and in 1854 entered into a Treaty of Friendship with the U.S., to be followed by treaties with Britain, Russia, the Netherlands and France. Emperor Komei initially refused his consent to these treaties and attempted to abdicate but was persuaded by his courtiers to consent subject to the demand that the Shogun perform his task of defending the country better in the future. The result of this crisis was that the political ruler, the

Shogun, subsided in public contempt towards extinction, whilst the Emperor became the focal point of popular dissatisfaction with the political administration. Throughout the country the slogan 'Revere the Emperor—Expel the Barbarians' became the dominant cry of the 1850s and early 1860s. In June 1863 the Satsuma and Choshu Lords commenced hostilities against foreign shipping and attempted to 'rescue' the Emperor Komei from the Shogun's power. In 1866 the last Tokugawa Shogun succeeded and on 30 January 1867 Emperor Komei died, ironically the final barrier to the overthrow of the Tokugawa Shogun whose power he had supported so long as it would attempt to expel the foreign encroachers. The Imperial Court allied itself with the Satsuma and Choshu Lords against the Tokugawa Shogun who on 9 November 1867 abolished his own position and retired his family from the Shogunal office with the declaration that:

> [I]f full authority is not vested in the Court alone, foundations of the state will be in jeopardy. If, however, the evil practices of the past are corrected and ruling authority returned to the Court, if extensive deliberations are carried out throughout the empire, the imperial judgment secured, and the nation sustained by harmony and co-operation by all, then I believe it is certain the nation will be able to rank with the other countries of the earth.[8]

The one hundred and twenty-second sovereign of Japan succeeded his father Emperor Komei at the age of fifteen on 13 February 1867, taking the name of the Meiji Emperor. He had been raised in the comparatively spartan simplicity of the Kyoto Court, trained in Confucian principles, Shinto ritual and literary skills. When he accepted the abdication of the Tokugawa Shogun in November 1867 he was deemed to be accepting restoration of the Emperor as the substantive ruler of Japan. In fact what was occurring was simply the passage of power to another group of political rulers legitimised by the supreme prestige of the Emperor. The dominant element in this group was that of the Satsuma and Choshu Lords who began the process of institutionalising a national system of Emperor veneration as the means of uniting the country while they undertook the task of reform and modernisation. In 1868 a Charter Oath was issued in the Emperor's name as the commencing point in modernisation, doing away with many official class distinctions, weakening the power of the rich Buddhist monasteries and modernising some customs. As part of this process the seat of the Emperor was removed from

Kyoto to Edo, which became 'the Eastern Capital', Tokyo. After advising his forebears of these changes at the shrine of Ise, Emperor Meiji began the first of his public tours which allowed ordinary Japanese citizens the first opportunity of seeing their Monarch since the court move to Kyoto twelve centuries previously. The government sent the Meiji Emperor on one hundred and two gyoko, or imperial excursions, outside of the capital during the forty-five years of his reign, compared with three imperial trips out of Kyoto by Emperors during the entire Tokugawa period. The leading government figure Inoue Kaoru said in 1878, 'the emperor's visiting all parts of Japan not only informs the people of the emperor's great virtue but also offers the opportunity of displaying direct imperial rule in the flesh, thus dispelling misgivings'.[9]

An Imperial Rescript of 1881 promised the development and implementation of a revised Constitution for Japan. This provoked a debate which has cautionary similarities to aspects of the constitutional debate occurring in Australia in the 1990s. The problem lay with attempts to define the imperial powers explicitly in written form. Ito Hirobumi was concerned to ensure that a balance should be struck between the powers of the Emperor and the powers of the government. In a speech in 1888 Ito Hirobumi declared that the Emperor must be the 'axis of the nation' and that without such an axis 'the State will eventually collapse when politics are entrusted to the reckless discussions of the people'.[10]

The last of the great Imperial tours throughout Japan was completed in 1885 when the system of cabinet government was implemented. The Emperor had fulfilled his role of promoting the concept of a central government in replacement of the Shogunate and could now recede 'above the clouds', leaving the Prime Minister and Cabinet to the task of running the country.

On 11 February 1889 the Meiji Emperor, dressed in Western military uniform, promulgated the new 'Constitution of the Great Empire of Japan' as a gracious imperial gift from the ruler to the ruled. In fact he was simply delivering a document prepared by a political oligarchy vesting Japan with attributes of 'civilisation' to equip it for dealing with the intrusive outside world. The form of polity which it was considered to have inaugurated was entitled rikkensei, constitutional government. It drew heavily on the prestige of the ancient Imperial House but was largely based on Prince Bismark's strongly centralised Prussian Constitution and implemented a two tier Parliament or Diet. Article One provided that 'the Empire of Japan shall be reigned over and governed by a line of Emperors unbroken by ages eternal'. An Imperial Household Ministry was established as one of the key Cabinet positions, placing the Emperor's person firmly under the control of the government. After the promulgation of the Constitution in 1889 the Meiji Emperor's appearances were reduced even further, and he was increasingly concealed from public view.

The final capping stone in the edifice of restored Imperial government came with the issue of the Imperial Rescript on Education in 1890. This focussed Japanese education on a sense of nationalism and nationhood which was epitomised by the Emperor and the venerable Imperial House. The Japanese people were enjoined to 'pursue learning and cultivate the arts, and thereby develop intellectual faculties and perfect moral powers', in order to 'guard and maintain the prosperity of Our Imperial Throne, coeval with heaven and earth'.[11] The Imperial Rescript on Education became the principal vehicle for shaping the Japanese character in the decades to 1945 and in the end was the means by which militaristic and ultra-nationalistic governments abused the status of the Emperor and the Imperial House to justify policies which led the nation to disaster.

Article 11 of the 1889 Constitution gave 'the Emperor . . . the supreme command of the Army and Navy'. That this role was symbolic is indicated by the outbreak of war between Japan and Russia in 1905 over Manchuria when the Emperor told his wife 'Diplomatic relations with Russia are to be severed. Although it is against my will, it is inevitable'.[12] When the Meiji Emperor died on 30 July 1912 he was buried amidst genuine national grief at Kyoto according to resuscitated Shinto rites. He was the first Emperor of Japan since the Heian era to exercise any form of substantive power, and even that was progressively eliminated from 1885 as the formal institutions of constitutional democracy took shape, leaving him as the remote symbol of national feeling and cultural identity. Having served his purpose he had been retired 'above the clouds' in the late 1880s and 1890s; his departure from the mortal realm altogether marked the last reign of an Emperor of Japan with more than a symbolic role.

The unstable mental health of the Taisho Emperor, and the retiring disposition and scientific interests of his son Hirohito as Crown Prince, Regent and Emperor, contributed to the already reduced role of the Imperial House in actual government after 1912. The Imperial Household lived in seclusion within Tokyo's

Imperial Palace Compound. At his accession in 1926 Emperor Hirohito took the reign name of 'Showa'—'Enlightened Peace'.

The refusal of the Western powers after World War I to accord Japan equal status contributed significantly to the ultra-nationalistic path down which it headed in the 1920s and 1930s. One of its vehicles was a strengthened focus on the Shinto religion and use of the Emperor cult to bind the nation in support of the dangerous adventurist path its increasingly militaristic government was exploring. From total isolationism Japan had gone in fifty years to the notions of the Greater East Asian Co-prosperity Sphere. Controversy still continues about the true role of the Showa Emperor in these events. After 1931 the Imperial Household Ministry allowed only photographs of the Emperor in military uniform to be released. He rarely appeared in public and on his journeys streets were closed and blinds lowered. However, the reality was that his year largely revolved around twenty-one annual religious ceremonies, such as the New Year Festival, and cultural events such as the Imperial Poetry Party. The Emperor had 'reserve powers' under the 1889 Constitution but he did not use them to arrest the worsening situation, abiding instead strictly by his role as constitutional figurehead and leaving the task of government to those who had command of the Diet.

Emperor Hirohito only emerged from his semi-cloistered situation in the months before Japan's final defeat. After the bombing of Tokyo in March 1945 he was highly visible in visiting damaged areas, much as King George VI was in London during the Battle of Britain. On 22 June 1945 the Emperor convened a meeting of his government and suggested that it find a way to bring the war to an end and avoid further suffering of the Japanese people. Peace feelers were then put out, only to be followed by the tragedy of Hiroshima and Nagasaki, and the Allied demand for Japan's unconditional surrender. On the day the atom bomb was dropped on Nagasaki, 9 August 1945, Emperor Hirohito instructed the Japanese War Cabinet to 'bear the unbearable' and unconditionally surrender. This was the ultimate exercise of the Emperor's reserve powers. The one Japanese precondition for surrender was that the monarchy be preserved as the symbol of the continuity of Japan as a nation.[13]

The United States Secretary of State, James Byrnes, stipulated that the final form of government in Japan must be decided by the will of the Japanese people. On 14 August 1945 the Emperor instructed Cabinet that the war must end immediately and on 15

August he gave his first radio broadcast. This was the first time all but a handful of his subjects had heard his voice, now almost incomprehensible in his use of the archaic court language, telling them that:

> Should we continue to fight, it would not only result in an ultimate collapse and obliteration of the Japanese nation, but it would also lead to the total extinction of the human civilisation . . . This is the reason why we have ordered the acceptance of the provisions of the Joint Declaration of the Powers . . . Submit, ye, to Our Will.[14]

Having symbolised the regime which took Japan to the brink of extinction, Emperor Hirohito proved the worth of his role as the means for providing continuity, compelling the recognition of defeat, smoothing the path for peaceful military occupation under General MacArthur, the acceptance of a new Constitution and the commencement of construction of a resuscitated state in which worship of the Emperor would not be the focus of national consciousness. At his meeting with General MacArthur on 17 September 1945 the Emperor assumed personal responsibility for the war. MacArthur recognised that the Emperor provided the perfect rallying point around which a non-militaristic Japanese nation in alliance with the West could be constructed. Suggestions that the Emperor should abdicate in favour of his young son, Crown Prince Akihito, or be tried as a war criminal, were shelved. Instead the semi-divine Emperor was used as the means of de-deifying himself and legitimising the process of demobilisation and constitutional renewal.

On 1 January 1946 the Emperor, on his own initiative, issued an Imperial Rescript renouncing his divinity and ending the concept of the superiority of the Japanese people. The 1889 Constitution was replaced on 3 May 1947 by a new Constitution in which sovereignty was transferred from the Emperor to the people. Article 1 provides that 'The Emperor shall be the symbol of the State and of the unity of the people, deriving his position from the will of the people'. By Article 3 the advice and approval of the Cabinet must be given for all acts of the Emperor in matters of State, and the Cabinet is responsible for all such actions to the Diet. Article 4 specifically provides that the Emperor 'shall not have powers related to government'. By Article 7 the Emperor is given a number of tasks to perform in matters of State on behalf of the people, which he can perform only with the advice and approval of Cabinet. These tasks include:

(1) promulgation of laws, cabinet orders and treaties;
(2) convocation of the Diet;
(3) dissolution of the House of Representatives;
(4) proclamation of general elections; and
(5) performance of ceremonial functions.[15]

Whilst the Americans thought this signified a fundamental change to the situation of the Emperor under the Meiji Constitution, it in fact only emphasised what the constitutional and actual power of the Emperor in government had been before 1947.

The Diet was upgraded to be the highest organ of State, and the Prime Minister and Cabinet were made responsible to the Diet rather than the Emperor. The Emperor was reduced to a purely symbolic role similar to that which the office had occupied for centuries before the Meiji Restoration. The significant theoretical difference which the American-imposed Constitution introduced was that the 'people' constituted the Head of State of Japan, not the Emperor, who was technically reduced to a symbol carrying out a restricted range of specific duties effectively as the delegate of the sovereign people of Japan.[16] An Imperial Household Law was promulgated on 15 January 1947 setting out strict succession to the throne by primogeniture in the male line of the Imperial lineage. The Imperial Household Ministry was reduced to the level of an Agency of the Prime Minister's Department. The Emperor was sent on an extensive series of tours of his reduced realm. His previous complete isolation rendered these visits uncomfortable events until the Emperor grew used to mixing with his people. As had occurred with the Meiji Emperor, so with the Showa Emperor, once these visits had served their purpose of accustoming the Japanese people to the new system of government the Emperor increasingly was confined to the grounds of the Imperial Palace and left to his academic researches. The event which most dramatically signified the transition which had occurred was the marriage of Crown Prince Akihito to a commoner, Michiko Shoda, in 1959.

Whilst the Japanese Emperor has a formal role in constitutional life in signing legislation into law, and carries out formal Head of State duties on behalf of the people at home and abroad, the Emperor and the Imperial House have avoided becoming popularist. The Emperor and his family appear to derive their major role in Japanese life as the symbols of Japanese culture and continuity. In this they carry on what has always been a significant part of their role throughout history. Members of the Imperial family have pursued serious academic research and a number of them, including Emperor Hirohito and his brother Prince Mikasa, have achieved genuine distinction in their respective fields. The Showa Emperor himself observed that 'the traditions of our Imperial House are not military. They are cultural and scholarly'.[17] Until his death Emperor Hirohito continued to devote himself to the major religious ceremonies which have always been part of the Japanese Emperor's role and purpose. Following the accession of Emperor Akihito in November 1990 these traditions have been continued, particularly the New Year's ceremonies and the Harvest Festival on 17 February each year when the Emperor harvests rice and offers it up as a sacrifice to the deities for whom he continues as High Priest. These, however, are not state duties under the Constitution but private duties of the Imperial House. The most important of the Emperor's religious activities occurs on 27 November of each year when he invites the goddess Amaterasu to dine with him. This involves the Emperor in a solitary night-long vigil alone with the spirit of his ancestress the Sun Goddess. Surrounded by one of the most highly sophisticated and technology-conscious trading nations in the late twentieth century world, Japan's monarchy continues as a practical method of providing a Head of State and at the same time is an evolving symbol of the deepest mystery in the life and consciousness of a people.

3. The Monarchy in Norway—Importing a Dynasty and Preserving a Nation

There could be no greater contrast to the Japanese monarchy than that of Norway's monarchy. Japan's Imperial House has reigned for two thousand years. Norway's Royal Family has fulfilled its role for less than ninety years. Yet both of them have been able to meet the changing needs of the nations they serve in some of the sorest trials of the twentieth century. This different example of a modern, low key but popular and effective monarchy shows how even the most egalitarian of nations can establish its own monarchy and have its national life enhanced and protected by so doing.

The Norwegians had been linked with Sweden for ninety-one years. In 1814 they had secured from Sweden a Constitution which provided them with internal independence under the rule of the King of Sweden, Carl XIV Johan, who only a few years earlier had been one of Napoleon's most successful Field Marshals, Jean Bernadotte. As the nineteenth century progressed the Norwegians pressed for greater control of their own affairs. In 1884 the Norwegian Parliament, the Storting, was able to secure full control over the King's Norwegian Cabinet, with a Prime Minister sitting in the Storting and presiding over the Cabinet. A second Prime Minister, the Statsminister, and two other Cabinet Ministers, were based in Stockholm to handle Norwegian Government affairs with the King. The growing significance of the Norwegian merchant fleet in world shipping had led to demands for the establishment of a separate Norwegian consular service. This, in turn, created pressure for a separate foreign policy which significantly reduced the rationale for a United Kingdom of Sweden and Norway.

In 1905 a coalition government was formed in the Storting under the leadership of Christian Michelsen, a prominent shipowner, who used the demand of the Storting for a separate Norwegian consular service as the means of bringing to a head the constitutional crisis with Sweden and the King, Oscar II. The Storting passed the consular legislation twice, and King Oscar vetoed the legislation on each occasion. Under the Norwegian Constitution, if the Storting passed it a third time the consular legislation would become law without the King's consent. In anticipation of the approaching breach, the Norwegian Ministers in Stockholm returned to Norway, the Storting passed the consular Bill a third time and deadlock resulted. Prime Minister Michelsen announced that King Oscar had effectively abdicated his royal functions in respect of the Norwegian Crown and the Storting voted to repose the royal duties in the Cabinet until the matter could be resolved. At the same time the Norwegian Government offered to accept a junior member of the House of Bernadotte as sovereign of a separate Norwegian Kingdom. Sweden rejected the Norwegian actions and the two countries hovered on the brink of war for three months. The Norwegians held a plebiscite which overwhelmingly rejected the continuance of the constitutional union with Sweden.

In this atmosphere in which Norway had effectively renounced its constitutional monarch and seemed unlikely to receive a substitute monarch as a parting gift from King Oscar, two alternative models were considered for independent Norway's Head of State. The first was to find an acceptable candidate as replacement King; the second was to adopt a republican form of government.

Norway had not had a resident monarch for at least four hundred and fifty years and the nation had a strong egalitarian tradition. Republicanism therefore had some degree of support, reflected in Bjornstjerne Bjornson's anti-monarchical drama of 1877, 'The King', and in the satirical novels of Alexander Kielland in the 1880s.[18] Whilst the forces which represented this strand of opinion were gathering during the confrontation with Sweden, other forces were pursuing the possibility of candidates for the throne. Within this group consensus was quickly reached that the ideal candidate would be thirty-five year old Prince Carl of Denmark, son of Crown Prince Christian of Denmark (later Christian X), maternal grandson of King Carl XV of Sweden and Norway and son-in-law of King Edward VII of the United Kingdom. Prince Carl had been educated as a naval officer and served in the Danish Navy. Initial informal contact with Prince Carl drew a negative response to the prospect of his becoming King of Norway in these circumstances. He eventually agreed that he would accept an offer on the basis that it was made as the result of a vote of the Norwegian Storting, that the King of Denmark, his grandfather, would agree and that King Oscar II would refuse to provide a candidate from the House of Bernadotte. Norwegian Prime Minister Michelsen favoured the candidature of Prince Carl as the one most likely to win acceptance in Norway and to ensure international recognition. Outstanding issues with Sweden were resolved by the drafting of the Treaty of Karlstad in September 1905. King Oscar indicated both that he would not put forward a Swedish candidate for the Norwegian throne and that he would accept the candidature of Prince Carl of Denmark.

The Norwegian Parliament was opened in October 1905 by Prime Minister Michelsen in the absence of a monarch and ratification of the Treaty of Karlstad was debated. Outside the Storting the debate over monarchy versus republic grew rapidly. The Labor Party favoured a republic to be implemented by plebiscite. A group of forty-four prominent citizens including the Chief of the General Staff, Haakon Hansen, and the senior Admiral, Christian Sparre, signed an appeal for the introduction of a Norwegian republic. One of the contentious parts of the debate revolved around whether the Storting should be able to make the decision or whether the people should decide by means of a plebiscite. The Norwegian Cabinet favoured an election of the King by a three-quarter majority of the Storting.[19] Prince Carl himself, however, strongly favoured the issue being settled by plebiscite, on the twofold basis that the people should be allowed to choose and also on the ground that implementation of the monarchy and election of the King by the Storting could easily be overturned by a similar vote of the Storting in the not too distant future.[20] The Government put the proposal of a Norwegian monarchy with Prince Carl as King to a plebiscite on 12 and 13 November 1905 and eighty-seven point nine per cent of voters agreed.[21] Whilst the debate during the plebiscite barely focussed on the personality of Prince Carl or his suitability for the position, the candidate was prepared to accept the result as a proper basis for the foundation and development of a new Norwegian monarchy. The result of the plebiscite was ratified by the Storting on 18 November 1905, with the unanimous support of the Government, the Labor Party and the Liberal Party. The President of the Storting then conveyed the unanimous resolution to the King of Denmark by telegram, and shortly after received the acceptance from Prince Carl of his election as King of Norway, taking as his throne name Haakon VII.[22]

In late 1905, barely five months after the breach with King Oscar II and Sweden, King Haakon VII was sworn in as King of Norway in the Storting in a simple ceremony where he took an oath to the Norwegian Constitution. The new monarchy began with few of the traditional appurtenances of a Head of State as there had been no resident Head of State beforehand. The economic conditions of Norway prevented the monarchy from being endowed or salaried in any but the simplest manner. Whilst the salary which was provided for during the lifetime of Haakon VII was acknowledged to be greater than might be awarded to a President, it was also accepted that under a republic retired Presidents would need to be given pensions and facilities which would not be needed in the case of the King. From the start, the style of the Norwegian monarchy was dictated by the strong egalitarian traditions of the Norwegian people.

The very fact that the Government had played a critical role in implementing the new Norwegian monarchy, coupled with the constitutional restrictions placed upon the King's role as Head of State, left no doubt in anybody's mind as to the strictly symbolic role which the King was to play in Norway.

As Norway had an established Christian church the King and Queen were required by the Constitution to have a coronation which took place on 22 June 1906. Prime Minister Michelsen together with the Bishop of Trondheim placed the crown on the

King's head. The coronation and the royal tour, which took place throughout the country before and after it, aroused genuine enthusiasm amongst the Norwegian people and the King was clearly able to secure ready acceptance and popularity.

The first true test of how the King would adapt to the political environment came in mid 1907 when he had to commission as Prime Minister another shipowner, Gunnar Knudsen, who had been a leading republican in the debates of 1905. This passed without difficulty and indeed the King went out of his way to show that he was as much at the service of the new Government as he had been at that of the previous one.[23] In 1910, in the absence of a clear candidate for Prime Minister, the King had to engage in exclusive consultations with the President of the Storting and others before issuing an invitation to Wollart Konow to form a government.[24]

The period between the First World War, in which Norway remained neutral, and the Second World War was a period of political instability in Norway, marked by a long series of short-lived minority cabinets. Militant worker unrest in the wake of the 1917 Bolshevik Revolution in Russia only added to the feeling of instability. This particularly impacted on the Norwegian monarchy because the Labor movement now adopted an openly hostile stance towards it.[25] In this atmosphere the simplicity of the Norwegian Monarch's lifestyle was amplified as was its 'Norwegian' nature.

In 1927 the Norwegian Labor Party emerged from a general election as the largest single party in the Storting, though without a majority. The King followed established precedent in the steps taken to form a government. As a result the King commissioned Alfred Madsen, leader of the Labor Party, to attempt to form a government. Alfred Madsen did so but put forward Christopher Hornsrud of his own party as the nominee for Prime Minister. Although this first Norwegian Labor Government lasted for only a short period, due to its difficulties in the Storting, the King's conduct in regard to it effected some change in the attitude of the Labor Party to the monarchy. It continued for some time after to maintain token protests of its republican stance but the King was no longer identified by the Labor Party with its opponents.[26] The King's Silver Jubilee was celebrated in 1930 amidst popular demonstrations in support of the Norwegian monarchy.

The outbreak of the Second World War in Europe saw Norway adopt a position of neutrality. From the outbreak of war, however, a series of incidents arose between Norway and Germany over shipping rights in the Baltic Sea. The Soviet invasion of Finland on 30 November 1939 gave an indication of what the other Scandinavian countries might expect from either the Soviet Union or Germany in a period of international conflict. Attacks by a German submarine on British shipping within Norwegian territorial waters also brought pressure from the Allies. In fact Germany had been preparing since 23 January 1940 for the invasion of Norway in spite of its earnest efforts to maintain neutrality.

On 8 April 1940 a German battle cruiser attempted to penetrate Norwegian defences in the sea off Oslo and war commenced between Norway and Germany. The Government and the Storting withdrew from the capital shortly before bombing raids commenced. Invasion forces had landed at several different points in the country. The Government resigned to allow for a government of national unity to be formed from all parties in the Storting and the King and the Crown Prince commenced an active role in meeting with the Government and military leaders. Advancing German troops forced the further tactical withdrawal of the Government and the Storting, and the Storting voted to confer emergency powers in the Government to protect the safety and future of the country.[27] Cabinet authorised the King to meet with the German Ambassador and at this session the German Government demanded that the King dismiss the Norwegian Government and appoint a new Government under Vidkun Quisling. The King refused and the German Ambassador stated that continuance of hostilities would thereafter be the King's responsibility.

The King reported the meeting to the cabinet negotiating committee and advised it that, whilst the Government must form its own attitude on the conduct of national affairs, he would abdicate for himself and his family if the Government yielded to the German demands.[28] The Government rejected the German demands and the King issued an appeal to the nation to support the decision which he and the Government had taken. The Quisling 'government' had already been put in place in Oslo and Quisling now demanded the return of the King to the capital. The King refused and was almost immediately subjected to a bombing attack by German aircraft. The Prime Minister advocated withdrawal of the Government into Sweden but the King and several of the Cabinet Ministers opposed this. The decision was made to withdraw to another location in Norway. At the age of sixty-eight, amidst the snows of winter, the King emerged as the focal point of Norwegian resistance to German oppression. The Allies launched a military venture against the Germans and were briefly successful together with Norwegian forces in capturing Narvik, a major iron ore mining town. However, pressures on the Allies on the Western Front shortly compelled withdrawal of these forces from Norway and the Norwegians were left to face the Germans alone. Cabinet met on 7 June 1940 and decided that the King, Crown Prince and Government should withdraw from Norway on the British cruiser 'Devonshire' in order to establish the Norwegian Government in exile in London, stating:

> The King and the Government of Norway will in this time of struggle be the free advocates for the national demands of the Norwegian people. They will as far as is practicable maintain the independent life of the Norwegian kingdom, so that none of the rights which appertain to a free State shall be lost.[29]

German pressures on remaining Storting leaders in Norway were countered by the response from the exiled Government that King Haakon VII ruled Norway by virtue of a plebiscite of the people and that any attempt to replace him and his Government would be a breach of the Norwegian Constitution.[30] In the crisis and events which followed it became clear that popular support throughout Norway was in favour of resistance and that to the Norwegian people the living symbol of their resistance and desire to reassert independence was their King. The King broadcast by B.B.C. to Norway on 3 July, concluding that:

> The liberty and independence of the Norwegian people are to me the first commandment of the Constitution, and I consider I am obeying this commandment and watching over the interests of the Norwegian people best by adhering to the position and the task which a free people gave me in 1905.[31]

Thereafter by means of such broadcasts the King took an active role in guiding the Norwegian people on how to handle the difficult task of surviving under rule by a puppet government of Germany. On 25 September 1940 the Quisling 'government' issued an order deposing King Haakon VII.

In London the King and the Government in exile took an active role in the Allied campaign against Germany. On 24 April 1943 five thousand Norwegians paraded through London and gathered in the Albert Hall to celebrate the King's seventieth birthday.

On 7th June 1945, the fifth anniversary of his exile, King Haakon VII returned to Norway to be received by an enormous outburst of national rejoicing. The pre-war Storting reconvened and following established constitutional convention the King was referred by the President of the Storting to the Labor Party leader, Einar Gerhardsen, who was commissioned to form a government until fresh Parliamentary elections could be held. In the political frictions which occurred at this time it was the King and the Crown Prince who provided the focal point of national unity and celebration. The King made extensive tours throughout the country and was greeted everywhere by large and enthusiastic crowds as he spoke on the need for national unity in order to reconstruct the war-ravaged nation.

Following fresh elections the King commissioned the Labor interim Prime Minister Gerhardsen to form a permanent government and on 25 November 1945 the King opened the new Storting. Norway had returned to constitutional normality. Labor Governments continued throughout the remainder of King Haakon VII's reign and the relationship between King and Government was good. The King, whilst expressing his opinion freely in private consultations with his Ministers, withdrew from the active role which he had of necessity played in the critical war years and returned to the normal ceremonial role of a constitutional monarch. When the King died on 20 September 1957 he was mourned deeply and sincerely by the Norwegian people. He left behind him a legacy of stable constitutional monarchy. He had shown, in the most dramatic and testing circumstances possible, that a nation can adopt a non-national as its monarch and that in doing so it can provide itself with a vivid national symbol able to ensure continuity and legitimacy in the face of even the most terrible threats to the survival of a nation.

4. Australia's Constitutional Monarchy—Representing the Crown and Representing the People

Australia has had a constitutional monarchy since 26 January 1788 when the Colony of New South Wales was proclaimed with King George III as King and Captain Arthur Phillip as Governor-in-Chief and Captain-General. The Commonwealth of Australia has been a constitutional monarchy since 1 January 1901 with the coming into force of the *Commonwealth of Australia Constitution Act* 1900 under Queen Victoria as the first Queen of

Australia. During the debate about Australia's form of government under a federation, both in the Constitutional Conventions of the 1890s and in the surrounding arguments in political circles, the possibility of Australia becoming a republic was considered and rejected. At a series of referendums in the Australian States in 1899 and 1900 the Australian people chose a form of constitutional monarchy which is embodied in the Commonwealth of Australia Constitution. As the recent Republic Advisory Committee Report notes, the form of government Australia has had since then may properly be described as a 'heptarchy', consisting of seven separate monarchies, those of the six States and that of the Commonwealth.[32] Associate Professor Gerard Carney elsewhere in this book gives valuable and detailed consideration to the State forms of constitutional monarchy and their present relationship with the Commonwealth Constitution.[33] The following consideration of Australia's constitutional monarchy will be confined to the Commonwealth level.

The preamble to the Commonwealth Constitution makes it clear that what the Australian people and the Australian States assented to in 1899 and 1900 was 'to unite in one indissoluble Federal Commonwealth under the Crown of the United Kingdom of Great Britain and Ireland, and under the Constitution hereby established'.[34] By Recital 2 of the Commonwealth Constitution the provisions of the *Commonwealth of Australia Constitution Act 1900* referring to the Queen 'shall extend to Her Majesty's heirs and successors in the sovereignty of the United Kingdom'.[35] By this means the sovereignty of the Crown of Australia has passed by inheritance with the Crown of the United Kingdom from the first Queen of Australia, Queen Victoria, to the present Queen of Australia, Queen Elizabeth II. The powers of the Queen of Australia are clearly defined and few:

(1) Her Majesty constitutes one of the three elements of Parliament, the other elements being the Senate and the House of Representatives;[36]

(2) She appoints a Governor-General as her representative in the Commonwealth of Australia with 'such powers and functions of the Queen as Her Majesty may be pleased to assign him or her';[37]

(3) She may assent to, or withhold assent from, any legislation which the Governor-General at his or her discretion has reserved for the Queen's pleasure;[38]

(4) She may disallow any law within one year from the Governor-General's assent, 'and such disallowance . . . shall annul the law from the day when the disallowance is so made known';[39] and

(5) She may authorise the Governor-General to appoint any person to be his or her deputy or deputies.[40]

In recognition of the Queen's formal role in the constitutional structure every senator and every member of the House of Representatives, before taking his or her seat in Parliament, must subscribe before the Governor-General to an oath or affirmation of allegiance to the Queen in a form specified in the Schedule to the Constitution.[41] Pursuant to the *Australia Act* 1986 (Cth) the Queen is able to exercise any other powers and functions vested in her under the Commonwealth Constitution only when she is actually present in Australia.[42] It is generally recognised that the last occasion on which the Australian Monarch attempted to exercise a stance under any of these Commonwealth powers independently of the advice proffered by the Australian Prime Minister was when King George V queried the appointment of a former politician and distinguished High Court Chief Justice, Sir Isaac Isaacs, as Australia's first native born Governor-General in 1930.[43] Since the adoption of the *Statute of Westminster* 1931 by Australia in 1942 the Australian Monarch has acted only in relation to the Australian Crown on the advice of the Australian Government.[44] The passing of the *Australia Acts* by the United Kingdom and Commonwealth Parliaments in 1986 recognised formally what had been the case by convention since at least 1930, that Australia's constitutional monarchy was and is independent of any power other than that of the Commonwealth of Australia. The one nexus between the Australian monarchy and any other nation is the requirement that the title to the Australian monarchy descends by inheritance with the Crown of the United Kingdom.[45] By the Commonwealth Constitution, the Queen of Australia must be the Queen of the United Kingdom. The Queen of Australia, by virtue of the Constitutions of the Australian States, is also separately Queen of each of those States and by convention those States refer to her as Queen of Australia, the title accorded to her by the *Royal Style and Titles Act* 1973 (Cth). It is the requirement that the Crown of Australia must be linked with the Crown of the United Kingdom which is the central objection of the Australian Republican Movement. Beyond that point one encounters a divergence of views on the hopes and expectations of committed republicans from a change in the Commonwealth Constitution. It is essential to bear in mind that this is the single core issue upon which all Australian republicans agree—it is their one fundamental objection to the present system of Australian constitutional monarchy.

In relation to Australia, beyond the Queen's limited powers, which are confined solely to the appointment and removal of the Governor-General on the advice of the Australian Prime Minister, the Commonwealth Constitution puts in place a form of monarchy which is distinctively Australian and which might more appropriately be styled a 'Governor-Generalcy'. The Governor-General is appointed by the Queen of Australia upon the advice of the Australian Prime Minister, who has been appointed by the preceding Governor-General because he or she is the person who commands the majority party in the House of Representatives, whose members have been elected by the Australian people. The will of the Australian people is thus filtered through the House of Representatives to the Prime Minister who chooses the only candidate to be presented to the Queen of Australia for her consent to his or her appointment to the office of Governor-General in which the Constitution vests almost the full plenitude of the power of the Crown of Australia. The Governor-General is therefore more properly seen not simply as the representative of the Crown but also as the representative of the people. Certainly Governors-General, at least since Sir Zelman Cowen's tenure, have seen themselves as 'representing the Australian people to themselves'.[46] We may see in this certain similarities with the 1947 Japanese Constitution by virtue of which the Japanese people are made the 'Head of State' and the Emperor exercises his duties as their representative. The powers conferred by the Commonwealth Constitution on the Governor-General are extensive. The Govenor-General:

(1) may summon, convene, prorogue and dissolve the Parliament;[47]
(2) may assent to Bills or reserve Bills for the Queen's assent;[48]
(3) exercises the executive power of the Commonwealth;[49]
(4) chooses the members of the Federal Executive Council;[50]
(5) appoints Ministers of State and settles upon the administrative arrangements for government Departments;[51]
(6) is the Commander in Chief of the armed forces of the Commonwealth;[52]

(7) in Council, appoints the Justices of the High Court and may remove these upon an address from both Houses of Parliament;[53]
(8) in Council, appoints members of the Inter-State Commission when such a body exists and may remove these upon an address from both Houses of Parliament;[54]
(9) may appoint deputies for himself or herself;[55] and
(10) may approve laws changing the Commonwealth Constitution if such changes have been approved by a majority of the electors in a majority of the States in a referendum.[56]

By convention the Governor-General exercises all of these powers upon the advice of the Prime Minister of the Commonwealth of Australia who, in turn by convention, has been chosen by the Governor-General as the leader of the party commanding the support of a majority in the House of Representatives. The Governor-General has extensive reserve powers, amongst which is the power to remove a Prime Minister in an emergency.[57] However, such is not an issue to do with republicanism—it is an issue to do with the Australian Constitution whatever our Head of State system may be. It is as much or as little a problem under a monarchy as it would be under a republic. Indeed, it is argued that whereas the conventions which govern the use of these powers seem reasonably clear and accepted according to the monarchical Westminster traditions, it is probable that if Australia was to become a republic a new system would evolve.

Apart from these formal and extensive constitutional powers the Governor-General has inherited the traditional role of the Crown in ceremonial and public life. The opening of Parliament and the Governor-General's address are the key ceremonial duties of the Governor-General. Beyond them lies a myriad of activities in opening ceremonies, civic tours, travelling the country and meeting the people. Unfortunately many champions of a republic, be they journalists, writers or politicians, completely undervalue this element of the Governor-General's role. It is a vital one valued by the community at a grass roots level and must form part of the Head of State's key functions no matter what choice Australians make on their constitutional future. The Governor-General, from the time of Sir Paul Hasluck's tenure in 1971, has also been allowed by the Australian Government to represent Australia internationally.[58] It has been open to Australia to increase this international role of the Governor-General and to ensure that the Governor-General is accorded full Head of State status. This has occurred in relation to the visit by the present Governor-General, the Hon. Bill Hayden AC, and Mrs Hayden, to Japan for the funeral of the Showa Emperor and the enthronement of Emperor Akihito. The problem that appears to exist in regard to the extent to which the Governor-General is allowed a high national and international profile, which accords with the role as our resident Head of State in the absence of the Queen, is that politicians do not want to share the limelight with such a person. Internationally our Prime Ministers and Ministers for Foreign Affairs have generally been eager to focus media attention on themselves by undertaking major overseas tours. Domestically as well, political leaders prefer to ensure that at high profile public events they are the centre of attention rather than the Governor-General. A major flaw in the republican case, particularly given the nature of some of the politicians who champion that cause, is that a President would be in no better situation than the Governor-General. The problem lies not in the nature of whether we are a constitutional monarchy or a republic but, rather, what role will the Prime Minister allow the resident Head of State outside of the strict allocation of duties and functions under the Constitution? This issue should be settled and a clear understanding documented. This can be done under our present Constitution and it should be done.

The remaining issue which, in this brief traversal of Australia's system of constitutional monarchy, needs to be touched upon is one addressed at the outset—the dignity of the Crown and its capacity to represent the continuity of our history, investing the Head of State role with a depth of symbolism which would be absent under a republic. In all other areas most rational and sincere republicans are divided by only a thin line from rational and sincere constitutional monarchists—hence such intense and earnest debate about the documentation of the reserve powers and the checks and balances which protect our constitutional freedoms. The one element which no sincere monarchist, however rational a constitutionalist he or she may be, can accept with a republic is the absence of a monarch. Since Federation the Crown of Australia has been held by a succession of remarkable, revered and well-loved people. Queen Elizabeth II is admired by most and beloved by many for the exemplary manner in which she has performed her duties for forty years and for what she represents, not simply of this country's links with Britain but its links with the values and traditions of western civilisation. It is not argued that those who are deeply committed monarchists form a majority of the Australian population—but there is a very large element drawn from almost every age, racial, ethnic and religious background, who have very intense feelings in favour of a monarchy in general and Queen Elizabeth II in particular. These people will feel utterly bereft if Australia abandons an element of monarchy in its constitutional system. When the principles of multiculturalism extol the rights of minorities to preserve their cultures within Australia it seems extraordinarily unjust to treat as worthless or of little account such a strong body of feeling, which embodies such a key feature in human history and which is so widely understood around the world, particularly in our own region. The great strength of Australia's present system of government is that it combines the useful vestiges of monarchy in retaining the Queen of Australia in a limited role, with a form of republicanism, the 'Governor-Generalcy', with extensive powers to supervise Australia's vigorous political process. This 'Crowned Republic' of the Commonwealth of Australia ought to satisfy all but the most extreme monarchist and republican positions. The events of the last few years seem to indicate that it is unacceptable to a small but vocal republican minority. Some form of change seems likely—it is the nature, extent and direction of change which is completely uncertain. In exploring the options Australians must be open-minded, analysing what is best and valuable from the system we have; what we may wish to borrow from other systems or invent for ourselves; and to pursue the consideration of options for change with no foregone conclusions as to the outcome. Above all, the pursuit of these matters must take place in an even-handed manner aiming for consensus and avoiding acrimony which otherwise will cripple our Head of State system for generations. While this debate is allowed to continue in a positive and constructive manner the present system, with the Queen of Australia and Governor-General's roles as they are presently fulfilled, should be accorded full respect and dignity, not being subjected to an insulting process of denigration and whittling away by attrition. The time for change from our present form of constitutional monarchy will be when the Australian people have indicated their choice in the only manner possible, by referendum under the Commonwealth Constitution. However, there are changes which we may develop and implement to improve the present system without referendum.

5. Australia's Head of State System—Options for the Future

In determining the way forward in Australia's Head of State debate only two serious obstacles present themselves. First, the insistence by the present champions of an Australian republic that Australia cannot share its Head of State with another country; and secondly, the insistencence by the champions of Australia's constitutional monarchy that some real element of monarchy must be retained in Australia's Head of State system.

All the other issues, such as the mode of nomination and selection of resident Head of State, removal of resident Head of State, duties of resident Head of State, documentation of reserve powers and sources of constitutional advice for resident Head of State, may be addressed equally with reference to the present Governor-Generalcy or a Presidency. None of these need divisive debate and none of them require a referendum with reference to the Governor-General. What should not be insuperable obstacles are the constitutional impediments, both Commonwealth and State, to Australia making a significant change from its present form of constitutional monarchy. If the Australian people seriously want to change from the present Head of State system to another then they should not be held captive by constitutional barriers: the means to achieve constitutional change must be found and placed within their grasp.

The two areas that may be considered in terms of options for the future of the Australian Head of State are reforming the present system and moving towards a new system.

A. Reforming the Present System

As the recent public debate has demonstrated, there is a real need for the role of the existing Australian Head of State system to be better understood by the public and for its functions and duties to be better documented. Significant improvement in this regard may be achieved by the establishment of a small Head of State Commission, to be chaired by the Governor-General and to consist of the Prime Minister, the Speaker of the House of Representatives, the President of the Senate, the Chief Justice of the High Court, the Chief of Staff of the Armed Services, a recently retired Governor-General and possibly the Chairpersons of the Australian University Vice-Chancellors Council and the Aboriginal and Torres Strait Islander Commission, with the role of developing legislation and policy to document the issues as clearly as is practicable, including the following:

- the eligibility criteria for the position of Governor-General;
- the method of receiving nominations for the position of Governor-General from the Australian people;
- the method of selecting one candidate from nominees for the position of Governor-General;
- the method of formally choosing the person whose name is to be presented by the Prime Minister to the Queen of Australia for her appointment of the person as Governor-General of Australia;
- the formal constitutional duties required of the Governor-General;
- the principal reserve powers to be exercised and guidelines on the manner and circumstances in which they may be exercised;
- the civic and representational duties to be undertaken by the Governor-General nationally and internationally;
- the form of address and ceremonial to apply to the Governor-General;
- the relationship of the Governor-General to the State Governors (by negotiation with the States);
- the mechanism by which the Governor-General may seek emergency constitutional advice, preferably from the High Court;
- the grounds for removal and means of removal of the Governor-General, which should match the means by which the Governor-General's name was selected for presentation by the Prime Minister to the Queen; and
- the role of the Queen of Australia and the duties to be undertaken by the Royal Family in Australia.

In regard to these issues it is suggested that the following options be considered:
- people who have held elected political office in the previous five years should not be eligible for nomination as Governor-General;
- nominees should have achieved national prominence in some field of endeavour;
- nominees should clearly be able to handle both the significant constitutional duties and also the civic and representational duties in a thorough and dignified manner which reflects credit on the Australian people;
- the Head of State Commission should select only one candidate from eligible nominees for approval by Cabinet;

- following approval of Cabinet the candidate selected by the Head of State Commission should be presented for confirmation of the nomination by a joint sitting in the Great Hall of Parliament House in Canberra of either all members of the Commonwealth Parliament, or all members of all Australian Parliaments if the Governor-General is to have a formal constitutional relationship with the State Governors;
- the term of office should be eight years;
- the Governor-General should be installed in office in the Great Hall of Parliament House, Canberra, in a major public event which reflects the symbolic dignity of the position as representative of the Crown and representative of the Australian people; and
- these principles should be incorporated in a Head of State Act.

B. Moving Towards a New System

The task of reforming the present system should commence immediately. In tandem with that process the means of reviewing and exploring options for constitutional change should be found. It is essential that this be handled in a manner which pursues consensus and which allows any change which may result to receive wholehearted support by the Australian people. The proposals put forward by Senator Cheryl Kernot on 31 October 1993 have much to commend them in dismissing the minimalist republican position and proposing that the issue of constitutional reforms, including the Head of State system, should be handled by the Constitutional Centenary Foundation in a five year programme.[59] If this programme is implemented then the following matters should be considered:

- The need for a permanent Australian Constitutional Commission to be established as the focal point for educating the public about the Commonwealth Constitution and handling consideration of the need for ongoing constitutional reform;
- Presentation of issues such as that of the Head of State must be handled in an even-handed manner—deep public anger and bitterness must not be permitted, as has occurred in the past, to result from elements of the media, politics and the intelligensia arrogating to themselves the right to dictate how the Australian people must think and feel about such sensitive issues as the Head of State.
- Once proposals for a package of major constitutional change have been prepared over the next five years, preparation should

be made for direct election by the Australian people of an Australian Constitutional Convention to be held at least two years after the celebration of the Centenary of Federation in 2001, allowing a proper and united celebration of that important national birthday to occur free from rancour over such sensitive issues as the Head of State.
- In exploring options for the future the Constitutional Centenary Foundation and any Constitutional Convention must bear in mind that there is a strong element of the Australian people who want to keep some form of constitutional monarchy. Therefore options for future change must include a constitutional monarchy as one of the choices available. The recent monograph 'Heads of State' prepared by the Constitutional Centenary Foundation canvasses only republican models when there are many excellent models of constitutional monarchy to consider, not the least of which is the one presently enjoyed.[60]
- If it is decided that the issue of sharing our Head of State with another country is the fundamental problem which outweighs all other factors, including the fact that our present system of Australian constitutional monarchy effectively combines both monarchical and republican elements in a uniquely Australian way, then acknowledgment must be given of the significance and validity of the monarchist element amongst the Australian people by allowing a referendum to contain a choice between a President and a resident Monarch. The case study on Norway shows that a strongly egalitarian nation without a recent tradition of resident monarchy has been able to adopt a suitable person to assume the position of resident Monarch. Norway and Belgium are two examples of nations which have benefited significantly from this being done and with having their national life protected and enhanced by the process. The means by which this could occur include the following:

(a) Identification of a suitable candidate, amongst whom might be included Prince Harry, Prince Edward, Princess Anne and the Duke of Gloucester.

(b) Introduction by a Regency Act of the Commonwealth and State Parliaments assented to by the Queen by means of which the Queen assigns all of her duties as Queen of Australia to a Regent selected from suitable candidates who would reside in Australia and who would exercise the full plenitude of powers of the Crown of Australia and the States including the right to appoint the Governor-General if such a

position is to be retained—this could occur before the centenary of Federation or, indeed, before the Olympic Games in 2000, if desired.
(c) During the lifetime of the present Queen, after the Regency had been assessed for a worthwhile period of years, the Australian people could be presented with a threefold choice:
  (i) Do Australians wish to have a Head of State who is not also the Head of State of another country?
  (ii) If the answer to the first question is no, then the present system of Australian constitutional monarchy would be retained.
  (iii) If the answer to the first question is yes, then do the Australian people wish to have:
   — a republican form of Head of State indirectly elected by Parliament; or
   — a constitutional monarchial form of Head of State with the Regent becoming King or Queen of Australia invested with all of the present powers of the Crown and the Governor-General. It must be emphasised that if this option is to be pursued it would have to be on the basis that the resident Regent/Monarch would be accommodated and remunerated no differently from the present Governor-General and that no greater trappings or dignity would surround the position than apply in respect of the Governor-General other than the use of the present royal titles and form of address in respect of the Monarch and the children of the Monarch.

Conclusion

The concept of monarchy is well understood and respected in our own part of the world, as it is in Europe. The monarchy is the oldest institution in the life of Australia and it reflects the continuity of our history. It provides a practical means of providing a Head of State free from political association and not requiring regular and expensive elections for the position of President, or pensions and benefits for retired Presidents. The dignity which surrounds the Crown reflects deeper needs than those represented by a President. The present system of Australian constitutional monarchy has served this nation well and can continue to do so into the future. It can be improved but it should not be jettisoned without good reason. If that good reason is, in the collective mind of the Australian people, the difficulty of sharing our Head of State with another nation then the principles of constitutional monarchy still require valid consideration in the choice which the Australian people are offered. A low-key localised monarchy may provide a popular symbol of national unity and the aspirations of the Australian people. We must be open-minded as we consider the way in which we should move forward.

Notes

1. W. Bagehot, *The English Constitution* (London: Oxford University Press), 67.
2. Office of the Governor of Victoria, *The Governor of Victoria*, 2.
3. Quoted by Sir Harold Nicholson in *King George V, His Life and Reign*, 61–63.
4. Article III Jushichi Kempo in W.G. Aston—*Constitution of Nihongi* (Charles E. Tuttle & Co., 1972), vol.2, 129.
5. Aston, *supra* note 4, Book XXV vol.II.
6. Quoted in J.M. Packard, *Sons of Heaven: A Portrait of the Japanese Monarchy* (Queen Anne Press, 1988), 171.
7. *Id.* 175.
8. *Id.* 199.
9. Quoted in C. Gluck, *Japan's Modern Myths* (Princeton: Princeton University Press, 1985), 75.
10. *Id.* 76.
11. *Imperial Rescript on Education* quoted by C. Gluck, *Id.* 121.
12. Packard, *supra* note 6.
13. *Id.* 295.
14. *Id.* 296.
15. The Constitution of Japan, set out in Kyoko Inoue, *MacArthur's Japanese Constitution* (Chicago: University of Chicago Press, 1991), 275.
16. See the discussions of the subtleties of these distinctions in Inoue, *Id.* 190–194, 205–219.
17. Quoted in S.S. Large, *Emperor Hirohito and Showa Japan* (London: Routledge, 1992).
18. T. Greve, *Haakon VII of Norway* (New York: Hippocrene Books, 1983), 16.
19. *Id.* 28.
20. *Id.* 30.
21. *Id.* 32.
22. *Ibid.*

23. *Id.* 62–63.
24. *Id.* 63.
25. *Id.* 87.
26. *Id.* 94.
27. *Id.* 133.
28. *Id.* 135.
29. *Id.* 149.
30. *Id.* 150.
31. *Id.* 152.
32. The Report of the Republic Advisory Committee, *An Australian Republic: The Options* (Canberra: A.G.P.S., 2 vols., 1993), vol.1, 124.
33. G. Carney, 'Republicanism and State Constitutions' in M.A. Stephenson and C. Turner (eds.) *Australia: Republic or Monarchy* (Brisbane: University of Queensland Press, 1994).
34. Preamble to *Commonwealth of Australia Constitution Act* 1900.
35. *Id.* Recital 2.
36. *Id.* Chapter I, s.1.
37. *Id.* Chapter I, s.2.
38. *Id.* Chapter I, ss.58, 60.
39. *Id.* Chapter I, s.59.
40. *Id.* Chapter VII, s.126.
41. *Id.* Chapter I, s.42.
42. *Australia Act* 1986 (Cth) s.7(4).
43. H. S. Nicholas, *The Australian Constitution* (Sydney: Law Book Co., 1952), 68.
44. *Statute of Westminster (Adoption) Act* 1942 (Cth).
45. *Commonwealth of Australia Constitution Act* 1900, Preamble and Recital 2.
46. A private conversation between Sir Zelman Cowen and the author, 11 February 1993.
47. *Commonwealth of Australia Constitution Act* 1900, Chapter I, s.5 and Chapter II, s.57.
48. *Id.* Chapter II, s.58.
49. *Id.* Chapter II, s.61.
50. *Id.* Chapter II, s.62.
51. *Id.* Chapter II, s.64.
52. *Id.* Chapter II, s.68.
53. *Id.* Chapter III, s.72.
54. *Id.* Chapter IV, s.103.
55. *Id.* Chapter VII, s.126.
56. *Id.* Chapter VIII, s.128.
57. R. D. Lumb, *The Constitution of the Commonwealth of Australia Annotated* (4th ed., Sydney: Butterworths, 1989), paras [067]–[070].
58. Sir David Smith, Occasional Paper 1—*Australian Constitutional Monarchy* (Sydney: 1992), 5.
59. Senator C. Kernot, *Press Release*, 31 October 1993.
60. Constitutional Centenary Foundation, *Heads of State*.

The British Influence on the Australian Constitution

A.A. Preece[*]

The extensive British influence on the development of the Constitution of the Commonwealth of Australia is undoubted. Also, much of the current constitutional debate, centred upon the question whether Australia should become a republic, is couched in terms of the need to cut such remaining constitutional links with the United Kingdom as may continue to exist. It has been argued by proponents of a republic that cutting these links, despite its being conceded that they are now extremely tenuous and largely symbolic, will have major beneficial effects. It is said that by making Australia 'fully independent' new energies will be released which will stimulate positive developments in constitutional and other fields.

Of course, many different views are held among republicans. Some argue directly that the need to make changes to the Constitution to bring about a republic is an appropriate opportunity for a major review of the Constitution. Of those who, to the contrary, argue for 'minimalist' changes to accommodate a republic, many still think that the change will stimulate new constitutional thinking. For example, it is thought that in determining constitutional issues courts will look less to Britain for analogies and more to the United States. Consequently, it is an appropriate time to examine the British influence in the development of the Australian Constitution.

The Achievement of Independence from Britain

The proposition that Australia needs to do more to become fully independent of Britain is highly controversial, since many would

---

[*] Lecturer in Law, University of Queensland.

regard complete independence as having been fully achieved certainly by the passage of the *Australia Act* 1986 by the United Kingdom Parliament. Others would argue that independence was achieved at an earlier time. The passage of the *Statute of Westminster* by the British Parliament in 1931 is seen by many as the crucial time, or its adoption in Australia in 1942.[1] Some would even argue that Federation in 1901 is the crucial time, since the Constitution established at that time by the passage by the British Parliament of the *Commonwealth of Australia Constitution Act* 1900 (UK), contained a provision for its own amendment in section 128 which may well have been held by the High Court to enable the remaining links with the United Kingdom to be eliminated.

Others place more emphasis on Australia's conduct in international affairs, such as the establishment of overseas diplomatic representation, or the fact that Australia felt competent to declare war on its own by 1942, as being crucial to the process of achieving full independence. It could even be argued that, as the representatives of the six colonies themselves essentially drafted the Constitution and that it was largely 'rubber stamped' in London after approval by referenda in the colonies, a large measure of *de facto* independence had been achieved by that time.

Indeed, the *Statute of Westminster* 1931 (UK) brought about a degree of interdependence between the United Kingdom and the Dominions, since provision was made for the Dominions to be consulted before the law relating to succession to the Crown was changed.[2] Such a procedure was adopted at the abdication of Edward VIII in 1936.[3] The participation of the Government of the Commonwealth of Australia in that process as well as popular approval in the 1890s of the draft Constitution containing monarchical elements, belie claims that the monarchy is a 'foreign' institution foisted upon Australia without its people's approval in any form having been given.

The Influence of British Constitutional Traditions on the Drafting of the Constitution in the 1890s

While it has always been conceded that British constitutional traditions played a major role in the drafting of the Constitution in the 1890s, it has also been maintained that other sources such as the American and Swiss Constitutions played a large emphasis. However, the author wishes to argue that the British influence on the final form of the Constitution, whether consciously recognised in the debates of the 1890s or not, is much greater than hitherto supposed. Indeed, it will be suggested that the Constitution is essentially a 'snapshot' of British constitutional practice of the 1890s, and that almost the only significant departures from this were those forced by the need to accommodate a federal system of government. Also the Constitution is a written constitution having superior force to ordinary law, which had no counterpart in British constitutional practice of that era.

Relevant Aspects of the British Constitutional Tradition

Britain has essentially enjoyed constitutional continuity since the 'Glorious Revolution' and revolution Settlement of 1688–1689.[4] This is an enviable record that not even the United States can fully match during the period of just over two centuries since the establishment of its Constitution, since there were certain extremely dubious actions by American authorities during the period of the Civil War of 1860–1865. As a constitutional offshoot of the British system, emanating from 1788, Australia has enjoyed constitutional and legal continuity since its inception, unless it can be argued that the High Court decision in 1992 in the *Mabo* case,[5] with its wholesale abandonment of legal doctrines such as *terra nullius* upon which the Australian legal system was based at its inception, is regarded as an extra-constitutional revolution Settlement.

The British 'Glorious Revolution' was the culmination and final settlement of the constitutional disputes of the seventeenth century, and related religious disputes going back to the Reformation. Traditionally religion has been regarded as playing the major role in these upheavals; however, they were essentially political. Religion was involved largely because it played such an important role in politics at that time. A certain amount of limited tidying up was carried out a little more than a decade later with the passing of the *Act of Settlement* 1700, so for the purposes of analysis it may be regarded as part of the constitutional Settlement. The 1689 constitutional Settlement has a number of key features which are reproduced in the Australian Constitution.

Constitutional Monarchy Based Ultimately upon Popular Consent

It may be argued that the monarchy had gradually become constitutional as opposed to absolute over a period of centuries, and that the monarchy was based on popular consent at and from the Restoration in 1660, since a Parliament was summoned which issued the call to Charles II to return. However, in 1660, the King was merely expected to respect the constitutional position which had been reached by 1641, whereas in 1689 the grant of the Crown to William and Mary by the Convention Parliament was clearly conditional upon their respect for the constitutional fundamentals designed to make arbitrary rule by the Monarch impossible.

In the latter part of the reign of Charles II and during the reign of James II, it was still possible for judges to be partisan, for juries to be stacked, and even for Parliament to be stacked. Accordingly, judicial independence and freedom of election to, and debate in, Parliament were secured in 1689.[6] Several alleged royal prerogatives assumed by James II were declared illegal: the suspending power,[7] the dispensing power,[8] levying of taxes or raising or keeping a standing army without consent of Parliament,[9] establishing special courts and commissions,[10] and grants of indemnities before conviction.[11]

In pre-Norman Anglo-Saxon times there was an elective element in succession to the throne, and there are still traces of this in the coronation ceremony. Even today, any person succeeding to the Crown must sign the declaration prescribed by the Bill of Rights of 1689.

The events of 1688-89 finally ended any notions of the divine right of kings to which such frequent appeal had been made by the Stuart Kings. The divine right of kings was a medieval doctrine evolved to aid the claims of kings and princes against the overlordship of the Pope. Paradoxically, an appeal was made to it in England by the Stuart Kings who were strongly suspected of a wish to restore the authority of the Pope in Britain.

The provisions of the Australian Constitution dealing with Executive Government (sections 61–70) are consistent with the conventions of constitutional monarchy evolved in Britain. The inability for the Executive Government to rule without Parliament, or to raise money without parliamentary approval, is ensured by the exclusivity of Parliament's power to legislate under section 52.

Parliamentary Privilege and Freedom of Election to Parliament Asserted

As mentioned above this was asserted in sections 8 and 9 of the British Bill of Rights.[12] The benefits of section 9 are entrenched in the Australian Constitution (sections 49 and 50). Section 8 of the Bill of Rights asserts freedom of election to Parliament. In this context it is interesting to note that in 1992 the High Court used the essential need for free speech as part of the process of proper Parliamentary elections as the basis for its invalidation of legislation attempting to restrict political advertising.[13]

Sovereignty and Supremacy of Parliament

The restriction of the monarchy to a constitutional role, meant that parliamentary sovereignty became the abiding feature of the British constitutional system in the years following 1689. The power of Parliament to make laws had been expanding for centuries. The time of Henry VIII is particularly significant as the dramatic legislation connected with the break with Rome, particularly the *Act of Supremacy* 1534, did much to dispel notions that there were limits on the power of Parliament to legislate. However, it was still possible in 1610, in *Bonham's* case[14] for the common law judges to argue that there were some common law legal principles that Parliament could not overturn. This notion of judicial review of legislation disappeared completely after 1689, but reappeared in the United States in 1804 in *Marbury v. Maddison*.[15] It exists in like fashion in Australia, and has recently shown signs of reappearing in Britain as a result of the supremacy of European law over domestic law of Member States.[16]

Religious Freedom Established to a Greater Extent Than Ever Before

Although much attention tends to focus on the lack of religious freedom for Catholics after 1689, the *Toleration Act* 1689, which formed part of the 1689 Settlement, granted much wider religious freedom than ever before. All the various Protestant sects achieved full toleration, although non-Anglicans remained subject to disabilities in the public service and the universities, though not in respect of election to Parliament, until well into the nineteenth century. Although the *Toleration Act* 1689 did not extend to Catholics, in practice they were allowed to observe their religion, particularly in private houses, the laws against them being invoked only in times of emergency such as the risings in support of the 'Old Pretender' in 1715 and 1745.[17]

A limited guarantee of religious freedom also exists as part of the Australian Constitution in section 116. The United States Constitution has a similar guarantee, the First Amendment to the Constitution and in the first article of the Bill of Rights of 1791. This operates more extensively than the Australian guarantee in that it has been extended by judicial decision in the United States.

Checks Upon the Exercise of Arbitrary Power by the Executive

The provisions of the Bill of Rights dealing with the above issue have already been mentioned in connection with the confinement of the monarchy to the constitutional road.

Securing of Judicial Independence

Following the untoward experiences of partisan judges and stacked juries, judges were to hold their commissions during good behaviour. This provision was strengthened in 1700 by the provision in the *Act of Settlement* 1700 that, in addition, judges might be removed only upon an address by both Houses of Parliament. Under this protection the judges, while surrendering the last vestiges of the concept that they could overrule Parliament, developed the common law extensively to protect the individual against arbitrary government.[18] Section 72 of the Australian Constitution is in almost identical terms to the relevant provision of the *Act of Settlement* 1700.

The Conservative Tone of the Settlement

The English people have been generally conservative rather than radical in political and constitutional outlook. One example of this is that even in times of apparently radical change, the 'radicals' have generally couched their appeal in terms of restoration of 'ancient rights and liberties' which the temporal government is alleged to have failed to maintain. Ever since *Magna Carta* allegations of breaches of its terms or failure to live up to its spirit have been possible. However, there have even been appeals at various times to earlier underlying Saxon freedoms said to have existed before the imposition of centralised monarchy at the Norman Conquest.

Although not expressed in the Bill of Rights, the implication of the Settlement is of individuals equal under the law with guaranteed basic rights, a unique concept in the world of 1689. A common thread runs from this thinking to that of Thomas Jefferson and the other founding fathers of the American Constitution almost exactly a century later. Such thinking underpinned the whole of the liberal enlightenment of the eighteenth century, led to a long period of pre-eminence of the English speaking countries who inherited these traditions, and has dominated western political thought until severely challenged in the 1960s. In tandem with these challenges, this pre-eminence has shown major signs of recent decline.

Main Developments in British Constitutional Practice Between 1689 and the 1890s

The genius of the constitutional Settlement of 1689 is demonstrated both by the fact that it has required no fundamental change in three hundred years, and that, by securing to the citizen an immensely greater status in law and liberty than existed until well into the nineteenth century in almost all other countries, it enabled unprecedented economic and social development in Britain during the succeeding period. The only major discord in this process was the disastrous quarrel with the American Colonies, leading to their independence. This was brought about almost exclusively by the failure of George III to observe the principles of the 1689 Settlement in relation to those colonies. Following upon the success of the colonists in the American War of Independence, no King was again able to contemplate any kind of backtracking on the 1689 Settlement. Ireland also presented problems from time to time, probably because the 1689 Settlement was never properly accepted and implemented. Ireland was the only part of the realm to witness a clash of arms in the period between 1688-1890, which may have been the major factor in causing religious bitterness to never fully heal.

The most significant changes since 1689 have been in the relationship between Crown and Parliament over the actual conduct of government and veto of legislation, and in the relationship between the two Houses of Parliament. The fact that the stage that particularly the latter development had reached by the 1890s was reflected in the Australian Constitution is a strong vindication of the 'snapshot' theory that the founding fathers copied the existing British practice in the 1890s.

Subsequent Changes in the Relationship Between the Crown and Parliament

Although formally nothing changed in the subsequent relationship between Crown and Parliament, the situation has been transformed by the development of the convention that the Crown acts only on the advice of ministers. William III had a very hands-on approach to government, Anne less so, and the arrival of the non-English speaking George I hastened the development of Cabinet Government and the concept of reliance on a parliamentary majority developed. The King could still strongly influence policy; George II was the last King to lead his troops into battle in the 1740s. The attempt by George III to take back more power into his hands led ultimately to disaster and has never again been tried.

The Crown must still assent to legislation today. However, in 1800 George III was still able personally to veto the emancipation of Catholics as part of Pitt the Younger's scheme for the Union of Ireland with Britain. Pitt resigned over the issue. By 1829 George IV could not resist this move for it had become clear that a veto could result in the government's resignation, followed by an election in which all parties would be united against the King on this issue. Since 1829 the Crown has not attempted to veto legislation except on the advice of the Prime Minister.

Subsequent Changes to the Relationship Between the Two Houses of Parliament

The legislative powers of both Houses were essentially equal in 1689, although the House of Commons was seen as the initiator of the vote of supply for the Government. Accordingly, the principle was established that budgetary measures must originate in the House of Commons, and could not be amended in the Upper House. For two centuries the Lords did not exercise their right to reject, as opposed to their lack of right to amend, a budget until the rejection of the Lloyd George budget in 1909 which led to the restriction of their powers under the *Parliament Act* 1911.

The co-equal legislative powers of the two Houses, subject only to the exclusive right of the Lower House to propose and amend money Bills, being the understood position in the 1890s is exactly reflected in section 53 of the Australian Constitution. Interestingly, the restriction of the powers of the Lords to reject money Bills, contained in the *Parliament Act* 1911, was essentially copied in relation to the Upper House in New South Wales in 1933.[19]

However, certain conventions developed regarding the veto of legislation by the House of Lords. Towards the end of the reign of Queen Anne the terms of the Treaty of Utrecht, ending the long wars of the Spanish Succession against France, were narrowly rejected in the House of Lords. Following this, passage of the legislation was secured by the creation by Queen Anne of the necessary, fairly small, number of Tory peers. This precedent was to have momentous consequences more than a century later. While the years 1710–1714 were a time of particularly sharp political division, generally in the eighteenth century sharp disagreements were rare since each House of Parliament largely represented the landed interests.

However, by 1832, the House of Commons had become unrepresentative of the great new towns and cities produced by the Industrial Revolution, and pocket and rotten boroughs had proliferated, hence the presentation of the Great Reform Bill in 1831. This Bill was rejected by the Lords, but after a general election had confirmed a Commons majority for the Bill, the House of Lords was forced to pass it by the threat of a mass creation of Whig peers to secure its passage. Accordingly, it became the convention that the House of Lords' veto could be overcome by a successful appeal to the people on the issue at a general election.

This procedure was followed in 1909–1911 to pass first the Lloyd George 1909 budget, and subsequently the *Parliament Act* 1911, two elections in 1910 being necessary to effect this process. After the rejection of the budget and its subsequent re-instatement, the Government of the day decided to put an end to the veto once and for all through the Parliament Bill. On the other hand the other major exercise of veto power by the House of Lords, the rejection of the second Irish Home Rule Bill in 1894, was initially a victory for the Upper House. The Government did not immediately call an election on the issue but was soundly defeated a year later in 1895 so the veto was regarded as having been endorsed by the voters.

It is highly significant that the Australian Constitution was framed after the English convention was developed but before the *Parliament Act* 1911. The provisions in section 57 of the Constitution for resolving deadlocks between the two Houses appear to be a translation of the current British convention on the matter. An election is required before the Senate can be overridden. Of course, with an elected Upper House there can be no exact parallel to the threat to create peers, so the joint sitting is substituted as a means whereby the House of Representatives, being more numerous, is likely to prevail.

An interesting sidelight on this matter is that the powers of the Canadian Senate, originally contained in the *British North America Act* 1867 (UK), were equal to those of the House of Commons, save that money Bills had to originate in the Lower House.[20] The lack of restriction on amending money Bills in the Senate may have stemmed from the lesser prominence of this convention in 1867 than its significance a generation later. The lack of any procedure for removing deadlocks may have stemmed from a lack of perceived need owing to the appointed nature of the Senate, or from the strong visibility of the United States example which also may have influenced the approach taken to the amendment of money Bills. What is fascinating is that in 1982 the powers of the Canadian Senate were in some respects reduced to a delaying power somewhat similar to that of the House of Lords by the new constitutional arrangements established by the *Canada Act* 1982.[21]

Other Examples of British Influence on the Australian Constitution

Numerous examples of the copying of British practice in the Australian Constitution have already been given. The overall tone of the Australian Constitution like that of the Settlement of 1689[22] is conservative. This in itself is an example of British influence. As for the rest of the Constitution, sections 1-50 set up a Parliament consisting of two chambers and the Crown, represented by the Governor-General, according to the British pattern. Section 80 is a guarantee of trial by jury, which has its origins in article 11 of the Bill of Rights of 1689, and is influenced by the Sixth Amendment to the American Constitution, itself inspired by the Bill of Rights of 1689. Remaining provisions are concerned with the federal system, which has no exact counterpart in Britain. However, here it is the United States experience which is drawn upon heavily, and since, as is argued below, the American Constitution is largely a 'snapshot' of British constitutional practice of the late eighteenth century, the British influence, albeit indirect, is strong here also.

The only major non-British import seems to be the lifting of the Swiss referendum requirement for the approval of constitutional amendments in section 128. In this respect Australia did not follow the United States, where amendments are proposed by a two-thirds majority of both Houses of Congress and ratified by the legislatures in three-quarters of the States (or by conventions).[23] However, the state of communications in 1787 as opposed to that in the 1890s may have accounted for this difference, as it may of Australia being in advance of the United States in adopting popular election of senators as opposed to State appointment. The United States adopted this practice in 1913 by virtue of the ratification of the Seventeenth Amendment. Equal representation of the constituent parts of the Federation in the Upper House, follows the United States, and is very common in federal systems. Vestiges of this existed in England as far back as the Middle Ages in the equal representation of each county in the House of Commons via the two 'knights of the shires'.

Parallels with the Establishment of the Constitution of the United States

A 'snapshot' theory of adoption of British constitutional practice can also be applied to the American Constitution drawn up in 1787, and its First Ten Amendments, known collectively as the Bill of Rights, added in 1791. The Bill of Rights is very much an embodiment of certain key features of the Settlement of 1689,[24] broadened to encompass the expansion of rights by judicial decision in the eighteenth century as in *Entick v. Carrington*.[25] The Eighth Amendment of the American Bill of Rights of 1791, dealing with excessive bail and fines, and cruel and unusual punishments, is an exact copy of article 10 of the Settlement of 1689. The Second Amendment, concerning the right to bear arms, has great similarities to article 7 of the Settlement of 1689.

The 1791 Bill of Rights went further in certain areas, for example, in respect of freedom of speech (First Amendment) and quartering of soldiers (Third Amendment), probably prompted by prior experiences. However, even these were entrenching only existing common law rights as part of the Constitution, a process then thought impossible in Britain. This is also probably the reason why certain provisions of the 1689 Bill of Rights were not reproduced in 1791. In this category are the first two articles dealing with the suspending and dispensing powers. These were regarded in 1787 as having been effectively expunged from the system by desuetude during the previous century, and anyway were essentially contrary to the provision in article VI that the Constitution and the laws made 'in Pursuance thereof' were to 'be the supreme Law of the Land'. This omission may not have been made if the founding fathers had foreseen the arbitrary manner in which President Lincoln suspended *habeas corpus* in the Civil War. Congressional approval was not obtained until much later, and after some notable opponents had been banished from Congress. The Sixth Amendment guaranteeing trial by jury is directed at the same evil as article 11 of 1689. The right to petition is secured by the First Amendment and by article 5 of 1689. All the other provisions of the Bill of Rights of 1689 are effectively secured by provisions in the main body of the American Constitution.

What is of particular interest is the way in which the relationship between the main organs of government is almost exactly a codification of British practice of the time. The years 1760–1782 were the era of personal rule by George III. How did the Americans go about establishing executive government? Some wanted to make George Washington king, as many had wanted to make Oliver Cromwell in the 1650s in England. Both suggestions were quickly quashed by the respective proposed monarchs. What the Constitution does is to establish a President the Head of the Executive. That is an 'elected King'! The relationship of the two legislative chambers in America, essentially equal, but with money Bills originating in the Lower House and no provision for deadlocks, reflects the pre-1832 position in Britain.

A major feature of the American Constitution is checks and balances. This may arise from a belief that such a balance of power between the three branches of government (legislative, executive and judicial) was the essence of the 1689 Settlement, and later subverted by the personal rule of George III. Hence the President's veto power over legislation is checked by the provision for an override by a two-thirds majority of each House. The ultimate check is impeachment. For the judges this is merely a variation on the *Act of Settlement* provisions. For the President it has no direct precedent but, perhaps, is implicit in the Settlement of 1689, as William and Mary were granted the Crown on condition that they ruled in constitutional fashion.

The Future

The constitutional Settlement of 1689 in Britain, and its offshoots in the former British Colonies, has stood the test of time remarkably well, being tested strongly by the American War of Independence, but emerging triumphant at its conclusion, on both sides of the Atlantic. It suffered minor damage in the American Civil War. However, since the radicalism of the 1960s it has suffered considerable damage. To the contemporary apostles of 'political correctness' it is anathema, as they wish to elevate minority rights and favoured group rights above those of the individual. For example, freedom of speech is to be curtailed in the name of restraining vilification of certain favoured minority groups. Changes are made in criminal procedure to unduly disadvantage those charged with certain offences which are the particular target of the politically correct.

It may be more than a coincidence that while the English speaking peoples grew to be so pre-eminent in the two and a half centuries following 1689, they have suffered major declines relative to other nations since the early and mid 1960s. What is even more remarkable is that this relative decline is not uniform but seems to be greater with increased advances of political correctness. To wit, the relative economic decline has arguably been greatest in the United States, almost as much as in Canada and least in Britain. Britain is where the 1689 Settlement has been least successfully attacked to date, whereas the United States has had large parts of its Constitution effectively rewritten by a radical Supreme Court. Canada had the misfortune to have a new Constitution drawn up in 1982 in the middle of this politically correct era. The recent jurisprudence of the Australian High Court suggests that we are on the verge of following the United States' example.

Notes

1. *Statute of Westminster Adoption Act* 1942 (Cth).
2. *Statute of Westminster* 1931 (UK), ss.1, 4.
3. *His Majesty's Declaration of Abdication Act* 1936 (UK).
4. The reader may wonder why the date of the Glorious Revolution and related events is sometimes given as 1688 and sometimes as 1689. The explanation is that William of Orange landed with an army at Torbay on 5 November 1688. The adoption of the constitutional Settlement including the Bill of Rights occurred on the following 12 and 13 February, which we would regard in modern styling as 1689. However, at that time the new year commenced on Lady Day, 25 March, and this continued until the enactment of the *Calendar (New Style) Act*, 1750, by which, as from and after 31 December 1751, the legal commencement of the year was changed to 1 January. For simplicity, the date 1689 is used in this article to refer to the time of the Bill of Rights 1688 (adopted 13 February 1688 old style) and related constitutional Settlement—see *Halsbury's Laws of England*, vol 10, (London: Butterworths, 1985), 44.
5. *Mabo v. Queensland (No. 2)* (1992) 175 C.L.R. 1.
6. See Bill of Rights 1689, ss.3, 7, 8 and 11.
7. *Id.* s.1.
8. *Id.* s.2.
9. *Id.* ss. 3 and 6.
10. *Id.* s.4.
11. *Id.* s.12.
12. The history of s.9, which asserts parliamentary privilege has been eloquently recounted by Sir Clarrie Harders as part of a recent article, 'Parliamentary Privilege—Parliament versus the Courts: Cross-

examination of Committee Witnesses' (1993) 67 *Australian Law Journal* 109, particularly 112–116.
13. *Australian Capital Television Pty Ltd v. The Commonwealth* (1992) 177 C.L.R. 106.
14. (1610) 8 Co Rep 113b, 118a; 77 E.R. 646, 652.
15. (1803) 1 Cr. 137.
16. *R. v. Secretary of State for Transport* (1989) 3 C.M.L.R. 1; *R. v. Secretary of State for Transport* [1990] E.C.R 2433. [1990] 2 A.C. 85; *R. v. Secretary of State for Transport* (No.2) [1991] 1 A.C. 603.
17. See G.M. Trevelyan, *History of England* (London: Longmans, Green, 1956), 474.
18. See *Entick v. Carrington* (1765) 19 How. St. Tr. 1030, 1066; (1765) 2 Wils. K.B. 275, 292; 95 E.R. 807, 818 holding general warrants illegal and part of the whole John Wilkes saga of the later 1760s.
19. *Constitution Act* 1902 (NSW), s.5A, added by Act No.2 1933, s.5. This enables Bills appropriating revenue for the ordinary annual services of government to be enacted without the concurrence of the Legislative Council.
20. *British North America Act* 1867, s.53.
21. See *Canada Act* 1982, s.47, allowing the Senate only 180 days delaying power in relation to certain amendments.
22. See *supra* note 4 above.
23. U.S. Constitution, Art. V.
24. See *supra* note 4 above.
25. (1765) 1a St. Tr. 1030.

The American Republic

Keith A. Cline[*]

The Constitution of the United States delineates the institutional structures and functioning of the central government.[1] The Constitution separates the power of the central government into three distinct branches: the legislative, the executive and the judicial branch. These institutional branches remain intact after more than two hundred years. However, the operations and interactions of such have changed dramatically since the Republic's founding.

I. Constitutional Development

A. *The Articles of Confederation*

The thirteen American colonies declared their independence from Britain in 1776, and the Revolutionary War confirmed that independence as fact by 1781. The States banded together as a loose confederation with a weak central government in 1777, largely to collectively oppose the British. The States adopted The Articles of Confederation and Perpetual Union as their unifying document. The drafters of the Articles sought to avoid the emergence of an American despot in place of the colonial governors whom they were attempting to overthrow. They purposely avoided creating a separate executive officer who might attempt to consolidate power and rule by fiat. Instead, the Articles directed the full body of the Congress to serve as 'the executive'

---

[*] Postgraduate scholar, Faculty of Law, University of Queensland.

when in session. During congressional recesses an executive committee of the States would operate under the direction of one member serving no more than twelve months.

The Articles did not empower Congress to enforce congressional directives, and the States were often hostile toward the central government and would refuse to comply with congressional 'requests'. After the Revolutionary War some States even began printing and circulating their own currencies. The States also established tariff systems directed against the goods of other States. The governing impotence of Congress to act on behalf of any national interest became obvious. Thus in 1787, the Congress resolved that delegates chosen by the States should meet to revise the Articles.

B. The Constitutional Convention

Fifty-five delegates from twelve States participated during the four months of the Constitutional Convention that met in Philadelphia through the summer of 1787.[2] The delegates readily agreed that a stronger central government was necessary, but they debated the form that government should take. One delegate from New York openly declared himself to be an admirer of the British monarchy and House of Lords.[3] However, he understood that the American people would be reluctant to accept a monarchy after violently rejecting just such a form of government so recently. Pragmatically, Alexander Hamilton embraced the republican philosophy and became an influential apologist for the proposed Constitution that emerged from the Convention.

A republican form of government became the preferred model early in the Convention. James Madison, a delegate from Virginia who later became the fourth President of the United States, offered this general definition of a republic:

> A government which derives all its powers directly or indirectly from the great body of the people; and is administered by persons holding their offices during pleasure, for a limited period, or during good behaviour.[4]

Madison persuasively promoted the republican form to the other delegates arguing, 'The mass of citizens should not be without a voice in making the laws which they are to obey, and in choosing the magistrates who are to administer them'.[5]

The delegates' mistrust of human motives in the political process led them to incorporate institutionally-based separation of powers in the Constitution.[6] That is, the powers of the central government were to be shared and exercised among three distinct branches of the government: a legislative branch consisting of two chambers would be responsible for making laws; an executive branch would enforce those laws; and a judicial 'checks and balances' branch would interpret those laws through a system of justly appointed courts. The Constitution also provides a system of 'checks and balances' between the separate branches of government. For example, the Senate checks the majority votes in the House of Representatives. The Constitution requires a majority vote in both Houses of Congress for a Bill to become a law. Even then, the President may veto the Bill. Congress may override the President's veto with a two-thirds affirmative vote for the Bill in both chambers. Further, the President must seek Senate confirmation of his or her appointments and treaties.

The delegates adjourned the Convention in September 1787. Governor Robert Morris, a delegate from Pennsylvania, drafted the proposed Constitution in its final form. The Constitution was then presented to the States for consideration. By August 1788, ten States had ratified the Constitution resulting in its adoption.[7] The effective date for the Constitution was set as 4 March 1789.

II. The Three Branches of the Central Government

A. *The Legislative Branch*[8]

Article I of the Constitution places all the law making powers of the central government in a body of elected representatives collectively called the Congress of the United States. The Congress consists of two separate Houses, the House of Representatives and the Senate.

1. The House of Representatives

Each member of the House of Representatives is elected to serve two-year terms of office by voters in the State where the representative resides. To serve as a representative, a person must be at least twenty-five years old, a citizen of the United States for at least seven years and currently living in the district from which he or she is elected. The district residential requirement is waived in sparsely populated States such as New Mexico and North Dakota. Originally, each State had one representative for every thirty thousand people. If a State had less than thirty thousand citizens, that State was allocated one seat in the House of Representatives. The maximum number of members in the House of Representatives is fixed at four hundred and thirty-five. Therefore, each Representative now represents approximately six hundred thousand persons. This cap attempts to keep the House of Representatives from growing so large as to be cumbersome and ineffective.

The House of Representatives has the exclusive power to impeach public officials of the central government. An impeachment is the accusation of wrongdoing against an official that may result in the official's removal from office. An ordinary majority vote of the House of Representatives is sufficient to impeach, at which point, the Senate has the sole power to try all impeachments. Two-thirds of the Senate must be present for an impeachment trial to commence, and conviction requires a two-thirds vote for such by those present. The House of Representatives has impeached only one President of the United States. A substantial majority in the House of Representatives impeached President Andrew Johnson in 1868, but the Senate acquitted him with one vote less than the two-thirds necessary to convict. President Richard Nixon chose to resign in 1974 in order to avert an inevitable impeachment, and probable conviction, on the eve of impeachment proceedings in the House of Representatives. Several lesser officials have been impeached by the House and subsequently convicted or acquitted in the Senate. The Senate's severest punishment upon impeachment and conviction is the loss of the official's office and a bar on that person ever serving as an officer of the central government. If the official has broken criminal laws, the official may also be subject to the jurisdiction of regular criminal courts.

2. *The Senate*

The United States Senate consists of one hundred members. Two senators are elected from each State and serve for a six-year term of office. The Vice-President of the United States serves as the presiding officer of the Senate, but only votes to break a tie. If the Senate conducts a trial on an impeached President, the Chief

Justice of the Supreme Court presides over the trial in the Senate. The inequity of the Vice-President, who is next in line for the office of President, presiding in such circumstances is obvious. To serve as a Senator, a person must be at least thirty years old and a citizen of the United States for at least nine years. He or she must also live in the State from which elected. Until 1913, members of the Senate were selected by the various State legislatures. The Seventeenth Amendment to the Constitution changed the method of selecting Senators to popular election.

3. Making Laws

Federal laws begin as Bills, and may originate in either House of Congress. However, tax Bills must originate in the House of Representatives. The Founding Fathers thought that such a requirement on revenue raising Bills would provide a popular check on potential misuse of the power to raise and expend money.[9] The Senate may amend tax Bills. When a member in the House of Representatives introduces a Bill that receives a majority vote in its favour, the House then sends the Bill to the Senate. If a majority of the Senate votes in favour of the Bill, the Senate then sends the Bill to the President of the United States. If the President signs the Bill, the Bill becomes a law. The President may veto the Bill and send it back to the House where it originated with accompanying objections. If the Bill originated in the House of Representatives, and the President sends it back there, a two-thirds vote by the House is necessary to send the Bill back to the Senate. If the Bill receives the two-thirds favourable vote in the House of Representatives, the House sends the Bill to the Senate along with the President's objections. If a two-thirds favourable vote in the Senate results, the Bill becomes law without the President's signature.

Both Houses of Congress have several committees that are interest-specific. For example, both Houses have committees made up of representatives or Senators in their respective Houses which study and advise the full House on issues such as appropriations, defence and the judiciary. These committees study the Bills in their area of expertise and recommend passage of those Bills of which they approve. This division of labour allows members of Congress to specialise in certain interest areas. Such specialisation provides depth to the debate on highly complex Bills and reduces the time lost on conflicts of minutiae that would inevitably result during consideration before a full House.

4. Congressional Powers

The Constitution enumerates the expressed powers of Congress in Article I, Section 8. These powers include the power to tax, to borrow money, to regulate commerce, to coin money, to establish post offices, to protect patents and copyrights, to establish all federal courts subordinate to the Supreme Court (which is set up by the Constitution), to declare war, to raise an army, to govern the District of Columbia and the city of Washington. Section 8 includes a catch-all necessity clause that provides the basis of Congress' implied powers 'to make any laws necessary and proper' to exercise Congress' expressed powers. Article I, Section 9 specifies powers denied to the Congress. These denied powers include making laws relating to the migration or importation of slaves (until 1808), and suspending the writ of *habeas corpus* except under revolutionary conditions. Congress may not pass a Bill of Attainder that punishes a singular individual without a right to trial. Likewise, Congress cannot make an *ex post facto* law that would criminalise otherwise non-criminal activity that occurred before the law was passed. The Constitution denied Congress the power to collect direct taxes not in proportion to the States' population until the Sixteenth Amendment provided for income tax.

The Tenth Amendment to the Constitution provides, 'The powers not delegated to the United States by the Constitution, nor prohibited by it to the States are reserved to the States respectively, or to the people'. A Chief Justice of the United States Supreme Court ruled that these residual State powers include, 'An immense mass of legislation which embraces everything within the territory of a State not surrendered to the general government; all of which can be most advantageously exercised by the States themselves'.[10]

B. The Executive Branch[11]

The President of the United States is the Chief Executive charged with effecting the enforcement of federal laws. To serve as President or Vice-President a person must be at least thirty-five years old, be a natural-born citizen of the United States, and have lived in the United States for at least fourteen years. The President and the Vice-President serve together for four-year terms. The Twenty-Second Amendment limits persons serving as President to a maximum of two terms in office. The Vice-President is sworn in as President if the President leaves office for any reason during mid-term. Reasons for departure could include removal through impeachment (which almost happened to Andrew Johnson), resignation (Richard Nixon) or death (Abraham Lincoln, John Kennedy). A Vice-President sworn in as President may appoint a new Vice-President to fill the open office. However, a majority in both Houses of Congress must confirm the appointment.

1. Electing the President

The Constitution formally calls for an indirect election of the President using an Electoral College. Each State has a number of electors equal to the number of congressmen representing that State. These electors, in aggregate throughout the United States, comprise the Electoral College.

Originally, each State legislature chose its State's presidential electors. Now, however, the electors are themselves voted for by the people in every State during the primary elections. Primary elections are held a few months before the general election to elect candidates who will represent a particular political party during the general election. When voters go to the polls during the general election, they vote for the President and Vice-President by name. In reality, however, they are voting for the electors of the presidential candidate's party. Custom and convention dictate that all electoral votes of a State be awarded to the presidential and vice-presidential candidate (running together) who win a majority of votes in that State. The votes are counted by both Houses of Congress, sitting together, on 6 January. If, after the count, no presidential candidate has a majority of electoral votes, the House of Representatives elects the President from the three front runners for presidency (in terms of elector vote count). Each State has one vote, and two-thirds of the States suffice for a quorum. A majority of all the States is required to elect the President. The oath of office is usually administered by the Chief Justice of the Supreme Court on 20 January.

2. Presidential Power

The office of the President of the United States has changed dramatically from the first Washington administration to the current Clinton administration. George Washington was a widely respected military leader called upon to become the first Chief Executive of an emerging nation. The office of President has evolved significantly since that time. Bill Clinton, two hundred and three years later, was inaugurated into arguably the most powerful and highest profile political position the world has yet known.

The Constitution provides the basis for presidential power, but it is only a starting point. Article II enumerates the few specific powers of the Chief Executive including the President's power over the armed forces as Commander-in-Chief, the power to require written opinions from his Cabinet members, and the power to grant reprieves and pardons. The President, with the advice and consent of the Senate, may make treaties with foreign countries, and appoint ambassadors and Supreme Court justices.

The President has a constitutional duty to inform Congress as to the 'state of the union' from time to time. This duty has transformed into an annual late January media frenzy as the President delivers his or her 'State of the Union' address to a joint session of Congress. The President may also convene either or both Houses of Congress in times of national emergency. The President may also adjourn Congress in the unlikely event that the two Houses cannot agree on when to adjourn. The President is required to receive ambassadors and other officials from foreign countries. The President must sign all commissions for people to become officers of the United States. Most importantly, the President must see that the laws of the United States are carried out faithfully.

The constitutional outline for the President has changed little since 1789. The presidential role in the political spectrum has, however, dramatically altered in the last two hundred years. An esteemed presidential scholar has written: 'The whole picture is a hundred times magnified. The outstanding feature of American constitutional development has been the growth of the power and prestige of the Presidency'.[12] Another noted presidential authority has written that the presidency, formally an equal branch of the government, has become an imperial institution.[13]

Presidential personalities and temperament have factored into the evolution of the presidency. George Washington was content as a symbolic head of this new nation. Thomas Jefferson was an unabashed political force leading his party. Andrew Jackson was the first President to declare his mandate as the nationally elected leader by the people and the most legitimate representative for the majority of the nation. Abraham Lincoln responded as a forceful national leader in a time of crisis. Woodrow Wilson was the first internationalist, and Presidents since have continued to develop and maintain complex foreign relation strategies.[14]

Presidents no longer wait for Congress to initiate legislation. Presidents often send proposals to the Congress to start the Bill-to-law process. Franklin Roosevelt's New Deal agenda required only that Congress keep up with a legislatively vibrant and idealist executive administration. Bill Clinton's Healthcare Plan is a social program on par with those of the New Deal. Hillary Clinton, the President's wife, has directed the development of the Healthcare Plan. Eleanor Roosevelt set a strong precedent for First Lady involvement in contemporary issues, and Hillary Clinton seems to be expanding the traditional role of First Lady into an extra-constitutional political appendage to the presidency itself.

3. Removal from Office

Any civil officer of the United States government, including the President and Vice-President, may be impeached and removed from office if the Senate convicts that officer of treason, bribery, or other high crimes and misdemeanours.

C. The Judicial Branch[15]

Article III of the Constitution vests judicial power in the Supreme Court of the United States and such inferior courts as Congress may ordain and establish. Currently there are three regular federal courts: these are, the Supreme Court, the Courts of Appeal, and the District Courts. Congress has established four other types of federal courts that hear only certain types of cases. These are the Court of Claims, the Court of Customs and Patent Appeals, the Court of International Trade and the Tax Court.

1. Jurisdiction of the Federal Courts

The federal courts' jurisdiction extends to all cases of law (criminal, civil and cases of equity) mentioned specifically in the Constitution, as well as cases involving federal laws and involving United States treaties. Federal courts also hear cases involving foreign representatives, admiralty and maritime issues, and cases in which the United States is a party. Federal courts are also called upon to resolve disputes between two or more States, between citizens of different States, and disputes in which citizens of the same State claim lands granted by different States.

2. The Supreme Court

Nine justices sit on the Supreme Court. The President appoints all the justices. The Senate has the power to confirm or deny the President's appointments. The justices are appointed for life. The President appoints one justice to serve as the Chief Justice. Seven men and two women currently serve as Supreme Court justices. The Supreme Court interprets the meaning of the Constitution and determines whether laws passed by Congress are consistent with its language. A former Chief Justice of the Supreme Court tellingly confessed, 'We are under a Constitution, but the Constitution is what the judges say it is'.[16]

The Supreme Court exercises original jurisdiction over cases involving ambassadors, public ministers, and consuls. It also has original jurisdiction over cases that involve a dispute between States. Its appellate jurisdiction includes all cases mentioned in the Constitution and certain classes of cases specifically defined by Congress. The Supreme Court may exercise appellate jurisdiction only when one party to the case is not content with a lower court judgment and appeals that judgment to the Supreme Court. The justices of the Supreme Court vote on whether to accept a case on appeal. Most of the cases accepted involve a question of constitutional interpretation and may involve extremely politicised issues requiring urgent resolution.

3. Judicial Review

Chief Justice John Marshall forcefully enunciated the principle of judicial review when ruling on a case in 1803.[17] In that case, the Supreme Court ruled an Act of Congress unconstitutional for the first time. Controversial arguments have raged since about the validity of Chief Justice Marshall's assertion that the Supreme Court may review and pronounce acts of the other branches of government to be in contravention of the terms or spirit of the Constitution. Chief Justice Marshall's rationale for judicial review has been the cornerstone allowing this doctrine of constitutional intervention to develop a foundation of legitimacy through time and acquiescence. Academic arguments abound that cite the non-democratic features of the Supreme Court and the violation of the separation of powers, but the American people seem to accept the Court's self-determined mandate.

Conclusion

The delegates to the Constitutional Convention determined to create a republican form of government that could exist on a large geographic scale. The year was 1787, and the delegates could scarcely imagine the growth of the Republic that their Constitution would facilitate. The United States has since survived the Civil War, two World Wars, the Cold War, natural disasters, political catastrophes and significantly increased world exposure and demands. The Constitution has endured. The Constitution of the United States of America survives with only twenty-seven amendments to its original form, and serves as a memorial to the Founders' determination to create a republican governmental structure sufficiently adaptable to the exigencies of an unfathomable future.

Notes

1. The central government referenced throughout this article is the national government whose seat of power is Washington D.C. The States have delegated certain powers and responsiblities to the central (i.e. federal) government through the Constitution.
2. Rhode Island did not participate in the Constitutional Convention and was the last state of the original thirteen to ratify the resulting Constitution.
3. Alexander Hamilton asserted that the British monarchy was the best model, but he understood American reluctance to embrace another monarchy so soon after the Revolutionary War. See R. A. Dahl,

Democracy in the United States (4th ed., Boston: Houghton Mifflin Co., 1981), 11.

4. J. Madison in the *Federalist* No. 39. See B. F. Wright (ed.), *The Federalist Papers* (Cambridge, Mass.: Harvard University Press, 1961).
5. J. Madison quoted in R. Hofstadter, *The American Political Tradition* (London: Cape, 1962), 6.
6. J. Madison cited the French political theorist Montesquieu as an influence when he wrote in the *Federalist* No.47, 'The accumulation of all powers legislative, executive and judicial in the same hands, whether of one, a few or many, and whether hereditary, self appointed, or elective, may justly be pronounced the very defnition of tyranny'. See Madison, *supra* note 4, 336.
7. 'The ratification of the conventions of nine states, shall be sufficient for the establishment of this constitution between the states so ratifying the same.' The *Constitution of the United States of America*, Article VII.
8. The *Constitution of the United States of America*, Article I, Sections 1–9.
9. R. Hofstadter, W. Miller, D. Aaron, *The American Republic, Volume One to 1865* (Englewood Cliffs, New Jersey: Prentice–Hall, Inc., 1959), 245.
10. *Gibbons v. Ogden* (1824) 9 Wheaton 1.
11. The *Constitution of the United States of America*, Article II, Sections 1–4.
12. C. L. Rossiter, *The American Presidency* (2nd ed., New York: Harcourt, Brace & World, 1960), 77.
13. A. M. Schlesinger, *The Imperial Presidency* (Boston: Houghton Mifflin, 1973), 418.
14. See Dahl, *supra* note 3, Chapter 6.
15. The *Constitution of the United States of America*, Article III, Sections 1–2.
16. Quoting former Chief Justice of the Supreme Court Charles Evan Hughes. See *Hofstadter et al., supra* note 9, 248.
17. *Marbury v. Madison* (1803) 1 Cranch 137.

The German Republic

Isolde Turwitt–Fieber[*]

The German Republic has existed since its proclamation by Philip Scheidemann from the Reichstag building in Berlin on 9th November 1918. Upon proclamation of the republic, the Kaiser abdicated, as did the heir to the throne. These acts were sufficient to transfer the Reich into a republic because, under pressure from the American President, Woodrow Wilson, the German Constitution had already been changed abruptly on 28th October 1918, from a non-democratic constitutional monarchy to a parliamentary democracy with a monarchical head. The State authority had been transferred from the monarch to the people.[1] In 1919 the monarch's function as Head of the German State was transferred, by a generally elected National Assembly,[2] to the first Reichspräsident, Friedrich Ebert.

The Weimar Constitution (Weimarer Reichsverfassung (WRV)) was proclaimed on 14 August 1919. Its first sentence stated: 'The German Reich is a republic'. As the relationship between the Executive, the Parliament and the Head of State is determinative in any governmental system, the position of the Reichspräsident became a central issue during the extensive consultations which took place regarding the Constitution. The result was a Constitution which combined a parliamentary system with a very strong President in terms of political power. The National Assembly chose a combination of the advantages of the French and the American systems.[3] The President was to be elected by universal suffrage (Article 41 WRV) for a period of seven years

---

[*] Visiting Scholar.

and could be re-elected indefinitely (Article 43 WRV). The memory of imperial power, and therefore concepts from the constitutional monarchy echoed in the new Constitution. There were remarkable monarchical features in the structure of the new parliamentary system itself, particularly in the provision of extensive presidential powers. The Reichspräsident was given the power to appoint and remove the Chancellor and the ministers and to dissolve the Parliament, and vast powers for emergency decrees were delegated to him. According to Article 48 WRV he was empowered in times of what he determined to be 'public disturbance' to take 'necessary measures'. These included the overruling of State laws, the abrogation of all civil liberties, the making of national laws by decree, the enforcement of law by the army and the establishment of exceptional courts and jurisdictions.[4]

The misuse of these vast constitutional powers was prevented only by the power of the Reichstag to impeach the President (Article 59 WRV) and the power of the people to recall him (Article 43 Abs. 2 WRV). On the other hand, the provision of a veto by majority vote of the Reichstag on all presidential decrees under Article 48 WRV was an ineffective check on presidential power because the President could dissolve the Reichstag according to Article 25 WRV and afterwards enact the same decree again.[5] The simultaneous existence of parliamentary, presidential and plebiscitarian elements resulted in a de-stabilised parliamentary system which was unable to resist its own elimination later under the Third Reich.

For the *Federal Republic of Germany*, Article 20 of the Basic Law (Grundgesetz (GG)) continues the tradition of almost all written constitutions in that it encapsulates the main principles underlying the organisation of the State's political and governmental structure in one section. Article 20 Abs 1 GG states: 'The Federal Republic of Germany is a democratic and social federal state'. The republican principle is not now expressly stated, partly because— for linguistic reasons—it became part of the name of the State, and partly because in 1949, at the time the article was framed, it was no longer a political issue.

The following sections of the Basic Law of the Federal Republic of Germany are specifically republican: Article 20 Abs. 2 GG states that all State authority emanates from the people. It shall be exercised by the people by means of elections and voting and by separate legislative, executive and judicial organs. Articles 38, 39, 54, 63, GG are premised upon the principle that all State organs including the President of the Federal Republic of Germany are elected only for a limited period of time. Article 79 Abs. 3 GG contains the so-called eternal guarantee of the basic principles by providing:

> An amendment of this Basic Law effecting the division of the federation into Länder, the participation in principle of the Länder in legislation, or the basic principles laid down in Articles 1 and 20, shall be inadmissible.

In 1949, the Parlamentarische Rat (Parliamentary Council) acting as a constituent assembly, decided that even a republic needed a Head of State.[6] Any tendencies, arising from historical reasons, to eliminate the office of the Head of State were overcome.

Some members of the Parlamentarische Rat were of the opinion that the President of the Federal Parliament (Bundestag) or a presidium consisting of the Federal Chancellor (Bundeskanzler) and both Presidents of the Parliament and the Federal Council (Bundesrat) could fulfil this function.[7] However, they were satisfied when they realised that the majority wanted to restrict the political powers of the President and to eliminate his direct election, thereby setting aside the double sovereignty which comes with such election. The parliamentary system tends to favour politically experienced and balanced personalities, whereas in direct elections, personalities able to mobilise masses of people are frequently chosen. The superfluous legitimation which comes from a direct presidential election encourages political activity and can lead to a latent opposition towards the Parliament.

The principles underlying Articles 54 to 61 GG dealing with the election, position and removal of the Bundespräsident are based on a new concept, namely, that the President does not belong to the Executive or the Government, and does not rank equally with the Parliament. Neither does he belong to the legislature. The Constitution provides that the Bundespräsident shall be elected without debate by the Federal Assembly, consisting of the members of the Federal Parliament and an equal number of people who shall be elected by the State Parliaments according to the principles of proportional representation. The office is limited to five years. Re-election is possible only once. The person who gains the majority of votes of the members of the Federal

Assembly is elected. In case this majority cannot be reached by any of the candidates within two ballots, the person who gains the majority of votes within the next ballot is be elected. As a relic from monarchical times, any gross misconduct by the Bundespräsident is dealt with by impeachment, rather than removal. The constitutional powers of the Bundespräsident are to be found throughout the Basic Law. The President has an integrative, representative and a political and legislative reserve function.

Integrative function: The Bundespräsident like other 'sovereigns has three rights: the right to be consulted, the right to encourage, the right to warn'.[8] The Basic Law does not give him (to date, no woman has been elected) any authority beyond the limits of the office's expressly-stated constitutional powers. It depends fully on the President's personality to fill the position with subjective authority. This is the difference between the monarchical and the presidential Head of State. The Crown, as the symbol of the State and its traditions, confers objective integrative powers, regardless of the powers which the Constitution expressly grants to the monarch.[9] The Bundespräsident does not have the constitutional right to decide on the national anthem, national flag, national colours and other national symbols.

Representative function: The Bundespräsident represents the Federal State internationally. He concludes treaties with foreign States on behalf of the Federal State. He accredits and acknowledges foreign ministers. Treaties, which govern the federal political relations or relate to federal legislative powers, need the approval or co-operation of the competent federal organ in the form of a federal law.

Political and legislative reserve function: One of the most essential decisions of the Parlamentarische Rat was to remove the Federal President from the tensions between Parliament and the Executive. The Federal Chancellor is the person who determines the political guidelines (Article 65 GG), which makes him the political leader of the State. The directions and decrees of the Federal President must be countersigned by the Federal Chancellor or the competent Federal Minister to be valid. Article 63 GG provides for the Federal Chancellor's election by the Federal Parliament on advice of the Bundespräsident. As a general rule, the Bundespräsident will suggest the person who will have the support of the majority in the

Federal Parliament. However, he is not constitutionally bound to do so. He cannot impede a quick election since, according to Article 63 Abs. 3 GG, the absolute majority of the Federal Parliament can elect its own candidate if the President's candidate could not gain the necessary majority. In that event, the President must appoint the Federal Parliament's candidate (Article 63 Abs. 2 GG).[10] If no candidate gains the absolute or relative majority, a Minderheitenkanzler (Chancellor of the minority) may be elected. In this case, the Bundespräsident then has to decide whether to appoint the Chancellor or to dissolve the Parliament (Article 63 Abs. 4 Satz 3 GG). Thus a crisis of the parliamentary system activates the reserve function of the Bundespräsident.[11]

This principle also governs the constructive vote of confidence case (konstruktives Mißtrauensvotum). According to Article 68 GG, the Bundeskanzler (the Federal Chancellor) can ask the Parliament for a vote of confidence. If the result is a vote of no-confidence, for example where the Federal Parliament is unable to agree upon and elect a new Federal Chancellor, the Federal Parliament may be dissolved by the Bundespräsident. The reserve power of the Bundespräsident expires as soon as the other organ of government, namely the Federal Parliament, masters the crisis.[12]

According to Article 82 Abs. 1 Satz 1 GG, the Bundespräsident is the so-called State notary, as he engrosses all statutes. The engrossment includes the President's signature on the original document beneath a statement by him that the Act came into existence in a process according to constitutional law. There is much debate as to whether the President, at the same time, has the right to examine the substantive law of the new Act to determine whether it is compatible with the Constitution.[13] The prevailing legal opinion is that the Bundespräsident ought to have this right.[14]

To date, each of the Presidents of the Federal Republic of Germany has discharged his presidential duties with a dignity appropriate to the highest office of State. Richard von Weizsäcker, the present Bundespräsident, considers it his main task to take part in discussions on major contemporary issues, not by providing his own answers and remedies, but by encouraging others to pose the relevant questions and to work out their solutions.

The German States (the Länder) do not have their own State representative like the Bundespräsident, but the Länder are forced by the Basic Law in Article 28 Abs. 1 GG to be republics:

The constitutional order in the Länder must conform to the principles of republican, democratic and social government based on the rule of law, within the meaning of this Basic Law.

Any constitutional provision which does not conform to these principles would be void according to Article 31 of the Basic Law. Article 28 GG therefore forces the Länder to be homogenous but not uniform. In the post-1871 German Empire, monarchies as well as three republics, Hamburg, Bremen and Luebeck, co-existed. Therefore, it is not self-evident that the Federal and State systems must all be republican. Today it is of even less importance whether Federal States are monarchies or republics. The political cohesion on which modern States, whether confederations (for example, Australia, the United States, Germany) or unitary States (for example, Great Britain, the Netherlands, Belgium, Spain), are founded does not depend on such States being republics as opposed to being monarchies. Rather it rests upon adherence to the principles of democratic government such as those enunciated in Germany's Basic Law. Those monarchies which have survived have done so because the monarch has resigned from the executive function within the State so that the monarch's function has been restricted to that of State representative. The integrative function of this role for the State should not be underestimated. Even in a republic the President must achieve political recognition as representative of the State before his or her integrative power can compare to that of a monarch who symbolises the nation's history and traditions. On the other hand, the integrative function of a monarch may be negligible in States (perhaps including Australia) where the citizens have diverse ethnic origins so that the monarch's symbolic linkage to the nation's history and traditions is less effective as a force for political cohesion.

Notes

1. W. Apelt, *Geschichte der Weimarer Verfassung*, 2. Auflage 1964, s.32 ff.
2. *Id.* s.69 ff.
3. G. Anschuetz, *Die Verfassung des Deutschen Reichs* vom 11. August 1919, 14. Auflage 1933, s.241 ff.

4. H. Schneider, 'Die Reichsverfassung' vom 11. August 1919 in *Handbuch des Staatsrechts der Bundesrepublik Deutschland* Bd 1, s.3 Rn 65 ff.
5. *Id.* Rn 67.
6. K. Schlaich, 'Die Funktionen des Bundespräsidenten im Verfassungsgefuege' in *Handbuch des Staatsrechts der Bundesrepublik Deutschland* Bd 11 s.49, Fn 210.
7. Eschenburg/Benz, 'Der Weg zum Grundgesetz' in *Eschenburg (Hg.), Geschichte der Bundesrepublik*, s.492.
8. W. Bagehot, 'The English Constitution', in *The Works*, vol IV, (Hartford: 1891), 112.
9. J. Isensee, Republik—'Sinnpotential eines Begriffs' (1981) *Juristenzeitung*, s.1 ff.
10. He has to appoint the federal ministers chosen by the Federal Chancellor (Art. 64 GG), federal judges and civil servants (Art. 60 GG) and members of the Bundesbank (s.7 Abs. 3 BBankG) as well.
11. BVerfGE 62, 1/Decision of the Federal Constitutional Court vol. 62, 1.
12. In this context see Art. 81 GG.
13. J. Mewing, *Die Pruefungskompetenz des Bundespräsidenten bei der Gesetzesausfertigung, insbesondere beim teilnichtigen Gesetz*, 1977.
14. Schlaich, *supra* note 6, s.49 Rn 33.

Representative Democracy, Federalism and Constitutional Revision

R.D. Lumb[*]

The last year (1993) has witnessed proposals for the revision of our constitutional system. Some popularity has attached to the minimalist theory[1] associated with the proponents of a change to the Head of State structure and the conversion of our Monarchy to a Republic. However, the problem of defining the reserve powers has been a major stumbling block for the Republic Advisory Committee. Others have proposed more wide-ranging changes such as the dismantling of the federal system and the reduction of the powers of the Senate.

Before any changes are made, there must be a dispassionate analysis of our constitutional fundamentals. These fundamentals are representative democracy, federalism, separation of powers and the monarchy. They are protected by the referendum mechanism embodied in section 128 of the Constitution and by section 15 of the *Australia Acts* (Cth and UK) 1986.

High Court decisions in 1992 have explored the underlying principles of our constitutional system. These decisions are the political advertising (*Australian Capital Television*)[2] and 'IRC contempt' (*Nationwide*)[3] cases. A right of political discourse or communication has been established as an implied right of the Constitution flowing from the principle of representative democracy. In the *Australian Capital Television* case,[4] the High Court held that this right was infringed by the *Political Broadcasts and Political Disclosures Act* 1991 (Cth) in its prohibition of political advertising on television and radio. In the *Nationwide* case, a provision[5] of the *Industrial Relations Act* 1988 (Cth) was

---

[*] Professor of Law, University of Queensland.

held to be invalid because it restricted the rights of citizens to criticize the workings of public institutions.

In *Nationwide*, Deane and Toohey JJ. list the doctrine of representative democracy together with the doctrines of federalism and of separation of powers as three basic foundations of our constitutional system.[6] In the view of these Justices, the modern cases establishing the latter two doctrines are *Queensland Electricity Commission v. The Commonwealth*[7] and *Harris v. Caladine*.[8]

Representative Democracy and Chapter 1 of the Constitution

The essence of the first doctrine, the doctrine of representative democracy, is formulated in this way:

> That doctrine can conveniently be described as the doctrine of representative government, that is to say, of government by representatives directly or indirectly elected or appointed by, and ultimately responsible to, the people of the Commonwealth. The rational basis of that doctrine is the thesis that all powers of government ultimately belong to, and are derived from, the governed.[9]

Deane and Toohey JJ. and other Justices consider that this doctrine finds expression in sections 7, 24 and 128 of the Constitution.[10]

In an earlier case dealing with electoral divisions, *McKinlay's* case,[11] the High Court had examined the concept of representative democracy. A basic holding in that case was that the principle of proportionality embodied in the second paragraph of section 24[12] required that the number of members chosen in each State reflect the State's population. This, in turn, required the use of up to date statistics in determining that population, and also that a forthcoming election be based on a redistribution following on any new determination of members where such up to date statistics required an alteration to the number of members for a State.

As to another major issue in that case, namely, whether section 24 mandated electoral divisions with an equal number of electors, the High Court (Murphy J. dissenting) considered that this was not a requirement of section 24. The Court relied heavily on history to reject the argument that electoral divisions should be numerically equal.[13] Stephen J. outlined three principles as flowing from section 24:

> Three great principles, representative democracy (by which I mean that the legislators are chosen by the people), direct popular election and

the national character of the Lower House, may each be discerned in the opening words of section 24.[14]

However, Stephen J. said that equality of electoral divisions was not a necessary consequence of any of these principles.[15]

The second and third principles are self evident: no intermediate electoral college (even though such a college may be of a democratic character) is to be interposed between electors and the choice of members of the House of Representatives, and population, as distinct from statehood, is established as the basis for selection of members of the Lower House. As to the principle of representative democracy, Stephen J. considered that the principle predicated 'the enfranchisement of electors, the existence of an electoral system capable of giving effect to their selection of representatives and the bestowal of legislative functions upon the representatives thus selected'.[16] The content of these elements was not fixed and indeed was fluid.[17] As to the extent of the franchise, some of the range of alternatives which would appear to be included within the concept were a minimum age prescription, a citizenship qualification and a gender prescription to which might be added a property qualification. Moreover, there would also be the question of identifying disqualifications based on incapacity or criminality.[18] The former, of course, reflected variations in the franchise of the various colonies at Federation, females having a right to vote only in a minority of States and property qualifications being required for some Upper Houses.[19]

Stephen J. also considered that the concept of representative democracy allowed for a variety of electoral systems including such matters as numbers and qualifications and disqualifications of members as well as different methods of voting such as proportional representation.[20] In relation to legislative functions he was more cautious, observing only that there was a wide range of legislative functions vested in a legislature in a federal polity.[21] Perhaps he could have added 'but confined mainly within those powers listed in section 51 of the Constitution'. Moreover, he did not specify which powers with respect to Bills were vested in a Lower House of the Federal Parliament and which were denied to the Upper House.[22]

As to electoral divisions Stephen J. made the following observation:

> It is no doubt true that something approaching numerical equality of electors within electorates is an important factor, together with much

else, in the attainment of what many will regard as representative democracy in its purest form, just as adult suffrage, free of discrimination on the grounds of race, sex, property or educational qualification, will likewise aid in its attainment. But neither of these in absolute form is necessarily imported in the Constitution by the selection of representative democracy as the chosen mode of government for the nation.[23]

However, in the same case several Justices did consider there were some limitations in relation to the size of electoral divisions. Mason J. considered that it was conceivable that variations in the numbers of electors could become so 'grossly disproportionate' as to raise a question whether the House of Representatives was structured according to section 24.[24] A more definite view was expressed by McTiernan and Jacobs JJ. when they referred to the concept of equality as being an objective but allowing for some departure from a uniform quota of electors.[25] (The margin in the *Commonwealth Electoral Act* 1918 at the time was one tenth above or below the quota.) In their view this did not deny the quality of choice which section 24 required. Specifically they accepted the possibility that 'gerrymandering' involving unnatural divisions would be inconsistent with the constitutional requirement.[26] McTiernan and Jacobs JJ. further considered that only universal adult suffrage could be described as a choice of the people.[27]

In the *Australian Capital Television* and *Nationwide* cases, various Justices cited with approval the general statements of Stephen J. on the incorporation of representative government into the Constitution.[28] For example, Gaudron J. states that representative democracy is 'as fundamental as federalism and as fundamental as the vesting of judicial power in an independent federal judiciary separate from the other arms of government'.[29]

The judgment of McHugh J. in the *Australian Capital Television* case[30] is particularly instructive in this respect. He notes both an historical and current basis for representative democracy as a constitutional implication. He takes account of the history of constitutional development in Great Britain and in the Australian colonies as well as current attitudes to political participation, association and communication, which established the foundation for the doctrine and for its application to federal elections.[31] In this light, sections 7 and 24 embody the right of the electors of Australia to choose the members of both Houses and elect their representatives by voting at periodic elections.[32]

Of particular importance to McHugh J. was the right of association and the associated right to create political parties: it was inconceivable the Parliament could prevent members of lawful political parties from being elected to Parliament.[33] In this regard, one might suggest that the incidental power conjoined with sections 29, 30 and 31 of the Constitution could be used as a basis to create rights in party members to play a role in the selection of Parliamentary candidates. It may be that the system of primaries which operates in the United States could come within the scope of Commonwealth legislative power as being derived from the concept of representative democracy.

Gaudron J. also emphasises the importance of the franchise as a concomitant of representative democracy. She points out that in section 7 senators are directly chosen by the people of a State, while members of the House of Representatives are directly chosen by the people of the Commonwealth.[34] However, Gaudron J. does not further develop this concept of representative democracy in terms of any restrictions on Senate powers *vis-à-vis* House of Representative powers.

Dawson J. considers that universal suffrage is not mandated by the Constitution because section 30 leaves to the Parliament the power to decide the nature and scope of the franchise. It is a political principle as distinct from being a principle of constitutional law.[35]

Electoral Divisions

In *McKinlay's* case,[36] Stephen J. questioned whether the procedures for a redistribution in the *Commonwealth Electoral Act* 1918 should be revised so as to make it a more accurate description of the electoral system as a choice of the people.

Since that decision, the Act has been amended to comply with the holding that the proportionality paragraph of section 24 required a determination of the number of members on the basis of up to date statistics and of a re-distribution giving effect to any new determination of members.[37] This would happen where population movements led to divergence from the electoral quota in divisions as between States, the consequence being that a redistribution must take place in one or more States. Under section 59 of the Act redistributions are required in these circumstances and also in circumstances when for a certain period of time more than one third of the divisions in a State have been malapportioned. The third requirement for a new redistribution is a temporal one: within thirty days of the expiry of a period of seven years from the last redistribution.

Section 66 of the *Commonwealth Electoral Act* 1918 is a complex section which describes the basis on which a redistribution takes place. The Redistributions Committee for a State or Territory in making a redistribution shall ensure that:

> [A]s far as practicable ... the number of electors enrolled in each Electoral Division in the State or Territory would not, 3 years and 6 months after the State or Territory had been redistributed be less than 98% or more than 102% of the average divisional enrolment of that State or Territory at that time.[38]

Subject thereto, it shall give due consideration in relation to each division to community of interest, means of communication, physical features and the boundaries of existing divisions.[39] Subject to these requirements a margin of allowance of one tenth more or one tenth less is allowed for the quota of electors in each division.[40] There is no doubt that these provisions comply with the *Nationwide* and *Australian Capital Television* principle of representative democracy.

The Right to Vote

As pointed out earlier, the overall thrust of several of the judgments in the *Australian Capital Television* and *Nationwide* cases is to adopt a contemporaneous interpretation of the right to vote even though this right is not expressed in the Constitution.[41] This seems to be a derivative from the doctrine of representative government as based on the recognition of adult franchise not restricted on a property or gender basis. To this extent, the fluid interpretation of the right by Stephen J. in *McKinlay's* case must be revised.

The *Commonwealth Electoral Act* 1918 gives effect to this right, the only requirements being age (minimum of eighteen years), Australian citizenship[42] and being enrolled.[43] Thus, if this entitlement was diluted by restrictions based on gender or on racial or national origin of Australian citizens, the question would arise as to whether representative democracy would be infringed and the likely opinion of the High Court in this respect would be that it had been. The disenfranchisement of persons under eighteen years of age, however, would be regarded as valid: intellectual maturity would appear to be an essential requirement for an informed choice.[44] Moreover, exceptions to the right to vote based on unsoundness of mind and serious criminal conviction and being under sentence would also appear to be valid.[45]

Electoral Methods

Representative democracy would also entail a diversity of electoral methods, whether first past the post, preferential voting or proportional representation. The combination of methods in the present system of Australian Government of preferential voting for House of Representative elections and proportional representation for Senate elections are clearly within the parameters of the concept.

Responsible Government

In the view of several judges in the *Nationwide* and *Australian Capital Television* cases, responsible government, that is, the responsibility of the executive to Parliament, goes hand in hand with representative democracy.[46] In the Australian system the winning of a majority of seats by a party or a coalition of parties, enables government to be formed by that party or parties. More difficult is the selection of the ministry where no party or coalition has achieved the necessary majority. In these circumstances a minority government is commissioned with all the problems associated with determining whether it will be a stable or viable government.[47]

One outstanding question is a situation where a party wins a majority of seats but another party or coalition of parties wins more than fifty percent of the popular vote.[48] In this situation the question of popular vote is disregarded: the number of seats is decisive. However, it may be pointed out that in South Australia some attempt has been made to grapple with this problem in relation to redistributions.[49]

Parliamentary Privilege

The Houses of Parliament and Members of Parliament are endowed with certain privileges under section 49 of the Constitution. Parliamentary privilege is an important protective mechanism for the achievement of the goals of representative democracy.[50] In this area the Speaker has a pivotal role.

Privileges of the House of Commons operate in Australia until changed by local legislation. The *Parliamentary Privileges Act* 1987 (Cth)[51] has modified some of these privileges. Section 16 of the Act affirms the traditional privilege of freedom of speech and proceedings in Parliament. This ensures that the Houses, their committees and members may carry out their duties free from harassment or legal action although the scope of this privilege has come under critical scrutiny.[52]

The Senate and Federalism

As we have seen, in both *Australian Capital Television* and *Nationwide* cases the members of the High Court linked together section 7 (composition of Senate) and section 24 (composition of House of Representatives) as incorporating the concept of representative democracy. Like section 24, section 7 embodies the principle of direct choice.[53] However, it provides that a State is to be treated as one electorate unless the Parliament otherwise provides.[54]

The system of choice initially provided for in relation to Senate elections was first past the post but a preferential system was introduced in 1919. In 1948 the present system of proportional representation was established.[55] Grouping of candidates is allowed according to political party designation. A method of voting 'above the line' by marking one box on the ballot paper (a group ticket vote) or voting for individuals 'below the line' by inserting marks in every box provide a variety of choice to the elector.[56] To be elected, successful candidates must obtain a quota, surplus votes being transferred according to the next available preference but with a reduced value. When this process is completed the candidates with the fewest votes are eliminated and their ballots are distributed to the remaining candidates until the final quota is attained.[57]

The proportional representation system raises a fundamental question of parliamentary democracy. The two party preferred system usually produces a clear cut result in terms of the formation of a majority government, while the proportional representation system produces an approximate equality of major party representation with independents and minor parties holding the balance of power. Where the system is used in Upper House elections, this does not produce instability in government unless of course the 'ultimate' power of the purse is exercised by the Senate.

Thus, political prudence and recognition of the conventions of responsible government will not bring down the government with a majority in the Lower House except in those circumstances, such as in 1975, where the Senate decides to exercise its ultimate power to reject or fail to pass a Bill appropriating monies for the ordinary annual services of government. That does not mean that the powers of amendment in relation to non-money Bills *and* the power to reject or to return a taxation Bill under section 53 requesting an amendment should not be exercised by the Senate in appropriate circumstances. It has a popular mandate to do so although it is of a different nature from that of the House of Representatives.

The requirement in section 7 that each State has an equality of members in the Upper House gives effect to the concept of State representation. It is a chamber in which, as Quick and Garran state, 'the States, considered as separate entities, and corporate parts of the Commonwealth, are represented'.[58] In practice, of course, party discipline has affected the freedom of senators to vote for individual State interests. However, there are a number of instances, where the interests of a State or States have been vitally threatened, of party discipline being breached.[59]

The effect of the *Territory Representation* cases[60] must also be considered in this respect. Even though the Federal balance may be disturbed by the appointment of Territory Senators, the disjunction of section 7 and section 122 is recognized by the Court in those cases. However, there may be circumstances in which the creation of additional Territory Senators (that is, in addition to the present two for the Australian Capital Territory and two for the Northern Territory) may be open to constitutional challenge.[61]

In the *Australian Capital Television* and *Nationwide* cases, the High Court did not consider what was the appropriate relationship between the two Houses but dicta in *Victoria v. Commonwealth*[62] suggest that the powers of the Senate are comprehensive and include a power to reject or fail to pass an appropriation Bill. As to Bills imposing taxation, the Senate may reject or return such Bills to the House requesting amendments. There are also the limitations on the House of Representatives arising from section 55 of the Constitution. In *Nationwide*, Deane and Toohey JJ. consider that representative government imports a *national* representation, while section 7, in requiring equal representation for the States, is an *exception* to this principle.[63]

Some commentators consider that the Senate is less representative than the House of Representatives in so far as there is no constitutional requirement that all its members (apart from a double dissolution) face the electorate at the same time as members of the House of Representatives. Section 13, indeed, embodies a rotation principle with only half of the senators retiring every three years.[64] However, the Constitution by spacing or 'staggering' elections for senators provides for a longer time span for the expression of voter choice in relation to the composition of the Upper House. This, indeed, is another aspect of the relations between two representative Houses: a concept of checks and balances may itself determine particular aspects of the relationship between them.

In the past there has been much criticism of separate Senate elections. However, one way of strengthening the 'States House' nature of the Upper House would be to hold such elections separate from House of Representatives elections. It must be remembered that State Governors issue the writs for Senate elections (section 12) and State Parliaments may make laws for determining the times of Senate elections (section 9). This may enable issues of particular importance to the States (for example, the *Mabo* legislation) to be highlighted in situations where otherwise (that is, at simultaneous elections) party politics and promises would predominate.

Section 128 of the Constitution

In *Nationwide*, Deane and Toohey JJ. referring to section 128 state that 'under the Constitution, those ultimate powers which the Constitution reserves to the people of the Commonwealth are exercisable by direct vote',[65] thus highlighting the importance of the will of a national majority in changing the Constitution. However, the additional requirement in section 128 of approval in a majority of the States is seen by them as a qualification which protects the position of the less populous States.[66] This requirement may also be seen as embodying the federal principle pursuant to which a majority of States through popular vote must give their assent to any changes, whether fundamental or non-fundamental, to the Constitution. Other Justices also highlight the importance of section 128 as the ultimate foundation of representative democracy in the Commonwealth of Australia.[67]

In effect, section 128 embodies both representative democracy and direct democracy: proposals are initiated by one or both Houses of Federal Parliament. Where one House does not agree, an interval of three months must lapse before the alteration Bill can be re-presented. The Bill with or without any amendments may then be submitted to the electorate for approval or rejection.[68]

Initiation of an alteration proposal by the Parliament has often been preceded by a report or recommendation coming from another body such as a parliamentary committee, constitutional convention (parliamentary) or constitutional commission.[69] The Constitution itself was drafted and approved by a fully elected constitutional convention before being submitted to the Parliaments of the colonies and to referenda in each colony.[70]

It may be pointed out that the United States Constitution, indeed, allows for alternative methods of initiation: proposal by Congress at the request of two thirds of the State legislatures or proposal by Constitutional Convention.[71] Indeed, if direct democracy is seen as applicable to both stages of the process— initiation and ratification—an elected constitutional convention would seem to be a natural concomitant of initiation, at least where fundamental changes are proposed. It would ensure that the right of initiation is not reserved for the dominant party in the House of Representatives at a particular time. At least, an elected constitutional convention might be considered as an alternative method to the present method. However, to be effective, such a method would require an amendment to section 128.[72] A statutory convention is a second best.

It is appropriate that, in light of the present debate on an Australian republic, proposals for fundamental changes such as the abolition of the monarchy should go to a Convention before being submitted to the electorate at a referendum. I would emphasise, however, that the agenda of such a Convention should be wide-ranging and include specifically the restructuring of our federal arrangements. This may be the only adequate method of ensuring an Australian consensus on such changes prior to the submission of any Bill to a referendum.

My tentative views would include provision for a Convention size of between one hundred and twenty and one hundred and fifty, and no *ex officio* or nominee members: the members of a Convention should be fully elected. An application for a Convention could be dealt with by a body of independent Commonwealth and State officers, or presiding officers of the

Parliaments. The most controversial question would be whether there should be equality of representation for the States or election of delegates on a population basis. I would suggest that the former, that is, equal representation of the States would be the only practicable way of securing all-Australia support. My other observation would be that it would be preferable for party designation not to appear on the ballot paper, that is, to have a non-partisan election of members of the Convention. I do believe that this Convention method would be a major way of securing an Australia-wide consensus without the intrusion of too much political interference in the formulation of proposals.

Other Issues: Separation of Powers and Monarchy

In relation to the doctrine of separation of powers, this involves questions of the independence of the judiciary and the exclusive investment in Chapter III courts of judicial power free from legislative or executive encroachment. Deane and Toohey JJ. state that ultimately this principle, like federalism, is subject to the amendment procedure of section 128.[73] However, in one respect the separation of powers doctrine operates at a higher level than the other elements because the High Court has the power of invalidating acts whether legislative or executive which it holds to be unconstitutional. Because this involves judicial power, it cannot be exercised at large, that is in a non-dispute situation, and the subject-matter with which the power deals must be justiciable. Therefore some political matters may be outside the jurisdiction of the Court.[74]

As to the Crown, the 'fount' of executive power, both Deane and Toohey JJ. recognise that the change in relationships between Buckingham Palace and Canberra has resulted in an Australian constitutional monarchy with formal executive power being vested in the Queen in right of Australia[75] but being exercised by the Governor-General on the advice of the Commonwealth Government.[76] This is, of course, subject to the exercise of reserve powers which give the vice-regal representative discretion to resolve constitutional crises.

In accepting the concept of a distinctly Australian citizenship the High Court in *Nolan v. Minister of Immigration and Ethnic Affairs*[77] emphasized the relationship between citizen and Crown as a relationship based on the recognition of the Monarch as Queen in right of Australia. This suggests that the Australian monarchy is a juristic entity: loyalty to the Queen in right of Australia is loyalty to the Crown as underpinning Australian institutions (including the Crown itself, representative government and federalism).

In the view of Deane and Toohey JJ. in *Nationwide* it would appear that the very existence and status of the monarchy is subject to the section 128 alteration procedure in so far as the monarchy is part of the legislative process (section 1) and the source of executive power (section 61).[78] However, Covering Clause 2 of the *Commonwealth of Australian Constitution Act* 1901 (UK), which recognises the continuation of the monarchy in Australia from 1901, is left by Deane and Toohey JJ. for future consideration.[79] The question must remain whether the monarchy as recognised in the Covering Clauses contained in the *Constitution Act* is within or outside the alteration procedure.[80]

There is also the question of the effect of the *Australia Acts* 1986 (Cth and UK), section 7, which recognise the existence of the monarchy in the Constitutions of the States. Section 15(1) of the Acts imposes a manner and form requirement, that is, unanimous approval of all State Parliaments and the Commonwealth Parliament for their repeal or amendment, subject to the qualification in section 15(3) that powers given to the *Federal Parliament* by a constitutional alteration Bill under section 128 are recognised.[81]

Conclusion

I will now try to summarize the 'Grundnorms' or 'rules of recognition'[82] of our system in the light of the High Court decisions to which reference has been made.

At the level of basic constitutional rules, representative democracy is a foundation even possibly a common law foundation[83] of the Constitution. It is partially incorporated into the Constitution in sections 7 and 24. As such, representative democracy is a pivotal principle which gives nourishment and support to the various sections of Chapter 1. In addition there are two other foundations: federalism and separation of powers. As to federalism, part of this concept is recognised in section 7, part in sections 53, 55 (separate subjects in a Bill imposing taxation) and 57, and is fleshed out in sections 51, 106, 107 and 108 and 109.

In the end result, there is in section 128 a basic 'rule of recognition' or 'Grundnorm' which reflects the representative democracy principle, that is that alteration proposals are made by the Houses of Parliament, and a direct democracy principle requiring ratification of alteration proposals by a national majority of electors, itself qualified by a federal principle which imposes the requirement that the proposal be also approved by a majority of electors in a majority of States. This principle is further qualified by the fifth and sixth paragraphs of section 128 which require approval by the affected State or States of a proposal which impacts on certain interests such as State boundaries or proportionate representation in the Federal Parliament or the minimum number of members in the House of Representatives. Where all States are affected by a proposal such as one to abolish the States or the Senate, approval by majorities in *all* States would be required for such proposals.

It is clear from the above analysis that it would be extremely difficult to accomplish the republican goal in one 'omnibus' referendum Bill. It would be just as difficult to achieve that goal with several proposals presented at the one referendum. In other words, there would have to be referenda on several occasions.

Presumably, however, overarching all such requirements for the alteration of the Constitution is the power of judicial review, with the High Court having the power to determine whether a 'successful' referendum (that is, one obtaining the requisite majorities) held under section 128 is valid, that is, in relation to its effect on the Covering Clauses and the *Australia Acts* 1986 (Cth and UK) and State Constitutions.

However, there is a conundrum here: a decision of the High Court on the validity of a constitutional amendment (or indeed any other type of decision) may itself be overridden by the same procedure, for example, by a referendum under section 128. Thus there is no single fundamental rule identifying a 'sovereign' in our constitutional system.

The issue of the relationship between judicial power and the other 'Grundnorms' of the Australian constitutional system gives rise to vital questions. If the doctrine of implied rights is extended beyond the area of representative government, a position which Deane and Toohey JJ. have supported,[84] it must then be asked whether the establishment of a partial bill of rights by judicial fiat intrudes on citizens' rights deriving from representative government and from their role in the constitutional amendment process. This question of reconciliation is a matter which is still to be addressed by the High Court.

This paper was presented at The University of Queensland T.C. Beirne School of Law Annual Symposium 1993.

Notes

1. See the Report of the Republic Advisory Committee, *An Australian Republic: The Options* (Canberra: A.G.P.S. 2 vols., 1993), vol.1, 116.
2. *Australian Capital Television Pty Ltd v. Commonwealth of Australia* (No.2) (1992) 177 C.L.R. 106 (cited hereafter as *ACTV*).
3. *Nationwide News Pty Ltd v. Wills* (1992) 177 C.L.R. 1 (cited hereafter as *Nationwide*).
4. Inserting Part IIID (ss.95-95U) in the *Broadcasting Act* 1942 (Cth). The ban applied during election periods: *ACTV* (1992) 177 C.L.R. 1, 125–126 per Mason C.J.
5. S.299(1)(d)(ii). The provision prohibited a person, by writing or speaking, using words which brought a member of the Commission or the Commission into disrepute.
6. (1992) 177 C.L.R. 1, 69–70 per Deane and Toohey JJ.
7. (1985) 159 C.L.R. 192.
8. (1991) 172 C.L.R. 84.
9. (1992) 177 C.L.R. 1, 70 per Deane and Toohey JJ.
10. *Id.* 71–72; see also Brennan J.,47; *ACTV* (1992) 177 C.L.R. 106, 137–38 per Mason C.J., 733–4 per Gaudron J., 742–4 per McHugh J.
11. *Attorney-General of the Commonwealth (ex rel. McKinlay) v. Commonwealth* (1975) 135 C.L.R. 1.
12. 'The number of members chosen in the several States shall be in proportion to the respective numbers of their people.' See generally G. Lindell, 'Proportionate Representation of States in the House of Representatives and Associated Issues—Some Recent Developments in Australia and the United States' (1988) 11 *University of New South Wales Law Journal* 102.
13. See, for example, the judgment of Gibbs J. (1975) 135 C.L.R. 1, 45–6.
14. *Id.* 56.
15. *Id.* 56–7.
16. *Id.* 56.
17. *Id.* 57.
18. *Id.* 56.
19. *Id.* 19 per Barwick C.J.
20. *Id.* 56.
21. *Id.* 56–57.
22. That is the problem of bicameralism: see below.
23. (1975) 135 C.L.R. 1, 57 per Gibbs J.
24. *Id.* 61.
25. *Id.* 37.
26. *Ibid.*

27. *Id.* 6.
28. See, for example, Brennan J. in *Nationwide* (1992) 177 C.L.R. 1, 46–47.
29. *ACTV* (1992) 177 C.L.R. 106, 210.
30. *Id.* 224 *et seq.*
31. *Id.* 227–228.
32. *Id.* 227.
33. *Ibid.*
34. *Id.* 209.
35. *Id.* 188.
36. (1975) 135 C.L.R. 1, 60.
37. See *Commonwealth Electoral Legislation Amendment Act* 1983. Where time is not sufficient to complete a redistribution because of circumstances such as an early election, provision is made for a mini-redistribution: *Commonwealth Electoral Act* 1918, s.76.
38. S.66(3)(a).
39. S.66(3)(b).
40. S.66(3).
41. *R. v. Pearson Ex parte Sipka* (1983) 152 C.L.R. 254 is authority for the view that s.41 of the Constitution (which guarantees a right to vote in federal elections to those enfranchised under State law) became spent when the Commonwealth enacted its own electoral legislation in 1902. But see *ACTV* (1992) 177 C.L.R. 106, 184 per Dawson J., 204 per Gaudron J; see also 149 per Brennan J.
42. *Commonwealth Electoral Act* 1918, s.93(1). It should be noted, however, that British subjects enrolled before the 26th January, 1984 are entitled to vote: *Commonwealth Electoral Act* 1918 s.93(1)(b)(ii).
43. *Commonwealth Electoral Act* 1918, s.93(2).
44. Cf. Stephen J. in *McKinlay's* case, (1975) 135 C.L.R. 1, 56.
45. *Ibid.*
46. *ACTV* (1992) 177 C.L.R. 106, 184 per Dawson J., 228–232 per McHugh J.: *Nationwide* (1992) 177 C.L.R. 1, 47–48 per Brennan J., 71–72 per Deane and Toohey JJ. who describe it as a possible fourth basic doctrine of the Australian constitutional system.
47. Examples are 1989–1991 in Tasmania and the current period in New South Wales with three Independents holding the balance of power in the Legislative Assembly.
48. This occurred in the federal election in 1990 with the Coalition parties obtaining 50.1 per cent of the two-party preferred vote and the A.L.P. 49.9 per cent.
49. *Constitution Act* 1934 (S.A.), s.83(1).
50. See generally, A.R. Browning (ed.), *House of Representatives Practice* (2nd ed., Canberra: A.G.P.S., 1989), Ch. 19.
51. Act No.21 of 1987.
52. e.g. s.16(3). See C. Harders, 'Parliamentary Privilege—Parliament versus the Courts: Cross-examination of Committee Witnesses' (1993) 67 *Australian Law Journal* 109.

53. 'The Senate shall be composed of Senators for each State, directly chosen by the people ... .'
54. As to Queensland, the power given to the Parliament of the State to divide the State into *divisions* conferred by the second paragraph of s.7 (which was subject to inconsistent Commonwealth legislation) is prevented by the *Commonwealth Electoral Act* 1918, s. 39.
55. J.R. Odgers, *Australian Senate Practice* (6th ed., Canberra: Royal Australian Institute of Public Administration, 1991), 140.
56. *Ibid.*
57. *Id.* 146.
58. J. Quick and R.R. Garran, *The Annotated Constitution of the Australian Commonwealth* (Sydney, 1901: Reprint 1976, Legal Books), 414.
59. Odgers, *supra* note 55, 8 *et seq.*
60. *Western Australia v. Commonwealth* (1975) 134 C.L.R. 201; *Queensland v. Commonwealth* (1977) 139 C.L.R. 585.
61. *Queensland v. Commonwealth* (1977) 139 C.L.R. 585, 601 per Gibbs J.
62. (1975) 134 C.L.R. 81, 121 per Barwick C.J., 143 per Gibbs J., 168 per Stephen J., 185 per Mason J.
63. (1992) 177 C.L.R. 1, 71–72.
64. See C. Howard and C. Saunders, 'The Blocking of the Budget and Dismissal of the Government' in G. Evans (ed.), *Labor and the Constitution: 1972–1975* (Melbourne: Heinemann, 1977), 251, 281.
65. (1992) 177 C.L.R. 1, 71.
66. *Id.* 72.
67. (1992) 177 C.L.R. 106, 139 per Mason C.J., 210–211 per Gaudron J. Mason C.J. considers that the *Australia Act* 1986 (UK) 'marked the end of the legal sovereignty of the Imperial Parliament and recognised that ultimate sovereignty resided in the Australian people', 138. Cf. Dawson J. 180–181.
68. The issue of Senate initiation of a constitutional alteration Bill which the House of Representatives fails to pass is discussed in R.D. Lumb, *Annotated Constitution of the Commonwealth of Australia* (4th ed., Sydney: Butterworths, 1986), 386.
69. See C. Saunders, 'Changing the Constitution' in B. Galligan and J.R. Nethercote (eds.), *The Constitutional Commission and the 1988 Referendums* (Canberra: Royal Australian Institute of Public Administration, 1989), 31.
70. See R.D. Lumb, 'Methods of Constitutional Revision in the Federal Sphere: an Elected Constitutional Convention?' (1992) 22 *University of Western Australia Law Review* 52, 55–8.
71. *Id.* 65.
72. *Id.* 68.
73. *Nationwide* (1992) 177 C.L.R. 1, 71.
74. G.J. Lindell, 'The Justiciability of Political Questions: Recent Developments' in H.P. Lee and G. Winterton (eds.), *Australian Constitutional Perspectives* (Sydney: Law Book Co., 1992), 180.

75. *Nolan v. Minister for Immigration and Ethnic Affairs* (1988) 165 C.L.R. 178, 186 per Mason C.J., Wilson, Brennan, Deane, Dawson and Toohey JJ. (referring to the *Royal Style and Titles Act* 1973).
76. *Nationwide* (1992) 177 C.L.R. 1, 70.
77. (1988) 165 C.L.R. 178, 186.
78. *Nationwide* (1992) 177 C.L.R. 1, 71.
79. *Ibid.* See L. Zines, *The High Court and the Constitution* (3rd ed., Sydney: Butterworths, 1992), 83, 272–274.
80. On this matter see G. Craven, *Secession: the Ultimate States Right* (Melbourne: Melbourne University Press, 1986), 160–1, who considers that they are outside the alteration procedure in s. 128. The Republic Advisory Committee has indicated the possible use of s.15(3) of the *Australia Acts* to overcome the problem. It would be a very messy way of achieving a republican goal as it would involve giving the Federal Parliament power to amend s.8 of the *Statute of Westminster* (1931). See Republic Advisory Committee Report *supra* note 1, vol.2, 298–303 (Acting Solicitor General's advice).
81. See generally Zines, *supra* note 79, 275. G. Winterton, 'An Australian Republic' (1988) 16 *Melbourne University Law Review* 467, 480. G. Lindell, 'Why is Australia's Constitution Binding? The Reasons in 1900 and Now, and the Effect of Independence' (1986) 16 *Federal Law Review* 29, 40. See also Mason C.J. in *ACTV* (1992) 177 C.L.R. 106, 139. R.D. Lumb, 'The Bicentenary of Australian Constitutionalism: The Evolution of Rules of Constitutional Change' (1988) 15 *University of Queensland Law Journal* 3, 27–32. See further Republic Advisory Committee Report, *supra* note 1, vol.2, 305–309 (Acting Solicitor General's advice).
82. See R.D. Lumb 'Fundamental Law and the Processes of Constitutional Change' in A.E. Tay and E. Kamenka (eds.), *Lawmaking in Australia* (Melbourne: Edward Arnold Australia, 1980), 76–81.
83. *Nationwide* (1992) 177 C.L.R. 1, 45 per Brennan J., citing Dixon, 'The Common Law as an Ultimate Constitutional Foundation' (1957) 31 *Australian Law Journal* 240, 245.
84. *Leeth v. Commonwealth* (1992) 174 C.L.R. 455, 483–487.

Republicanism and State Constitutions

*Gerard Carney**

While much attention has been focused on the Australian (or Commonwealth) Constitution in the current republican debate, little consideration has been given to State Constitutions and the impact republicanism may have on them. Can they remain monarchical with a republican Commonwealth? If a State decides to go the republican path, which constitutional path should it take? What legal obstacles are placed in its way?

The Report of the Commonwealth's Republic Advisory Committee[1] only briefly considered the States under paragraph six of its terms of reference: 'The implications for the States'. The Committee's main focus was on the options for a republic at the Commonwealth level. Given that Australia is a federation and that most assume that an Australian republic will replace the monarchy at both the Commonwealth and State levels, the Committee should have considered in some detail the effect of republicanism on the States. Instead, it concentrated only on the situation if one or more States wished to remain as a monarchy and the capacity of the Commonwealth to prescribe a republican constitutional system for the States.

For the Commonwealth to become a republic the necessary amendments to the Commonwealth Constitution, deleting the Queen and substituting at least an appointed Head of State or President, will need to be approved by a majority of Australian voters and by a majority of voters in a majority of States at a referendum pursuant to section 128 of the Commonwealth Constitution. Therefore, there is the possibility that the Commonwealth may become a republic when two States may not wish to embrace republicanism. Those States which agree to

---

* Associate Professor of Law, Bond University.

embrace it will need to amend their own Constitutions in order to convert to a State republic.

This paper examines the constitutional position in each of these potential situations. It begins with an outline of the current constitutional system (in so far as it is relevant to the republican debate) and then considers two main issues: first, the nature of a republican system of government at the State level; and secondly, the capacity of the Commonwealth to facilitate or impose republicanism at the State level. The arguments for and against republicanism are not at issue in this discussion.

The Current Position

The six Australian States provide in their respective Constitutions for a Westminster monarchical system. Each of their systems of government is based upon the principle of responsible government whereby the Government is responsible to the Parliament in having to have the support of the Lower House in order to form a government. The Queen through her State Governors performs two crucial functions in this system: first, in granting royal assent to Bills passed by the Parliament in order for them to become law; and secondly, as the head of the Executive (or Government) with the power of appointing and dismissing the members of the Executive (that is, Ministers). By virtue of the principle of responsible government, these powers are exercised on the advice of the ministry.[2]

Until the passing of the *Australia Acts* 1986 (Cth and UK) by both the Commonwealth and the United Kingdom Parliaments, any advice tendered to the Queen by a State was channelled via the United Kingdom Government. But the *Australia Acts* 1986 (Cth and UK) in finally recognising that the States are part of an independent and sovereign nation, provide for the direct tendering of advice to the Queen by the State Premier.[3] Further, by virtue of section 7(2) of the *Australia Acts* 1986 (Cth and UK), 'all powers and functions of Her Majesty in respect of a State are exercisable only by the Governor of the State'. There are two exceptions though: the power of appointing and dismissing the Governor remains vested in the Queen;[4] and when the Queen is personally present in the State, she is able to exercise those powers and functions vested in her.[5]

The distribution of powers between the Queen and the State Governor in each State reflects the similar distribution of powers between the Queen and the Governor-General under the Commonwealth Constitution. Because the Queen has the power of appointment and dismissal of the Governor-General and of the State Governors, she is formally the Head of State at the Commonwealth level and Head of State in each of the six States. The Commonwealth's Republic Advisory Committee has referred to Australia as a *heptarchy*—a nation of seven monarchies.[6]

The direct constitutional link between each State and the Queen through the State Governor means that there are no formal constitutional links between each of the State Governors and between the State Governors and the Governor-General.[7] This has important implications for any form of republican government which the States may adopt. This aspect will be considered further below.

Although the Queen is styled in Australia as the 'Queen of Australia' after this was assented to by the Commonwealth Parliament in 1973[8] and subsequently proclaimed by the Queen,[9] none of the States has sought to adopt a new style for the Queen in relation to their particular State, such as 'Queen of Queensland'.[10] There would seem to be no legal obstacle to the States adopting a specific style for their own State, especially in view of the 'patriation'[11] of the States by section 7 of the *Australia Acts* 1986 (Cth and UK). As the Queen is Head of State in each State then each State must have the capacity to prescribe her royal style and title for that State in the same way as the Commonwealth has done. Learned commentators who oppose this view do so on the basis that the Commonwealth has the exclusive power to prescribe the royal style and title of the Queen.[12] While this may be so in relation to the Commonwealth, it does not necessarily follow in relation to the States. However, before a State could prescribe a royal style and title for the Queen in that State, this would require the agreement of, and subsequent proclamation by, the Queen.

Most of the powers vested by the State Constitutions in the Crown are given to the Governor and not to the Queen. Since 1986 even those few powers vested in the Queen, such as the power of dismissing State judges[13] and the remaining royal prerogative powers, are now exercisable only by the Governor, except when the Queen is present in the State and except for the power of appointment and dismissal of the Governor which is exclusively vested in the Queen. Therefore, as in the case of the Governor-General at the Commonwealth level, each State

Governor is the *de facto* Head of State of that State. Furthermore, although neither the Governor-General nor the State Governors are subject to instructions from the Queen[14] each must by convention act upon the advice of his or her respective ministry.

The range of powers of a State Governor include the power to:

(i) grant royal assent to Bills either in the name of the Queen or in the name of the Governor;
(ii) summon and prorogue Parliament and dissolve the Lower House;
(iii) recommend to Parliament the passage of appropriation and taxation Bills;
(iv) appoint and dismiss Ministers;
(v) attend and preside over meetings of the Executive Council;
(vi) remove and suspend public officials;
(vii) remove Supreme Court judges upon an address from Parliament;
(viii) grant pardons; and
(ix) issue writs for Senate elections (Commonwealth Constitution, section 12); and appoint a temporary replacement Senator where the position of a Senator becomes vacant at a time when the State Parliament is not sitting (Commonwealth Constitution, section 15).

These powers (i) to (viii) are vested in State Governors or, in a few instances, in the Queen either by the relevant State Constitution Act,[15] by statute, or by letters patent. New letters patent were issued by the Queen on 14 February 1986 for all State Governors except the Governor of New South Wales. Subsequently, both in Queensland[16] and in New South Wales,[17] statutory provisions now provide for the office of Governor. All powers vested in the Governor, as with the Queen, are exercised only by convention on the advice of the Premier or appropriate minister.

Republican Options for the States

If a State decides to convert from a monarchical to a republican system of government, issues similar to those which are involved in the same conversion at the Commonwealth level will arise. There is, though, for the States a preliminary issue which does not arise to the same degree in relation to the Commonwealth. Is it necessary for a State to have a Head of State at all or any position equivalent to the State Governor? Given that it is only the

Commonwealth of Australia which is recognised as the nation state according to international law for ceremonial and diplomatic purposes, a Head of State is clearly required at the Commonwealth level.[18] The States, on the other hand, are not individual nation states and so the basis for having their own Head of State may be somewhat different.

As with many Heads of State including the Queen and the Governor-General, there would appear to be two roles currently performed by State Governors—constitutional and ceremonial. From time to time it is suggested[19] that the constitutional role of State Governors could be performed by the Chief Justice while presumably, the ceremonial role would be taken over by local politicians. As regards the constitutional role, the question arises whether that role performs a useful purpose as guardian of the constitutional system. Could it be dispensed with altogether? Similarly with the ceremonial role, is it worth the expense of such an office? Clearly, opinions may differ on the necessity for both of these roles and the benefit each provides the community in terms of political and social stability.

The ceremonial role calls for someone who is politically neutral yet who commands general public respect as the people's representative. Such a Head of State performs the important role of according due recognition to a host of achievements within the community in a manner which few politicians (if any) could emulate. While the Governor-General represents 'the Australian nation to the people of Australia',[20] the State Governor or Head of State represents the State to the people of that State.

The constitutional role of a State Governor is substantially similar to that of the Governor-General. As the above list of powers reveals, the Governor is an integral component of Parliament with the power of royal assent, and head of the Executive with the power of appointing and dismissing ministers. While these and the other powers of the Governor are exercised only by convention on the advice of the ministry, exceptional circumstances may arise which justify the exercise of certain powers without such advice. This is referred to as an exercise of *reserve power*. It is generally accepted[21] that the reserve power of a State Governor is likely to arise only in relation to the following situations:

- the appointment of a Premier, particularly when only a minority government can be formed;

- the dismissal of a Premier for illegal conduct, loss of support in the Lower House, or parliamentary denial of funds for the continued functioning of the Government;
- granting of an early general election by dissolving the Lower House.

As these powers are exercisable only by the Governor and not by the Queen, it is clear that the reserve power is vested only in the Governor. Whether the circumstances at the time justify an exercise of reserve power remains essentially *at the discretion of the Governor*. The dismissal of the Prime Minister, Mr Whitlam, by the Governor-General, Sir John Kerr, in 1975 for failing to secure supply, aroused considerable political and constitutional debate as to whether the circumstances justified the dismissal *at that time*.[22] Given the fact that the exercise of reserve power has occurred only on rare occasions,[23] the situation must be very exceptional before such power needs to be exercised without the advice of the ministry. In this respect, the State Governor as the Queen's representative, assumes the role as guardian of the constitutional system. It is significant to note that the dual nature of the Head of State at the State level, provides a further control mechanism whereby the Governor remains ultimately accountable to the Queen who acts only on the advice of the Premier. The Westminster system in Australia, therefore, creates this special tripartite relationship between the Queen, the Governor and the Premier at the State level and similarly between the Queen, the Governor-General and the Prime Minister at the Commonwealth level. The constitutional role also demands political neutrality in order for it to be effectively performed.

The case in favour of having a republican Head of State at the State level is significantly stronger if that office is intended to perform some guardianship role of the constitutional system — a role required by the very nature of the Westminster system of responsible government.[24] Such a role would presumably entail powers and responsibilities similar to those currently vested in the State Governors. The conventions regulating their use and the circumstances in which an exercise of reserve power is justified may be expressly incorporated in a republican constitution without denying to the Head of State an important constitutional role.

The case against maintaining a Head of State at the State level advocates the elimination of the constitutional role of Head of State by substituting detailed rules, justiciable before the courts or a special constitutional court, to resolve all future constitutional problems. Professor Winterton[25] advocates this approach, pointing out that it has been adopted in the States of Germany. Whether detailed constitutional rules can adequately resolve *all* future constitutional crises seems doubtful. Their weakness is in the impossibility of prescribing rules which will cover every possible situation and the delay which any judicial determination of those rules may inflict upon the resolution of the crisis. Such delay may be inimical to political stability when swift action is required to prevent further undermining of the political system by unconstitutional conduct.

An alternative to detailed rules is to vest the ultimate guardianship of the constitutional system of a State in an existing public official, such as the Presiding Officer of either House,[26] the Chief Justice or the President of a republican Commonwealth. None of these office-holders could perform the constitutional role of Head of State as well as a State Governor or a new Head of State. Presiding officers are political appointees and therefore lack the necessary neutrality, while the independence of the judiciary may be compromised if this role is given to the Chief Justice. The President may be put in a position of conflict of interest if acting as Head of State for the Commonwealth and the States. Also it would be impossible for the President to review all Bills of all seven Parliaments before giving assent to them as well as perform all the other constitutional and ceremonial functions.

There are models in republican federal systems with and without non-executive Heads of State at the State level.[27] In India, the States have a Governor to perform both constitutional and ceremonial roles.[28] On the other hand, the federal States of Austria[29] and of Germany[30] essentially leave the role of Head of State to the chief minister of each State, the *Landeshauptmann* in Austria and the *Ministerpräsident* or *Regierender Burgenmeister* in Germany.

The importance and demands of the ceremonial role of a State Governor should not be underestimated. As the *de facto* Head of State at the State level, the State Governor performs a significant role within the community in providing support for an enormous number of people and their projects which are designed for the public benefit. The political neutrality of the position confers upon the office of the Head of State considerable respect and influence and so provides a unifying force for the State. Those benefits for the State which derive from the position of Head of State would probably be lost if the position was disbanded and its ceremonial functions transferred to politicians or other public officials. They simply do not have the time to perform such a role nor could they perform it nearly as well.

The arguments in favour of maintaining a Head of State at the State level to perform a constitutional and ceremonial role seem overwhelming. If then, it is decided to replace the Queen as the formal Head of State in the States with a locally appointed Head of State but maintain the existing Westminster system of parliamentary and responsible government, then issues similar to those which have been considered at the Commonwealth level arise here:

(i) What title is to be given to the Head of State?
(ii) How is the Head of State to be appointed?
(iii) What are to be the powers and functions of the Head of State?
(iv) Grounds and procedure for removal of the Head of State?

(i) Title

The title must reflect the importance of the position as Head of State. The current title of 'Governor' is an option, given that it is the designation of the republican Head of State in each of the States of the United States and in the States of the Republic of India. Another option is 'Administrator' which was used in the provinces of South Africa and is currently used in the Australian States to describe the person, normally the Chief Justice, who assumes the powers of the Governor when the latter is absent from the State.

If the Head of State is to assume both constitutional and ceremonial roles, the preferable title would seem to be 'Governor' for several reasons: it reflects the importance of the office; it involves fewer constitutional amendments; it is used in other federal republics; and it assists in maintaining continuity with those conventions and traditions of a monarchical Governor. Those conventions and traditions are: political neutrality, guardianship of the constitutional system, and being the representative of the people of the State. Furthermore, it is the oldest title of public office in Australia and it would seem unfortunate not to preserve it as part of the historical evolution of Australia into nationhood.

(ii) Appointment

The process of appointment of a Head of State at the State level, as with the other issues following in (iii) and (iv), may be guided by the republican constitutional arrangements adopted at the Commonwealth level. Provided the people of each State are satisfied with the Commonwealth position, it would seem desirable to adopt similar arrangements at the State level to provide some consistency in the Australian constitutional system as currently exists. This would reduce public confusion over the nature of the constitutional system at both levels. Moreover, such consistency would enable each of the States and the Commonwealth to draw upon each other's constitutional experience in the development of appropriate conventions and customs.

As regards appointment of a Head of State at the State level, the situation is less complicated than at the Commonwealth level where the process for appointment of a President may have to take into account the wishes of the States. The options for appointment at the State level are:

- by the Premier (the current position in practice);
- by the State Parliament;
- by the people; or
- by the President of the Commonwealth (on the advice of the Premier).

The last-mentioned option closely resembles the current position whereby State Governors are appointed by the Queen on the advice of the State Premier. If the appointment was to be made by the President of the Commonwealth instead of by the Queen, a tripartite relationship would be retained as a further control mechanism, although possibly not one as effective as that currently in place. If the appointment was to be made by the President of the Commonwealth, only advice tendered by the Premier or by the State Parliament to the President would be acceptable to the people of that State. The position in both Canada and India, where the Provincial and State Governors are appointed by the federal Head of State on the advice of the Federal Government, would most likely not be accepted in Australia.

In India, the President of India appoints the Governor of a State on the advice of the Indian Government.[31] Consequently, certain State Governors have been accused of being puppets of the Federal Government.[32] Reinforcing the subservience of the States to the Federal Government is the power of 'President's rule'[33] in Article 356, whereby the President (on the advice of the Federal Government) can take over the Government of a State if the President is satisfied that the Government of the State cannot be carried on in accordance with the provisions of the Constitution.

In Canada, the Head of State in each of the Provinces is the Lieutenant-Governor who is appointed by the Governor-General in Council on the advice of the Prime Minister, not the Premier of the Province.[34] In practice, the Premier is consulted only if he or she is a member of the same party as the Prime Minister. Also, the appointee usually belongs to that party.[35] The Lieutenant-Governor, however, acts only on the advice of the Provincial Government and not on the advice of the Government of Canada.

It is unlikely to be acceptable to the Australian States that their respective Heads of State be chosen by the Commonwealth. Moreover, the position outlined above in Canada and India does not give full effect to the principle of responsible government at the State level since the local Head of State is ultimately accountable to the Federal Government. If it is desired to give recognition to the Australian federal system in the process of appointing the Head of State at the State level, then the formal appointment could be made by the President on the advice of the State Government after the State selection process has determined the appointee. This option is considered further below.

The process of appointment must involve the least degree of politicisation to ensure the neutrality of the position; must not create a situation in which the Head of State believes he or she has a mandate from the people to act as a rival to the elected government; and must not discourage eligible persons from accepting nomination to the position. These requirements seem to rule out direct and indirect appointment by the Premier and by the people.

The most desirable process appears to be an invitation to the people of the State to nominate to the Cabinet office suitable persons for appointment as Head of State, the selection and nomination of one person as Head of State by the Cabinet after consultation with the Leader of the Opposition and the leaders of the other minority parties, followed by ratification of that appointment by a two-thirds majority of the Parliament at a joint sitting. This proposal resembles one of the main options identified by the Commonwealth's Republic Advisory Committee for the appointment of a President.[36]

Eligibility for appointment as Head of State should include the stipulation that the nominee has not held elected office in Australia for a prescribed period of, for example, five years. The period prescribed must be sufficient to reduce the danger of the nomination of a prominent politician who may be unable to bring to the position the neutrality it requires. As a temporary disqualification on politicians, it still accommodates suitable nominees whose former political involvement, at least five years earlier, may have been only an incident in a successful career outside politics. It also allows those with extensive political experience to distance themselves from the current political scene to enable them to assume an apolitical role as Head of State.

The options for formal appointment of the Head of State after ratification by the State Parliament seem to be by the Parliament itself, by the Executive, or by the President of the Commonwealth. There are certain advantages which flow from the appointment being made by the President. One pre-condition would be that the States must have been involved in the appointment of the President such that the presidency is truly a federal office.[37] On this basis one can justify the role of the President in the appointment of Heads of State at the State level. While this role would be merely a formal one, acting on the advice of the State Premier after the State selection process has confirmed the appointee, it provides among all seven Heads of State a formal constitutional link which reflects the federal compact.

This constitutional link would also be advantageous in several other respects. There would be between the Premier, the Head of State, and now the President, the continuation of a tripartite relationship which, as noted above, can act as a control mechanism on the constitutional system. It would provide for consistency in terms of ceremonial custom in much the same way as has occurred through Buckingham Palace and it would facilitate the appointment of one of the Heads of State at the State level as the administrator of the Commonwealth when the President was absent from office. The only apparent drawback from the State's perspective of the appointment being made by the President is the precedence then to be accorded to the President over the Heads of State at the State level. This is currently not the case with the Governor-General and the State Governors. But this precedence is merely ceremonial and it reflects the paramountcy given to the Commonwealth Constitution over the State Constitutions by section 106 of the Commonwealth Constitution. The only alternative to the President of the Commonwealth making the formal appointment would seem to be an appointment by the State Parliament itself.

(iii) Powers and Functions

Here again, it seems desirable that the States follow the approach taken in relation to the powers and functions of the President. If these powers and the conventions governing their exercise are formulated in the Commonwealth Constitution, much of that formulation could readily be adopted for inclusion in a State Constitution. The particular issues which arise in relation to the powers of a Head of State at the State level include:

- Is it necessary to require the assent of the Head of State to Bills before they become law?
- Should the Head of State's powers be expressly exercisable *only* on the advice of the Premier or appropriate minister and that no advice from any other source be permitted? If not, which sources of advice are to be allowed?
- If the Head of State is to retain 'reserve powers', should these powers be defined and their exercise regulated?
- Should the powers of the Head of State and their exercise be justiciable before the courts?

The Commonwealth's Republic Advisory Committee[38] considered these issues in relation to the powers of the President of a Commonwealth republic. One of their main conclusions was that the Westminster conventions including those governing the exercise of the reserve powers must be expressly included in the Commonwealth Constitution.[39] There is no doubt that the same process must also occur at the State level.[40]

If the basic convention that the Governor must always act on the advice of the Premier or appropriate minister is to be codified, the issue arises whether this is to be an absolute rule thereby abrogating the reserve powers of the Governor, or whether the reserve powers are to be retained. This issue has already arisen in Queensland and Victoria where their respective Constitutions appear to adopt different positions. In Queensland, section 14(2) of the *Constitution Act* 1867 gives full scope to the reserve power by providing that ministers hold office at the pleasure of the Governor 'who in the exercise of his power to appoint and dismiss such officers shall not be subject to direction by any person whatsoever nor be limited as to his sources of advice'. However, clause 3 of the 1986 Victorian Letters Patent provides that, apart from the Executive Council, 'The Premier (or in his absence the Acting Premier) shall tender advice to the Governor in relation to the exercise of the other powers and functions of the Governor'. It has been suggested that this provision abrogates the reserve powers of the Governor.[41] On the other hand, it seems to provide only *who* is to advise the Governor.[42]

(iv) Removal

The procedure for removal of the Head of State requires careful consideration if the position is vested with a constitutional role, to ensure adequate security of tenure.[43] To simply empower the Premier to remove the Head of State would effectively deny that office of any capacity to act as guardian of the constitutional system. If the appointment process involves several parties as suggested above, namely, nomination by cabinet, or ratification by a special majority of both Houses with the formal appointment by the President or State Parliament, then to adopt the same procedure for removal would make the office of Head of State sufficiently secure from unscrupulous dismissal. The grounds for removal should also be specified to prevent arbitrary dismissal. The two grounds for removal of federal justices pursuant to section 72 of the Commonwealth Constitution of 'proved misbehaviour and incapacity' seem adequate grounds especially in view of their interpretation by recent judicial commissions of inquiry.[44]

Consequential Changes for Republican States

- Legislative provision will need to be made in South Australia, Tasmania, Victoria and Western Australia for those matters currently provided for by the Letters Patent in each State, especially the Executive Council.
- State Constitutions should vest in the Head of State the executive power of the State to ensure that all of the royal prerogative powers currently vested in State Governors are carried over to the new Head of State.
- Once all of the provisions required for the adoption of republicanism at the State level are incorporated in the State Constitution, the final issue is whether they ought to be entrenched by requiring a referendum to approve their amendment.

State Self-determination: How to Proceed?

The determination of all of these issues discussed above would be facilitated by following as far as possible their resolution at the Commonwealth level. Consistency between the constitutional systems of the Commonwealth and of the States should be the objective, at least in so far as the approach adopted is appropriate and conducive for stable and good government. This is a matter which will need to be assessed by the people of each State at a referendum along with those other matters peculiar to the States, such as the need for a Head of State at all and the process of formal appointment.

Legal Obstacles to State Republicanism

Of concern here are those legal obstacles to the enactment of constitutional changes required for conversion to a republic by way of *ordinary* legislation of the State Parliament. There would seem to be at least two legal obstacles to the elimination of the monarchy in State constitutional systems by a simple constitutional amendment:

(1) section 7 of the *Australia Acts* 1986 (Cth and UK); and
(2) entrenched 'manner and form' provisions in five of the six State Constitutions.[45]

(1) Australia Acts 1986

Section 7 of the *Australia Acts* 1986 (Cth and UK) provides:

(1) Her Majesty's representative in each State shall be the Governor.
(2) Subject to subsections (3) and (4) below, all powers and functions of Her Majesty in respect of a State are exercisable only by the Governor of a State.
(3) Subsection (2) above does not apply in relation to the power to appoint, and the power to terminate the appointment of, the Governor of a State.
(4) While Her Majesty is personally present in a State, Her Majesty is not precluded from exercising any of Her powers and functions in respect of the State that are the subject of subsection (2) above.
(5) The advice to Her Majesty in relation to the exercise of the powers and functions of Her Majesty in respect of a State shall be tendered by the Premier of the State.

The question here is whether section 7 prescribes a monarchical system for each of the States or whether it simply defines the relationship between the Queen and a State Governor for so long as the States maintain a monarchical system. If the former, then section 7 needs to be repealed before the States can adopt a republican system. If the latter, no repeal is required. The former view is supported by the assumption made in section 7 that the

Queen possesses certain powers and functions and by the exception in section 7(4) that the Queen may exercise her powers when personally present within the State. The latter view is advocated by Professors Winterton[46] and Zines[47] on the basis that section 7 *assumes* a monarchy but does not prescribe one. The Commonwealth's Republic Advisory Committee preferred the latter view but recommended the safer course of repealing section 7 to avoid any doubt.[48]

There are two mechanisms for repealing section 7 available under section 15 of the *Australia Acts* 1986 (Cth and UK), both of which require legislation of the Commonwealth Parliament. The first, pursuant to section 15(1), is by an Act of the Commonwealth Parliament passed at the request of or with the concurrence of *all* State Parliaments. If one State Parliament refuses to agree to the proposed amendment, then only the second method pursuant to section 15(3) is available. This requires an amendment to the Commonwealth Constitution pursuant to section 128 conferring on the Commonwealth Parliament the power to make the necessary amendment to, or repeal of, the *Australia Acts* 1986 (Cth and UK).

An argument has been raised[49] that an amendment by way of section 128 empowering the Commonwealth Parliament to amend or repeal section 7 of the *Australia Acts* 1986 (Cth and UK) by removing the Queen from the constitutional systems of the States requires by virtue of the final paragraph of section 128 the approval of the electors of *each* State because such an amendment affects 'the provisions of the Constitution in relation thereto'.[50] The better view, however, seems to be that 'in relation thereto' refers only to those provisions concerned with constitutional representation of the State in the Commonwealth Parliament and with the territorial limits of the State.[51] Furthermore, the Constitution referred to is not the State Constitution but the Commonwealth Constitution. Accordingly, it seems that the Commonwealth may be empowered to remove the paramount effect of section 7 of the *Australia Acts* 1986 (Cth and UK) if this is approved by a national referendum and in four out of the six States. Whether the Commonwealth can use section 128 to directly alter the constitutional system in a State is considered below.

(2) Entrenchment of a Monarchical System

All of the Constitutions of the six States contain 'manner and form' provisions[52] which prescribe special additional requirements for the enactment of laws amending or repealing certain constitutional provisions. These entrenched provisions either expressly prescribe the monarchical system for that State, or clearly assume that system. The special requirement common to four of the Constitutions[53] is that of approval of the proposed law at a State referendum, while another requirement in some of them is that an absolute or special majority must pass the Bill in each House.[54]

Whether these special 'manner and form' requirements are effectively binding in each case depends upon a number of complex legal principles, a detailed discussion of which falls outside the scope of this paper.[55] Suffice to say that the main basis for their enforcement is section 6 of the *Australia Acts* 1986 (Cth and UK) but this section operates only in relation to laws 'respecting the constitution, powers or procedure of the Parliament of the State'. Several State Constitutions[56] purport to entrench provisions which provide for the office of Governor and hence any Bill affecting these provisions may not satisfy the characterisation test of section 6. While there are, however, potential grounds[57] outside section 6 which may entrench these provisions, it is not necessary to consider those grounds because the very fact that a manner and form provision exists which refers to the requirement of royal assent by the Governor, sufficiently entrenches the monarchical system in that State. This is so provided the manner and form provision is doubly entrenched, that is, its special requirements apply to a law to repeal that manner and form provision itself.

As noted just above, the State Constitutions entrench the monarchical system either directly or indirectly. Direct entrenchment of the monarchical system by way of a referendum requirement is effected by the Queensland and Western Australian Constitutions. Each entrench those provisions which: define the Parliament as including the Queen;[58] vest the legislative power of the State in the Queen with the advice and consent of the Legislative Assembly in Queensland[59] and with the advice and consent of both Houses in Western Australia;[60] and require royal assent to be given to Bills passed by the Parliament in order to become law.[61] Since any repeal or amendment of those provisions would relate to the Constitution, powers or procedure of the Parliament, then they are effectively entrenched unless their repeal or amendment is approved by the electors at a referendum in each State. A further requirement is imposed in Western Australia—the Bill must pass both the second and third readings in each House by an absolute majority.[62] Both Constitutions also purport to entrench the office of Governor as the Queen's representative[63] but, as noted above, those provisions are probably not entrenched by virtue of section 6 of the *Australia Acts* 1986 (Cth and UK). Also, it is not entirely clear whether they are entrenched on grounds outside section 6. It is unnecessary to consider their status further because those other provisions concerned with the composition of Parliament which are effectively entrenched, mean that the Constitutions of these two States cannot be converted from monarchical to republican without the approval of the electorate in each State. This is, however, subject to whatever power the Commonwealth may have to directly alter the constitutional system of a State. The Victorian Constitution just manages to directly entrench the monarchical system by requiring that any alteration to the constitution of the Parliament which is defined as the Queen, the Legislative Council and the Legislative Assembly, be passed by an absolute majority in each House.[64] Significantly, no referendum requirement is imposed.

Indirect entrenchment of the monarchical system is effected by the Constitutions of New South Wales and South Australia. Both[65] require Bills repealing or amending certain provisions of their Constitutions to be approved by a referendum in the State before they can be presented to the Governor for royal assent. South Australia also requires that alterations to the constitution of both of its Houses be approved by an absolute majority in each House at the second and third readings.[66] These manner and form provisions and the provisions they entrench, unlike those entrenched in Queensland, Western Australia and Victoria, do not expressly prescribe a monarchical system. But they do assume such a system by referring to the role of the Governor in some provisions, and more importantly, by referring in their respective manner and form provisions to the requirement of royal assent after approval at the referendum.

It is important also to note that all of the manner and form provisions in the five State Constitutions considered so far are doubly entrenched and hence incapable of simple repeal by ordinary legislation of the State Parliament. Any law purporting to repeal or amend a manner and form provision itself must comply with the very requirements of that provision.[67] This, however, is not the position in Tasmania where, although there is a purported indirect entrenchment of the role of the Governor in section 41A by requiring a two-thirds majority of the House of Assembly to amend section 23, section 41A is not doubly entrenched and hence both section 41A and section 23 can be repealed or amended by ordinary legislation.

From the above survey, it can be seen that in four of the six States (New South Wales, Queensland, South Australia and Western Australia), a referendum of the people of each State will be necessary in order for those States to adopt a republican system of government. In Victoria and Tasmania no referendum is required by law although in Victoria the elimination of the Queen as part of Parliament must be approved by an absolute majority in both Houses. What remains to be considered is the capacity of the Commonwealth to override these entrenched provisions of State Constitutions with or without the consent of the State. This raises the whole issue of the Commonwealth's ability to interfere with the *institutions* of State government.

Republicanism: Within State Legislative Power?

Even if section 7 of the *Australia Acts* 1986 (Cth and UK) is repealed and the States manage to satisfy the requirements of relevant manner and form provisions, do the States have the legislative capacity to convert to a republican system? Prior to the enactment of section 7 in 1986, it was accepted that the States lacked the legislative capacity to eliminate the requirement of royal assent for the enactment of law.[68] This view was based first upon the States' incapacity to legislate repugnantly to Imperial legislation which assumed the monarchical system in the States.[69] Secondly, it was thought that the power given by section 5 of the *Colonial Laws Validity Act* 1865 (Imp) to 'every representative legislature ...[namely]... full power to make laws respecting the constitution, powers, and procedure of such legislature', did not include the power to alter the constitution of the legislature by eliminating the Crown. Although this power enabled a bicameral legislature to convert to a unicameral legislature,[70] the Crown was viewed as an indispensable component of the legislature.

Since the *Colonial Laws Validity Act* 1865 (Imp) no longer applies to the Australian States by virtue of section 3(1) of the *Australia Acts* 1986 (Cth and UK), there would seem to be no legal impediment to the States enacting the necessary constitutional changes for republican government. The basis of this power is the plenary power of each State Parliament to make laws for the peace, welfare (or order) and good government of the State. Of course, the amendments which eliminate the Crown will need to be given royal assent by the Governor.

Commonwealth Power

The next issue to consider is the capacity of the Commonwealth to abrogate State entrenched manner and form provisions and to otherwise alter the constitutional systems of the States with or without their consent. Whether the Commonwealth Parliament has either capacity depends upon finding in the Commonwealth Constitution a legislative power which enables the Commonwealth Parliament to change the constitutional system within the States and identifying any restrictions on the exercise of such a power. There are two potential sources of legislative power, section 51 (xxxviii) and section 128. Section 51 (xxxviii) can be used only with the co-operation of the State concerned and may enable the Commonwealth to assist a State to override an entrenched manner and form provision. Section 128, which depends not upon State co-operation but a successful national referendum, may empower the Commonwealth to actually alter the constitutional system of a State.

Section 51(xxxviii)

With the request or concurrence of the State Parliament, the Commonwealth Parliament could enact a law pursuant to section 51(xxxviii) repealing a State manner and form provision and/or the constitutional provisions entrenched by it, on the basis that their repeal could be effected only by the United Kingdom Parliament at the establishment of Federation. Professor Winterton[71] disagrees with this view because the States themselves had the power to repeal the manner and form provision by complying with its requirements. His view depends upon a broad notion of legislative capacity as encompassing even a fettered legislative power. However, he does accept that the Commonwealth could come within section 51(xxxviii) if it simply empowers the State to just *disregard* the manner and form provision.

However, there may be a difficulty in obtaining a valid request or consent from the State if the Act of the State Parliament by which the request or consent is given must itself comply with the manner and form provision. Whether such compliance is required depends upon the wording of the manner and form provision. It is arguable that none of the manner and form provisions in the State

Constitutions extend to request or consent laws of the States. For instance, section 7A of the *Constitution Act* 1902 (NSW) applies only to Bills which expressly or impliedly 'repeal or amend' certain sections. A State Bill which requests the Commonwealth to repeal or amend those sections does not itself effect that result. Any repeal or amendment is effected by the Commonwealth Act. It is true, though, that the State Act is an essential prerequisite for the Commonwealth Act and so it may be argued that the State Act purports to *indirectly* repeal or amend the entrenched provisions. But 'indirectly' in section 7A is most likely intended to mean that the *terms* of the State Act are simply inconsistent with the entrenched provisions and would override them according to established principles of statutory interpretation. 'Indirectly' is not used to refer to the legislative *process* as such. Less clear is the position in Queensland and Western Australia where their respective manner and form provisions apply to any Bill which 'expressly or impliedly *in any way affects*' the entrenched provisions.[72] It may be easier to establish that a State request or consent law indirectly *affects* those provisions by enabling the Commonwealth to repeal them, than to establish that the State Act indirectly *repeals* those provisions by enabling the Commonwealth to repeal them.

There are two potential restrictions on the Commonwealth's exercise of power pursuant to section 51(xxxviii) in the above circumstances: section 106 of the Commonwealth Constitution and the *Melbourne Corporation* principle. Section 106 provides:

> The Constitution of each State of the Commonwealth shall, subject to this Constitution, continue as at the establishment of the Commonwealth, ... until altered in accordance with the Constitution of the State.

It is still an unresolved issue[73] whether section 106 constitutes a restriction on the exercise of Commonwealth legislative power affecting the Constitutions of the States pursuant to sections 51 and 52 when both section 106 and those legislative powers are expressly 'subject to the [Commonwealth] Constitution'. Professor Zines[74] argues that section 106 is not such a restriction on Commonwealth power, preferring to rely for the protection of the States upon the general implication drawn from the federal nature of the Commonwealth Constitution known as the *Melbourne Corporation* principle. Section 51(xxxviii) which relies upon the consent of the State concerned may be in a different position from an exercise of other legislative powers so that section 106 is subject to section 51 (xxxviii). This was the position taken in *Port MacDonnell Professional Fishermans' Assoc. Inc. v. South Australia*[75] which upheld the validity of the *Coastal Waters (State Powers) Act* 1980 under section 51(xxxviii) and concluded that section 106 was subject to any law made pursuant to this legislative power. If section 106 is a restriction on Commonwealth legislative power, the manner and form provisions in question undoubtedly fall within 'the Constitution of the State' even within its narrowest meaning.[76] The other relevant restriction is the *Melbourne Corporation* principle which contains two limbs:

> [The] Commonwealth cannot in the exercise of its legislative powers enact a law which discriminates against or "singles out" a State or imposes some special burden or disability upon a State or inhibits or impairs the continued existence of a State or its capacity to function.[77]

Neither of these limbs is likely to apply to a law under section 51(xxxviii) which is made with the consent of the State concerned.

Section 128

The other possible basis by which the Commonwealth may directly or indirectly alter the constitutional system of the States is to rely upon the amendment provision, section 128 of the Commonwealth Constitution. This might be used to assist a State to remove entrenched monarchical provisions in its Constitution since the Commonwealth is not bound by section 6 of the *Australia Acts* 1986 (Cth and UK). Of greater concern is that section 128 might be used to impose upon the States a republican system by forcing the elimination of the Crown from that system. For whichever of these purposes section 128 is used, the same legal issue arises. To what extent can section 128 be used to alter the constitutional system of the States? Since Professor Lumb considers this issue in his paper, only an outline of the main arguments[78] will be given here.

The main argument for the view that the Commonwealth lacks this capacity to alter the constitutional system of the States relies upon the nature of the Commonwealth Constitution as 'a compact of States'[79] and that the creature of that compact, the Commonwealth, cannot alter the very parties to that compact (that is, the States) unless those parties agree to their own restructuring. This would require, presumably, a referendum in each State approving that restructuring or the vesting of such a power in the

Commonwealth. The counter argument is that the Commonwealth Constitution including section 128 is binding on the States and their people by virtue of section 106, and that section 128 empowers the Commonwealth Parliament and the people of the Commonwealth to change 'the relationship between the Commonwealth and the States and the constitutional arrangements of the States themselves'.[80] A further argument, based upon the penultimate paragraph of section 128, for requiring the consent of each State whose Constitution is to be altered by a Commonwealth constitutional amendment, was examined earlier[81] and rejected as this argument relies upon a misinterpretation of section 128.

The case in favour of section 128 being used to alter the constitutional system of the States relies upon the phrase in section 106 that the State Constitutions are 'subject to the [Commonwealth] Constitution'. It is argued[82] that section 106 incorporates the State Constitutions into the Commonwealth Constitution and as they are expressly subject to the Commonwealth Constitution this means that they can be directly amended pursuant to section 128. The last phrase of section 106, 'until altered in accordance with the Constitution of the State', appears simply to be there to ensure that the State Constitutions are not entrenched by section 128 but are still able to be amended by the State Parliament in the usual way.

Even if section 106 does not actually incorporate State Constitutions into the Commonwealth Constitution, section 128 might still be used to confer upon the Commonwealth Parliament the power to alter State Constitutions. In this way, the Commonwealth may acquire the legislative *capacity* to force the States to substitute their monarchical system for a republican one. The potential width of such a power may frighten voters and so reduce the chances of being approved at the section 128 referendum. The advantage of this approach, though, is that any restrictions[83] which may be derived from section 106 can be avoided by appropriate drafting of the amendment. Even if the Commonwealth can by a section 128 amendment alter the constitutional system of the States, such an amendment must be approved by a majority of voters nationally and in four States. If this approval is obtained there remains, however, the important issue: should the Commonwealth force onto the States a new constitutional system even if it has the power to do so? Might this not cause the collapse of the federal system?

A Mix of Republic and Monarchy?

If in the end republicanism is not voluntarily embraced by all Australians for both levels of government nor imposed upon those unwilling to embrace it, is it feasible both legally and practically for the Federation to be comprised of both monarchies and republics? What is at issue here is whether or not the conversion to republicanism must be 'a boots and all' affair. In other words, if one State (or even the Commonwealth) remains monarchical does this prevent the others from becoming republics?

If one accepts that the current Federation of six States and the Commonwealth are, within the constraints of the Commonwealth Constitution, independent of each other, and that there are seven Crowns, then there seems to be no reason in law why one or more of these entities cannot adopt a constitutional system which is different from the others whether this be a monarchy or republic, a parliamentary or a presidential system. Hence, we may have monarchical States and a republican Commonwealth, or even some republican States in a monarchical Commonwealth as was the case in the post-1871 German Empire.[84] These situations may be 'anomalous' but as Professor Winterton[85] points out so was the position before the *Australia Acts* 1986 (Cth and UK) whereby the States, in theory at least, retained colonial status while the Commonwealth had been upgraded to a Dominion.[86] Although there is now no apparent federation in the world with such a cocktail of different constitutional systems, it is difficult to understand the basis for the opposing view put forward by D.P. O'Connell[87] that it is 'impossible' to combine in the Australian Federation a republic and a monarchy.

Another view is that if the monarchy is abolished at the Commonwealth level so that the Queen is no longer Queen of Australia, then her role also ceases at the State level. The Australian Crown is removed altogether. Since this view is not based upon the incompatibility in a federal system of a monarchy and a republic, the Commonwealth's Republic Advisory Committee[88] recommended, for the avoidance of doubt, on the basis of the opinion of the Acting Commonwealth Solicitor-General[89] that if the Commonwealth Constitution is amended to provide for a Commonwealth republic, a provision should be inserted expressly allowing the States to retain their monarchical system if they wish.

Apart from the republican issue, there also seems to be no reason in law for requiring consistency in the type of constitutional system operating at the Commonwealth and State levels. A State may adopt a presidential system of government while the parliamentary system is retained at the Commonwealth level or vice-versa.[90] While the law may tolerate such differences within a federal system, do they threaten or weaken the federal relationship? If the difference is simply in terms of the Head of State, one a monarch, the other elected, this is unlikely. If the difference is in the system of government itself, the effect on the federal system is difficult to judge in the absence of overseas experience. More complicated co-operative arrangements between the Commonwealth and the States may result. Negotiations may be necessary at both the executive and legislative levels in order for effect to be given to agreements where one of the parties has adopted a presidential system of government.

There is much to be said in favour of consistency in a federal system. A lack of consistency in terms of Australia's constitutional systems may increase public confusion and hence reduce public confidence in government. This would be so in the case of a monarchical State within a republican Commonwealth but clearly more so in the case of a republican State in a monarchical Commonwealth.

Conclusion

Whatever the scope of Commonwealth power in relation to the constitutional system of the States, the adoption of republicanism at the State level must be resolved within each State by the political processes of that State. The future of the Federation will be at risk if a new system of government is imposed on the people of a State without their majority support.

If the States wish to become republics, every effort should be made to maintain consistency between the systems of government at the Commonwealth and State levels, as well as between the States themselves. There are cogent arguments for retaining in each State its own Head of State to perform a constitutional and ceremonial role similar to that currently performed by the State Governor as the *de facto* Head of State. This would be consistent with the uniquely individualistic character of the Australian States.

Notes

1. The Report of the Republic Advisory Committee, *An Australian Republic: The Options* (Canberra: A.G.P.S., 2 vols., 1993), vol. 1, 123–132, 148.
2. As Professor Winterton aptly puts it: 'It is the *government's* advice the Governor must act on, not the Premier's *personal advice*.' G. Winterton, 'The Constitutional Position of Australian State Governors' in H.P. Lee and G. Winterton (eds.), *Australian Constitutional Perspectives* (Sydney: Law Book Co., 1992), 302.
3. *Australia Acts* 1986 (Cth and UK) s.7(5).
4. *Id.* s.7(3).
5. *Id.* s.7(4).
6. Republic Advisory Committee Report, *supra* note 1, vol.1, 125. Cf L. Zines, *The High Court and the Constitution* (3rd ed., Sydney: Butterworths, 1992), 272.
7. Except the office of the Governor-General does co-ordinate for Australia the conferral of Australian honours and processes applications for the prefix 'Royal' and the use of the Crown insignia.
8. *Royal Style and Titles Act* 1973 (Cth).
9. On 19 October 1973 (see Commonwealth Gazette 1973, No. 152).
10. Although the oath of allegiance in the Second Schedule to the *Constitution Act* 1975 (Vic) refers to the Queen as 'lawful Sovereign of the United Kingdom and of this State of Victoria'.
11. See J.A. Thomson, 'The Australia Acts 1986: A State Constitutional Perspective' (1990) 20 *University of Western Australia Law Review* 409 , 425.
12. See Zines, *supra* note 6, 272; Winterton, *supra* note 2, 274.
13. For example, *Constitution Act* 1867 (Qld) s.16.
14. See Winterton, *supra* note 2, 282.
15. See R.D. Lumb, *The Constitutions of the Australian States* (5th ed., Brisbane: University of Queensland Press, 1991), 3–46.
16. *Constitution (Office of Governor) Act* 1987 (Qld) s.3. Section 13 suspends the Letters Patent for Queensland of 14 February 1986.
17. *Constitution Act* 1902 (NSW) s.9F.
18. See Republic Advisory Committee Report, *supra* note 1, 1, 47–51.
19. See Winterton, *supra* note 2, 275–6; suggested by Australian Labour Party soon after Federation.
20. Sir Ninian Stephen, 'Depicting a Nation to its People', *Weekend Australian*, 7–8 January 1989, 12.
21. See R.D. Lumb, *Australian Constitutionalism* (Sydney: Butterworths, 1983), 76–79; Winterton, *supra* note 2, 293ff.

22. G. Sawer, *Federation Under Strain* (Melbourne: Melbourne University Press, 1977).
23. Two recent case-studies of Queensland in 1987 and Tasmania in 1989, in B. Galligan, 'Australia' in D. Butler and D.A. Low (eds.), *Sovereigns and Surrogates: Constitutional Heads of State in the Commonwealth* (London : MacMillan, 1991), 85–97.
24. See P.W. Hogg, *Constitutional Law of Canada* (2nd ed., Toronto: Carswell Company, 1985), 212: 'A system of responsible government cannot work without a formal Head of State who is possessed of certain reserve powers'.
25. G. Winterton, *Monarchy to Republic* (Melbourne: Oxford University Press, 1986), 106–7.
26. *Ibid*. In Sweden, the Speaker performs this role.
27. Not a presidential system with an executive Head of State as in the United States.
28. Governors of the States in India are appointed by the President of India: Art. 155 *Constitution of India*.
29. See the case study by Professor B. Raschauer, 'Austria' in the Republic Advisory Committee Report, *supra* note 1, vol.2, 21, 46.
30. See the case study by Professor K. von Beyne, 'Germany' in the Republic Advisory Committee Report, *supra* note 1, vol.2, 53, 68.
31. Art. 155 *Constitution of India*.
32. A.G. Noorani, 'India', the Republic Advisory Committee Report, *supra* note 1, vol.2, 91–92.
33. *Ibid*.
34. *Constitution Act* 1867 s.58.
35. Hogg, *supra* note 24, 193 and note 13.
36. Republic Advisory Committee Report, *supra* note 1, vol.1, 66–69.
37. *Id*. 73–4.
38. *Ibid*.
39. *Id*. 81–116.
40. See Winterton, *supra* note 2, 333–4.
41. Galligan, *supra* note 23, 81.
42. Winterton, *supra* note 2, 288.
43. Cf. *Constitution (Office of Governor) Act* 1987 (Qld) s.3(2) (b) which requires the removal of the State Governor to be by instrument under Her Majesty's Sign Manual upon publication in the *Gazette*.
44. Queensland Parliament, 'First Report of the Parliamentary Judges Commission of Inquiry, 1989'; 'Ruling on Meaning of "Misbehaviour" by the Parliamentary Commission of Inquiry into The Hon. Mr. Justice Murphy' (1986) *Australian Bar Review* 203.

45. *Constitution Act* 1902 (NSW) ss.7A and 7B; *Constitution Act* 1867 (Qld) s.53; *Constitution Act* 1934 (SA) ss.8 and 10a; *Constitution Act* 1975 (Vic) s.18; and *Constitution Act* 1889 (WA) s.73.
46. Winterton, *supra* note 2, 277.
47. See *supra* note 6, 266.
48. Republic Advisory Committee Report, *supra* note 1, vol.1, 127.
49. This was a submission of Australians for Constitutional Monarchy to the Republic Advisory Committee, *supra* note 1, vol.1, 130–131.
50. Penultimate paragraph of s.128 of the Commonwealth Constitution.
51. This was the conclusion of the Republic Advisory Committee, *supra* note 1, vol.1, 130; it was also the view of the Acting Commonwealth Solicitor-General, see Report of the Republic Advisory Committee, *supra* note 1, vol.2, Appendix 8, paras 42–44.
52. See *supra* note 45 and the *Constitution Act* 1934 (Tas) s.41A.
53. NSW, Qld, SA, and WA, *supra* note 45.
54. SA s.8; Tas s.41A; Vic s.18; WA s.73.
55. See G. Carney, 'An Overview of Manner and Form in Australia' (1989) 5 *Queensland University of Technology Law Journal* 69.
56. Qld ss.11A and 53(1); Vic s.6; WA ss.50 and 73 (2); but NSW s.9A not entrenched.
57. See Carney, *supra* note 55, 86–93. There are three possible grounds: the principle of *The Bribery Commissioner v. Ranaisinghe* [1965] A.C. 172; reconstituted legislature; and s.106 of the Commonwealth Constitution.
58. Qld s.2A(1); WA s.2(2). See also *The Constitution Act Amendment Act* 1934 (Qld) s.3.
59. S.2.
60. S.2(1).
61. Qld s.2A(2); WA s.2(3).
62. S.73.
63. Qld ss.11A and 53(1); WA ss.50 and 73(2).
64. S.18.
65. NSW ss. 7A and 7B; SA ss.8 and 10a.
66. S.8.
67. See *Attorney-General for New South Wales v. Trethowan* (1931) 44 C.L.R. 394.
68. See *Taylor v. Attorney-General of Queensland* (1917) 23 C.L.R. 457, 474, 481; *Clayton v. Heffron* (1960) 105 C.L.R. 214, 251; *Re Scully* (1937) 32 Tas.L.R. 1, 42–45.
69. *Colonial Laws Validity Act* 1865 (Imp) s.2.
70. *Taylor v. Attorney-General of Queensland* (1917) 23 C.L.R. 457.
71. See *supra* note 25, 142.
72. Qld s.53; WA s.73.
73. See Winterton, *supra* note 25, 135–6.

74. Zines, *supra* note 6, 289–294.
75. (1989) 168 C.L.R. 340.
76. That is the formal *Constitution Act*. See Zines, *supra* note 6, 291.
77. *Commonwealth v. Tasmania* (1983) 158 C.L.R. 1, 128 per Mason J.
78. See G. Sawer, 'The British Connection' (1973) 47 *Australian Law Journal* 113; R.D. Lumb, 'Fundamental Law' (1978) 9 *Federal Law Review* 148; D.P. O'Connell, 'Canada, Australia, Constitutional Reform and the Crown' (1979) 60 *The Parliamentarian* 5.
79. See *supra* note 1, 130. The High Court in the *Engineers* case (1920) 28 C.L.R. 129, 142 did describe the Commonwealth Constitution in the following way: 'That instrument is the political compact of the whole of the people of Australia...'.
80. Republic Advisory Committee Report, *supra* note 1, vol.1, 131.
81. See note 49.
82. See Winterton, *supra* note 25, 141.
83. Suggested in R.D. Lumb, *The Constitution of the Commonwealth of Australia—Annotated* (4th ed., Sydney: Butterworths, 1986), 348. See also notes 73–75.
84. See G. Winterton, 'An Australian Republic' (1988) 16 *Melbourne University Law Review* 467, 470.
85. Winterton, *supra* note 25, 104–105.
86. *Statute of Westminister Adoption Act* 1942 (Cth).
87. D.P. O'Connell, 'Monarchy or Republic?' in G. Dutton (ed.), *Republican Australia?* (South Melbourne: Sun Books, 1977), 23, 38.
88. Republic Advisory Committee Report, *supra* note 1, vol.1, 125, 128–129.
89. See *supra* note 51, vol.2, Appendix 8, 305–307.
90. See Winterton, *supra* note 25, 107.

The Other Road to the Republic: the Separation of Powers

*Suri Ratnapala**

Introduction

The purpose of this paper is not to argue for or against the proposal to make Australia a 'republic' by severing its remaining constitutional links with the British monarchy. The aim rather is to consider whether there is an opportunity to make the Australian Constitution more republican than it now is whether or not these links are severed. It is argued that although the Australian Constitution is fundamentally republican, its republican attributes have been seriously undermined since Federation by the judicial attitudes towards one of its fundamental doctrines, namely that concerning the separation of powers. However, the present High Court by its recent decisions has shown a keen appreciation of the republican values which characterise the Constitution. The Court's attitude to the Constitution has kindled hopes for a judicial restoration of the separation doctrine and the consequent strengthening of Australian republicanism. It is urged that the revival of this doctrine be considered as an essential part of the republican issue.

The current debate on the republic, with its narrow focus on the links to the Crown, overlooks more substantial issues concerning republicanism in Australia. This is reflected in the recent Report of the Prime Minister's Republic Advisory Committee. The Committee states:

> Australia is, therefore, a state in which sovereignty resides in its people, and in which all public offices, except that at the very apex of

---

* Senior Lecturer in Law, University of Queensland.

the system, are filled by persons deriving authority directly or indirectly from the people. It may be appropriate to regard Australia as a 'crowned republic', a view favoured by some monarchists, in that the only Australian office incompatible with a republic is the monarchy. It follows that all that is required to make Australia completely republican is to remove the monarch; no other constitutional change is required.[1]

In fairness to the Committee, it should be noted that the Prime Ministerial terms of reference did not permit it to address the more substantive issues of republicanism. However, it is of concern that the Report gives the impression that a republic would be achieved simply by abolishing the monarchy. There is an implication here that in other respects Australia has achieved the republican ideal. This is not the case and there are more fundamental and pressing problems which should take precedence in a truly republican agenda. One such problem is the disenfranchisement of the Australian public and the decline of the rule of law which has occurred as a consequence of the non-implementation of the separation of powers doctrine.

This author's view on the matter differs from that of the Republic Advisory Committee which reports that: 'In this respect also, Australia is already republican since our governmental system is based on the separation of powers and has always adhered strongly to the rule of law, enforced by judicial review'.[2] While the separation of powers and the rule of law are fundamental to the Australian Constitution, this author disagrees with the suggestion that in these respects, the Constitution is in good health.

Representation, Separation of Powers and the Rule of Law— Cornerstones of Republicanism

Thomas Paine remarked in the *Rights of Man* that 'Republican Government is no other than government established and conducted for the interest of the public, as well individually as collectively'.[3] A republic may be defined as a constitutional arrangement in which the government is conducted for the public good (*res publica*). A republic does not require by definition a particular form of government, but certain forms are clearly more conducive than others to the achievement of the republican ideal. Indeed, it is doubtful whether a system of government will remain republican for very long unless it is democratic in nature. Madison regarded a republic as a 'government in which the scheme of representation takes place'.[4] Paine argued, a republic 'is not necessarily connected with any particular form, but it most naturally associates with the representative form, as being best calculated to secure the end for which a Nation is at expense of supporting it'.[5] The Republic Advisory Committee recognised that the rule of law and the separation of powers are necessary elements of a republican form of government. Clearly, the Committee was aware that representative democracy cannot be achieved without these constitutional attributes.

The monarchical element in the present Constitution of Australia serves as an institutional check on power. The Monarch and her representatives act on advice of responsible ministers except in relation to the 'reserve powers'. Yet, their formal participation in legislative, executive and prerogative acts places a salutary constraint on government and Parliament. The Monarch also has, to use Bagehot's classic formulation, 'the right to be consulted, the right to encourage, the right to warn'. As De Smith and Brazier show, this is not a vacuous privilege.[6] Thus, if the monarchical element of the Constitution is to be abolished, it is imperative that the remaining checks and balances in the Constitution be strengthened. In particular, the doctrine of the separation of powers needs to be restored as a bulwark of democracy and the rule of law.

Separation of powers serves the republican ideal in two ways. First, the tripartite separation of powers requires the legislative, executive and judicial powers to be kept, as far as practicable, in separate hands. Hence, it serves as a system of political checks and balances which prevents the dominance of any one branch of the government over the others. The doctrine militates against the pursuit of sectional interests at the expense of the public good. Secondly it promotes the representative principle.

The representative principle cannot be maintained without a degree of separation of powers. In its ideal form, the separation doctrine distinguishes the function of making law from the function of administering the law. Where these functions are united in the same hands, the law can be made at the point of its enforcement. The law may be made for the particular case. It is practical to achieve consensus concerning the law but wholly impractical, and indeed unjust, to determine individual cases by popular will. A representative body would have neither time nor necessary information to make enlightened decisions in particular cases, especially in the absence of a rule to guide its decision. This problem was noticed by Aristotle in relation to the city states. When the citizen body began to decide every detail, it ceased to express consensus but became the tool of demagogues.[7] By contrast the representative principle is eminently suited to the determination of general rules which guide conduct, that is, laws properly so called. The separation of legislative and executive functions serves republicanism by ensuring that officials do not make their own law but act within the law determined by a representative body.

The Weakening of the Separation of Powers: the Error of Neglecting the Legislative/Executive Division

The High Court's overall policy towards the separation of powers doctrine has been to keep judicial and non-judicial powers in separate hands while condoning the unification of legislative and executive powers in the hands of officials. This policy is fundamentally flawed. In a series of cases the Court has held that the Commonwealth Parliament could delegate its legislative power to the executive without significant limits. In the leading case of *Victorian Stevedoring and General Contracting Co. Ltd. v. Dignan*,[8] the High Court approved of the grant of legislative power to the Governor-General in Council to regulate the entire subject of the employment of waterside workers, including the power to determine who might be employed in Australian ports and what such employees would be paid. This power was not guided by any principles laid down by Parliament. On the contrary, the Act contained a 'Henry III Clause' which authorised the making of regulations contrary to existing Acts of Parliament. The width of the power prompted a leading commentator to observe: 'Because the Executive thus legislates, the Executive and the legislature are not separate in function'.[9]

The *Dignan* Case and other decisions which followed it, have abrogated the rule implied in the separation of powers doctrine that the legislative power should be confined to the legislature, with the executive, where necessary, being delegated the power to work out the detail of the law subject to principles settled by the legislature.[10] These cases are in accordance with the Court's policy of keeping the judicial and non-judicial powers separate while permitting the unification of executive and legislative power. This approach reflects the inadequacy of the Court's theoretical inquiry concerning the separation doctrine. The Court has emphasised correctly the instrumentality of an independent judiciary in preserving liberty. An independent judiciary is part of a system of institutional checks and balances. It reflects the constitutional fragmentation of powers which militates against tyrannical rule. However, there is a more vital link between judicial independence and liberty which the Court has neglected to consider.

In the ultimate analysis, it is the rule of law which generates liberty. In classical theory, the rule of law was distinguished from the rule of the prince. Where the rule of law prevails the prince is subject to the law. Where the rule of the prince prevails, the 'law' is the *voluntas principi*, the will of the prince as and when expressed. It is evident that the rule of law is impossible without a degree of separation of the law making and law enforcing functions. If one and the same act is legislative as well as executive/judicial, effectively, there is rule of the magistrate. The rule of law does not require that the government be excluded from the law making process. It does require that in the conduct of the administration, the government is subject to pre-established rules, even if they are of its own making. Naturally, the rule of law is more likely to prevail where the legislative and executive bodies are distinct. Where some persons are members of both the legislature and the executive branches, other constitutional devices are required to maintain the separation of the two functions. Judges preserve liberty by upholding the law. A constitution may guarantee liberty by a bill of rights. In this case, it is the preeminence of the law concerning fundamental rights which secures liberty. Where there is no bill of rights or in areas where a bill of rights has no impact, it is the supremacy of the law over capricious will which provides the stability of expectations which is the essence of liberty.

Apart from serving as a system of political checks and balances, the separation of powers doctrine contributes to the rule of law in two ways. First, by separating the law making function from the executive function, it makes government subject to the law. It prevents the law being equated with the government's capricious will. Secondly, by separating the judiciary from the other branches, the doctrine makes it less likely that the law, after it is made, is not corrupted to serve the momentary wishes of the government or a private party. The certainty of the law which the separation doctrine provides in this way secures the degree of predicability of state and private actions without which we would have no liberty.

The High Court's approach to the separation doctrine emphasises the second aspect of the doctrine's contribution to the rule of law. By insisting on the separation and independence of the judiciary, the Court has sought to strengthen the capacity of the judiciary to ensure the integrity and certainty of the law after the law is made. However, the Court has overlooked the fact that this capacity is diminished where the law is what the officials will it to be. By allowing the executive to make law in its unfettered discretion, the Court risks depriving itself of the standards by which the legality of executive actions may be adjudged. Herein lies the defect. In implementing one but not the other aspect of the separation doctrine, the Court failed to appreciate the integrity of that doctrine.

The power to create new rights and obligations may be conferred on the executive in two forms. The enabling statute may authorise an official to make laws in the nature of rules, such as regulations and by-laws. Although these are easier to make and unmake than Acts of Parliament, they nevertheless involve a degree of procedural formality which give them some constancy. Hence, this is the less pernicious form of executive law making. Courts have the opportunity to ensure that the executive, in its actions, observes the rules which it itself made previously. The courts may also question the validity of the rules themselves on grounds such as the failure to establish a certain and therefore observable rule of conduct.[11] Alternatively, Parliament may confer a wide discretion upon an official to alter legal rights and obligations in a particular case. This may be done directly by the Act or indirectly by the authorising of the making of delegated legislation which confers such discretion on an official.[12] According to the *Dignan* doctrine, such conferments of discretion need not be subject to standards. As Barwick C.J. asserted following *Dignan*, a legislative discretion conferred upon an official cannot be challenged on the grounds of 'width ... and the lack of discernible criteria by reference to which the propriety of its exercise could be tested'.[13] This is the most dangerous form of discretion as it is largely unreviewable.[14] By virtue of the Act, the law is what the official wills. The courts would strive to narrowly construe the empowering provisions.[15] However, where the language is unequivocal, the current doctrine would pose no impediment to the executive enjoying complete arbitrary power.

In *Dignan's* case, the High Court reasoned that the system of responsible government established by the Constitution had made the rule against delegation unnecessary.[16] This reasoning presupposed that under responsible government Parliament is a deliberative assembly which is capable of independently judging the actions of the executive. This might have been the case before the rise of mega political parties. However, the supposition has no foundation in modern party politics where party discipline holds sway and members of a majority party in Parliament have no incentive to bring down a government upon which they rely for their own political survival. In fact, as David Mullan pointed out at the Second Commonwealth Conference on Delegated Legislation, even parliamentary committees set up to scrutinise delegated legislation have proved ineffective for the task owing to the 'high degree of party discipline within Committees and the general politicisation of the process'.[17]

The High Court also feared that effective government would be impossible unless the executive possessed wide law-making power.[18] However, the experiences of countries such as the Federal Republic of Germany and the United States prove the contrary. These nations continue to implement the rule against delegation without impairing the effectiveness of their Governments. The German practice of the non-delegation principle is most instructive as that country also has a system of 'parliamentary government' under which a government which has lost the confidence of the legislature could be removed from office.[19]

The German Federal Constitutional Court has viewed the rule limiting delegations[20] as a requirement of the separation of powers and an essential condition for the rule of law. The Court has stated that 'a vague blanket provision which would permit the executive [branch] to determine in detail the limits of [the individual's] freedom conflicts with the principle that an administrative agency must function according to law'.[21] The Court stated further:

> [T]he judiciary's mandate to protect [the citizen] legally [from encroachment by the state] can only be carried out if the courts can review the implementation of the norm by the executive [agency] encroaching upon the citizen's legal sphere. For this reason as well [the statute] must adequately define the authorization for encroachment.[22]

The German Court recognised a crucial fact concerning the separation doctrine, which the High Court has consistently overlooked, namely, it is futile to insist on the separation and independence of the judicial branch when the legislative and executive powers are not separated. Where the executive makes law, it can validate its own actions leaving little or nothing to the courts to decide.[23] By failing to limit the law-making power of the executive, the High Court has sanctioned the practice whereby countless rules affecting citizens are made by officials unrestrained by any democratically established principles.

This argument is not meant to devalue the importance of separating judicial and non-judicial powers. It aims to show that one of the main objects of keeping judicial and non-judicial powers separate, namely the preservation of liberty, cannot be achieved fully without the complimentary division of legislative and executive powers. The latter division involves the recognition that unfettered power to make law belongs exclusively to the legislative branch and that the law-making power of the executive is limited to the elaboration or application of general principles enacted by the legislature. Under such an arrangement, the courts would have a realistic chance of subjecting the executive to principles settled by the popular assembly.

The Curtailment of the Right to be Heard by a True Court

The Constitutional separation of the judicature from the other branches of government gives effect to the principle that a person should not be deprived of his or her rights except by the decision of a competent and impartial court.[24] The rule of law is clearly in jeopardy where this principle is not implemented. The Constitution secures the independence of federal judges by guaranteeing their tenure and their remuneration.

The High Court's treatment of the separation of powers doctrine in Australia constitutes an attempt to keep judicial and non-judicial powers in separate hands while condoning the unification of legislative and executive powers in governmental authorities. As previously observed, this policy is fundamentally flawed in theory. In practice, it has been seriously compromised by the Court. The High Court regards the separation and independence of the judiciary as an indispensable condition for maintaining the federal character of the Constitution[25] and for securing the liberty of the citizen.[26] It follows logically that an independent judiciary will be to no avail if judicial decisions are made actually by non-judicial bodies which lack independence from the other branches of government. The High Court has also considered that the vesting of non-judicial power in the judiciary will compromise its separation and independence and hence undermine the values of federalism and liberty.[27]

From the analytic standpoint, the High Court's implementation of judicial separation has two broad aspects. First, the Court has sought to describe the concept of judicial power and to identify the various occurrences of it. Secondly, it has developed a number of 'rules of separation' which seek to ensure, subject to certain exceptions, that the judicial power of the Commonwealth will be vested exclusively in courts whose independence is constitutionally secured. In relation to both the concept of judicial power and the rules of separation, the High Court has committed errors which have seriously weakened the doctrine's capacity to serve its political ends.

Conceptual confusion attends the formulation of some of the rules of separation. In particular, the Court's willingness to permit the delegation of judicial functions to non-judicial officers of courts[28] and to allow Parliament to vest non-judicial powers in judges of federal courts in their personal capacities[29] gives cause for concern. However, the Court has committed more serious errors in the course of defining the concept of judicial power. In his celebrated definition of the concept, Griffith C.J. identified the basic elements of judicial power. A decision is judicial in character if it resolves a controversy between citizen and citizen or between state and citizen, the controversy concerns rights, liberties or property, and the decision is conclusive in effect.[30] However, in subsequent cases, the High Court has compromised the Griffith definition to the point that Parliament is able now to entrust non-judicial bodies with extensive adjudicative powers affecting the citizens' rights. The Court, thereby, has undermined the effectiveness of the rules of separation. In defining judicial power, the Court has advanced a number of highly questionable propositions. Of particular concern are the following:

1. *The theory of innominate powers*. The proposition that there is a class of innominate powers which may be vested in any branch of government at the election of Parliament.

2. *Chameleon-like power*. The proposition that identically defined powers may be classified as judicial when reposed in a court and as executive when vested in a non-judicial body.

3. *The factum theory*. The proposition that statutory authority to determine conclusively questions of fact is not judicial power because such decisions merely constitute *facti* upon which the statute operates to create new legal relations.

4. *The theory of provisional effectiveness.* The proposition that the authority to determine disputes concerning rights is not judicial power if such decisions are reviewable *de novo* by a court on appeal.
5. *The basic rights approach.* The proposition that the constitutional guarantee of a judicial inquiry does not extend to the determination of disputes concerning rights which the court does not regard as 'basic'.

Many of the decisions of the Court which relaxed the rules of separation and the decisions establishing the above propositions concerning the meaning of judicial power were not dictated by constitutional imperatives. They were results of expediency or unfortunate conceptual errors. These decisions have caused real uncertainty with respect to the constitutional right of the citizen to have disputes concerning vested rights determined by a true court. This uncertainty seriously jeopardises the liberty of the citizen which, in the Court's theory, is a primary concern of the separation doctrine. Hence, these decisions reflect a significant divergence between the theory and the practice of the Court with respect to the separation doctrine. Attention will be drawn to three glaring examples.

Innominate Powers

The High Court has advanced the alarming proposition that there exists a category of powers which may be assigned to more than one of the three branches of government because they are not distinctly legislative, executive or judicial. In the *Boilermakers'* case, the majority judgment endorsed the view expressed by the American writer Willoughby, that: 'Generally speaking, it may be said that when a power is not peculiarly and distinctly legislative, executive, or judicial, it lies within the authority of the legislature to determine where its exercise shall be vested'.[31] Similar observations have been made in *R. v. Davison*,[32] *The Queen Victoria Memorial Hospital v. Thornton*,[33] *Federal Commissioner of Taxation v. Munro*[34] and *Commonwealth of Australia v. Leeth*.[35] Professor Lane has termed this type of power 'innominate power'.[36] The subversive effect of this proposition on the separation doctrine is plain. The proposition means that in relation to certain activities of the State, Parliament is not bound by the constitutional division of powers but may itself determine whether a function is classified as executive or judicial. The proposition amounts to an abdication by the High Court of its constitutional responsibility to classify functions and to confine them to the appropriate branch of government. The High Court has compounded the problem by suggesting that there are chameleon-like functions which acquire their character from the nature of the agency to which they are entrusted.[37] Hence, according to this doctrine Parliament may classify the identical function differently, simply by its choice as to the repository of the power.

The belief in the existence of an innominate power results from two serious conceptual errors. The first is the failure to recognise the distinction between the concept of judicial power and the rules of separation. For convenience this will be called the concept/rule dichotomy. The second is the failure to appreciate the distinction between subject and function which occurs within the concept of power. This may be called the subject/function dichotomy.

Confusion of the Concept/Rule Dichotomy

The fact that a power is held to be judicial in character does not mean necessarily that it has to be exercised by a Chapter III court. The High Court has recognised certain exceptions to the basic rules which vest judicial power exclusively in Chapter III courts and which keep non-judicial power away from such courts. The relevant cases show that the High Court admitted these exceptions, not because the powers in question were 'innominate', but because their location was sanctioned expressly or by implication by the Constitution as exceptions to the general policy of separating judicial and non-judicial powers. For example, in *Re Nolan; Ex parte Young*[38] and *Re Tracey; Ex parte Ryan*,[39] the High Court considered that the power to try and to punish service personnel for military offences was judicial power of the Commonwealth but held that the power might be vested in military tribunals. This conclusion was based on the Court's reading of section 51(vi) interpreted in the light of historical and practical considerations. In *R. v. Richards; Ex parte Fitzpatrick and Browne*,[40] the High Court determined that the historical power of the Parliament to punish persons for contempts of Parliament was not prohibited under the Constitution. The Commonwealth Parliament enjoyed that power under section 49 interpreted in the light of historical reasons. Again, in cases such as *Queen Victoria Memorial Hospital v. Thornton*[41] and *R. v. Davison*,[42] the Court expressed the view that functions which ordinarily would be regarded as administrative in character, could be exercised by courts if they could be considered to be incidental to the exercise of judicial power. In doing so, the

Court was saying, in effect, that the rule against Chapter III courts exercising non-judicial power did not preclude the courts from making orders which were incidental to the effective performance of their judicial functions. These cases indicate clearly that the question concerning the characterisation of a power is not coterminous with the question whether a given power may or may not be validly located in one or the other branches of the State. Yet, the High Court has sometimes failed to appreciate this dichotomy.

For example, in the Second *BIO* case, Isaacs J. identified the power to determine the validity of parliamentary elections as an innominate power.[43] His Honour was alluding to the fact that under the Australian Constitution the power to make such determinations may reside in Parliament itself. The determination of the validity of an election to Parliament is, without any doubt, a judicial act. It satisfies the most stringent test of judicial power. It is hardly necessary to labour the point that such a decision must be made according to law and not according to discretion. The decision affects rights and it is conclusive in the technical sense. Thus, ordinarily, the power to make such decisions would 'clearly and distinctively appertain' to the judicial branch. However, section 47 of the Constitution expressly authorises either House of Parliament to exercise this power 'until Parliament otherwise provides'. Section 47 creates an exception to the rule of separation that the judicial power of the Commonwealth is vested in Chapter III. This exception no doubt is founded on the historical privilege of the Houses of the British Parliament to determine questions concerning the validity of its composition. It hardly matters whether the rule is founded on historical and theoretical grounds or is stated expressly in the Constitution. The fact is that the power may be exercised by Parliament not because it is 'innominate' but because it is expressly authorised by the rules of separation.

Confusion of the Subject/Function Dichotomy

The concept of power has two aspects: subject and function. According to the most appropriate dictionary meaning, a subject refers to 'that which is or may be acted or operated upon'.[44] In this sense a subject may be a person, a thing, or a specified action or activity 'towards which action or influence is directed'.[45] 'Function', in its etymological sense means 'the action of performing' and in general usage means 'the special kind of activity proper to any thing; the mode of action by which it fulfils its purpose'.[46] In the constitutional context, 'function' refers to the mode by which a subject of the law is treated. Hence, logically, it is nonsense to speak of an innominate 'function'. The Constitution recognises three such modes, the legislative, the executive and the judicial. Usually, more than one function or mode is employed in the regulation of a subject of the law. Thus, a crime may be defined by legislation, investigated by executive action and adjudicated through the judicial function. Here, the crime is the subject of action and, like all subjects, it is innominate. It can be dealt with legislatively, executively and judicially. The modes of dealing with it signify distinct functions. The High Court has sometimes confused subject and function. An example of an innominate power given by the Court is the power to deregister a trade-mark. Like all subjects, trade-marks may be dealt with legislatively, executively and judicially. It is the responsibility of the Court to determine which mode has been selected by Parliament in the statute under scrutiny.

The line between the judicial mode and the executive or legislative modes will sometimes be very thin. However, the court must construe the statutory provisions to determine on which side of the line a function falls. That is its constitutional duty. Unfortunately, in these difficult cases the High Court has taken the easy way out by saying that such powers are innominate and capable of being assigned to one branch or the other at the discretion of Parliament. If by 'power' the Court meant the 'subject' component of power, the decisions make sense. All subjects are innominate in the sense that they can be dealt with legislatively, executively or judicially. However, this is not what the Court meant. The Court suggested that the functions in question are innominate, hence capable of being entrusted to any one of the three branches. As has been seen, this is a logical impossibility. What is worse, the proposition gives Parliament a licence to subvert the constitutional separation of powers by ingenious legislation.

The 'Chameleon' Powers

The High Court has deepened the confusion concerning innominate powers by suggesting that there is a category of chameleon-like functions which may acquire a judicial or administrative character, depending on the nature of the authority in whom it is reposed. In effect, the doctrine permits Parliament to classify the identical power as judicial or administrative simply by determining which branch of government shall exercise it.

It is of utmost importance to distinguish the chameleon doctrine from the technique of statutory interpretation which the High Court, from time to time, adopts to resolve difficult problems relating to the classification of powers. Sometimes it is not clear from the terms of a statute whether the power conferred on a repository is judicial or non-judicial. Doubts may arise because it is not clear whether the authority is required to determine a controversy according to the pre-existing rights and duties, that is, according to established objective standards, or is authorised to resolve the matter by adjusting or modifying existing legal relations. The answer to this question will depend ultimately on the extent of discretion conferred on a tribunal and the manner in which it is expected to reach its decision. Where the statute does not yield an unequivocal answer to the question, the Court is justified in having regard to the nature of the body to which Parliament has committed the function for the purpose of determining the character of the power. Thus in case of doubt, the fact that a power is vested in the judiciary would indicate that Parliament intended the controversies to be determined in a strictly judicial manner. As Kitto J. stated in *R. v. Spicer; Ex parte Australian Builders' Labourers' Federation*:

> The reason for concluding in some such cases that the judicial character of the repository imparts a judicial character to the power is simply that the former provides a ground for the inference, which in those cases there is nothing or not enough in other considerations to preclude, that the power is intended and required to be exercised in accordance with the methods and with a strict adherence to the standards which characterise judicial activities.[47]

Thus, in *R. v. Hegarty; Ex parte City of Salisbury*, when Mason J. stated that 'A function may take its character from that of the tribunal in which it is reposed',[48] he was in fact applying this principle of construction. As he put it, 'if a function is entrusted to a court, it may be inferred that it is to be exercised judicially ...'.[49] The point to note is that the principle is applied when there is some doubt about the nature of the function, that is, the mode in which the act is to be performed or the decision taken by the functionary. In such instances, the character of the functionary determines the mode of action.

On the contrary, the chameleon doctrine does not have the effect of changing the nature of the function according to the nature of the repository. It simply changes the description of the function while the function remains essentially the same. Thus, in *R. v. Quinn; Ex parte Consolidated Foods Corporation*,[50] the identical function was considered to be administrative in the hands of the Registrar of Trade-Marks and judicial in the hands of the Justices of the High Court. In each case the criteria upon which the decision was to be made, hence also the mode of deciding, remained the same.

The Theory of Provisional Effectiveness

A key virtue of the Griffith definition of judicial power is that it ensures that only a court can *conclusively* determine our rights and liabilities. If a decision affecting rights is conclusive, it is judicial, hence must be taken by a court. An official may 'decide' that a person has violated the law. But nothing flows from it. The 'decision' is only an expression of official opinion.

According to the earlier understanding of judicial power based on the Griffith definition, a decision would be regarded as conclusive, and hence judicial, even if it could be appealed against. In other words the availability of an appeal does not deprive a decision of its judicial character. It is the reason why lower courts are considered to exercise judicial power even when their decisions are subject to appeal. It is the reason that it was considered impermissible to grant administrators the power to determine questions concerning existing rights subject to an appeal to a court.

However, certain rulings of the High Court appear to permit executive authorities to make what are, in effect, final determinations concerning existing rights. The Court has created this possibility by tinkering with the Griffith definition in two ways. First, it has allowed Parliament to confer on administrators power to make decisions having provisional validity with the onus on the aggrieved citizen to take the matter to the courts. Where the citizen fails to do so, the official's decision stands as a final determination of the dispute. For convenience, this position will be identified as the 'theory of provisional effectiveness'. Secondly, the Court has advanced what may be termed the 'factum theory' in terms of which Parliament may grant executive authorities the power to finally determine questions of fact involved in disputes concerning existing rights. The former theory is examined here.

In the Second *BIO* case,[51] the High Court concluded that a decision resolving a controversy concerning existing rights is not a judicial decision if it is capable of being reviewed on appeal by way of a complete rehearing. The Privy Council endorsed this view on appeal.[52] The decisions contradicted the earlier understanding of judicial power based on the Griffith definition according to which the availability of an appeal does not deprive a decision of its judicial character. This proposition is suspect when viewed in the light of historical practice. It is not unknown for purely judicial decisions to be made reviewable by way of a complete rehearing. The Quarter Sessions, and later, the Crown Court have always heard appeals from summary convictions by way of a complete retrial. It could hardly be said for that reason that the convicting justices were not performing judicial functions. However, the more fundamental objection to the proposition springs from the philosophical foundations of the separation of powers doctrine.

The proposition means that Parliament could entrust to the executive the function of determining the rights and duties of the citizen in the first instance, provided that the citizen is given the right to institute proceedings to have the matter re-examined by a court *de novo* in all respects. The far-reaching implications of this position have not been widely observed. It means that Parliament could potentially transfer to non-judicial bodies, which are subject to political interference, powers over many of our cherished rights provided only that we are given a right to institute actions to vindicate those rights. It hardly needs to be stressed that few people can afford the costs of litigating against the government. Hence, in practical terms, most decisions made by a non-judicial body under such a legislative scheme could be final and conclusive.

Under such laws, the executive could provisionally deprive the citizen of his or her rights, or declare him or her subject to liability moving the onus on to the citizen to prove otherwise in a court of law. Where the citizen fails to institute proceedings, the provisional decision will be binding. It would make no difference whether the citizen failed to challenge the provisional decision because he or she conceded its correctness or because he or she could not afford the cost of litigation! Clearly, such arrangements cannot be used to determine questions affecting certain types of rights without endangering long cherished principles of constitutional government. For example, the executive determination of criminal guilt, even on a provisional basis, would be obnoxious to the constitutional principle that a person shall not be deprived of liberty except on conviction by a competent and impartial court. The principle, which is associated most frequently with the thirty-ninth chapter of the *Magna Carta*,[53] is also enshrined in the *International Covenant on Civil and Political Rights* which Australia has ratified and seeks to implement through the *Human Rights and Equal Opportunity Commission Act* 1986.[54] The principle lies at the heart of the rule of law ideal. Any statutory scheme which places the onus on a citizen to institute action to establish his or her innocence would be a severe threat to the rule of law.

Hence, the proposition that a decision which is reviewable *de novo* by a court is non-judicial cannot be applied universally without imperilling the separation doctrine as a whole. The High Court has not considered this prospect and therefore has not given any indication of the proper sphere of operation of the principle. Perhaps when the High Court is called upon to address this issue, it will draw on historical precedents and its own notions regarding the value of the rights affected. Until the Court confronts this issue and supplies credible guidelines, Parliament's potential for enacting such legislative schemes will remain unclear.

The Misuse of the 'Basic Right' Test

The High Court has taken the view that the citizen's constitutional entitlement to have disputes affecting his or her rights finally determined by a Chapter III court is limited to cases where the right in question is a 'basic right'. The power to determine disputes concerning other rights may not be classified as judicial even though it satisfies every test of judicial power. The concept of a 'basic right' has a useful part to play in the implementation of the separation of powers doctrine. It could be used to ensure that the Parliament does not remove from the courts essentially judicial powers by formulating such powers in terms calculated to avoid their classification as judicial power. In other words, the concept of a 'basic right' could be used as a barrier against legislative and executive encroachments on the province of judicial power. However, the High Court has used the concept precisely to the contrary, that is, to allow such encroachments. It has used the concept to classify as 'non-judicial', powers which otherwise would be regarded as judicial.

In *R v. Quinn*[55] the Court determined that the function of deregistering a trade-mark was non-judicial in character, and hence capable of being performed by an administrator. The power to deregister trade-marks had been traditionally exercised by the courts both in England and in Australia. The power, *prima facie*, satisfied every test of judicial power. The decisions affected existing rights and they had to be made according to pre-established objective criteria. However, the judges had no hesitation in regarding the power as non-judicial. The reasons which the judges gave for their decision are particularly disturbing.

In the main judgment, Jacobs J. declared that the constitutional guarantee that the rights of persons would be 'determined by a judiciary independent of the parliament and the executive' extended only to what may be considered 'basic rights'. His Honour did not regard the rights conferred by a trade-mark as sufficiently important to be characterised as basic rights. Hence, the power of deregistration was not a judicial power.[56] The implication of this ruling is that the entitlement of a citizen to have a question affecting his or her rights determined by a court depends on whether the rights are 'basic' in the opinion of the High Court. If this is the case, the rule of law in Australia is clearly in jeopardy. Jacobs J. indicated that the question whether a right was 'basic' could depend on whether it had been historically protected by the courts. However, His Honour failed to apply this test in *Quinn*. In any event, the historical test is both unreliable and theoretically unsound. The value of rights changes with circumstances. Intellectual property had little relevance in feudal society. Today, it is of great commercial value. The Court's approach pays inadequate attention to the nature of the expectation created by the legislation. The obligation to make decisions according to objective criteria creates a correlative expectation in the community that the decision will be performed judicially and not arbitrarily. This expectation is defeated or placed under threat where the decision is entrusted to a body which is not independent.

The reasoning of Barwick C.J., though analytically different, was no less dangerous. His Honour emphasised that the rights affected by deregistration were rights 'derived from the very statute which gives the Registrar the power of removal from the register' and that they were rights 'given subject to a power of modification or destruction under the provisions of the statute itself'.[57] If taken to its logical conclusion, the proposition would allow Parliament to place even the most important rights beyond the purview of the courts simply by casting them in statutory form. Such a proposition strikes at the heart of the separation doctrine by negating its principal rationale. The modern era is characterised by extensive legislative reformulation of the law. Legislation constantly intervenes to modify or replace common law rules. One has only to look at the law of contract to appreciate the extent to which basic principles of common law have been modified by legislation. Statutes on industrial relations, fair trading, health and safety and civil rights have made far-reaching changes in this branch of the law. If the proposition stated by Barwick C.J. is treated as a general rule, then the enforcement of basic common law rights could be taken out of the reach of the courts by the simple expedient of replacing the common law rights with statutory rights exercisable subject to conditions being fulfilled to the satisfaction of a statutory authority.

Barwick C.J.'s approach contrasts sharply with that of the United States Supreme Court which permits Congress to vest federal judicial power in bodies other than Article III courts[58] only when the disputes concern 'public rights', that is, where government sues in its sovereign capacity to enforce public rights created by statute.[59] Accordingly 'wholly private tort, contract, and property cases, as well as a vast range of other cases' are exclusively within the purview of Article III courts.[60] In a later case, the United States Supreme Court, stated that even 'public rights' 'presumptively' belong in Article III courts.[61] Unless similarly qualified, Barwick C.J.'s proposition may sound the knell of the separation doctrine.

Reviving the Separation of Powers Doctrine as Part of the Republican Project

The formal severance of constitutional links with the British monarchy will not make Australia more republican than it is today. Under existing conventions, the Monarch acts on the advice of elected ministers except in relation to the reserve powers. If the Westminster system is retained in a transition to a republic, the Head of State who replaces the Monarch will play a very similar role. Such a transition will be culturally and emotionally important to many Australians but will have little constitutional significance. From the constitutional standpoint, republicanism is advanced by strengthening the power of the people. The representative principle and the rule of law which are the foundations of republican power cannot be sustained without enforcing the separation of powers in a meaningful way. In the author's opinion, the separation of powers doctrine has been mangled beyond recognition in Australia.

A true republic cannot be established in Australia without reviving the separation of powers doctrine. Theoretical errors and the demands of short term policy have been major causes of the decline of the doctrine. In cases such as *Polyukhovich v. Commonwealth*,[62] *Leeth v. Commonwealth*,[63] and *Chu Kheng Lim v. Minister of Immigration*,[64] the present Justices of the High Court have demonstrated a keen philosophical appreciation of the separation doctrine. Their erudition augurs well for the doctrine. However, the revival of the doctrine requires judicial courage. The task demands the abandonment of an attitude which has been entrenched for over fifty years. It involves limiting the powers of government and hence is likely to elicit protestations from both sides of politics. True republicans must hope that the Court will display in relation to the doctrine of the separation of powers, the type of valour that it showed in bringing down the *Mabo* ruling.

This paper was presented at The University of Queensland T.C. Beirne School of Law Annual Symposium 1993. An earlier version of this paper was presented in the Bert Kelly series of lectures conducted by the Centre for Independent Studies (1993) and published in Restoring The True Republic *(Sydney: The Centre for Independent Studies, 1993).*

Notes

1. The Report of the Republic Advisory Committee, *An Australian Republic: The Options* (Canberra: A.G.P.S., 2 vols., 1993), vol. 1, 39.
2. *Id.* 40.
3. T. Paine, *Rights of Man: Being an Answer to Mr. Burke's Attack on the French Revolution* (London and Toronto: J.M. Dent & Sons, 1906), 174.
4. J.E. Cooke (ed.), *The Federalist* (Middletown, Connecticut: Wesleyan University Press, 1961), 62.
5. Paine, *supra* note 3, 174.
6. S. de Smith and R. Brazier, *Constitutional and Administrative Law* (6th ed., London: Penguin, 1989), 114–115.
7. Aristotle, *Politics* (Oxford: Oxford University Press, 1916), 157.
8. (1931) 46 C.L.R. 73.
9. P.H. Lane, *The Australian Federal System* (2nd ed., Sydney: Law Book Co., 1979), 405.

10. *Panama Refining Co v. Ryan* (1935) 293 U.S. 388; *Schechter Poultry Corp v. United States* (1935) 295 U.S. 495.
11. *King Gee Clothing Co Pty Ltd v. Commonwealth* (1945) 71 C.L.R. 184; *Cann's Pty Ltd v. Commonwealth* (1946) 71 C.L.R. 210. See also D.C. Pearce, *Delegated Legislation in Australia and New Zealand* (Sydney: Butterworths, 1977), 209–211, 221–222.
12. See for example, *Munt Cottrell and Co Ltd v. Doyle* (1904) 24 N.Z.L.R. 417; *Cook v. Buckle* (1917) 23 C.L.R. 311.
13. *Giris Pty Ltd v. Federal Commissioner of Taxation* (1969) 119 C.L.R. 365, 374. See also *Murphyores Inc Pty Ltd v. Commonwealth* (1976) 136 C.L.R. 1, 19 per Mason J.
14. Pearce, *supra*, note 11, 173.
15. See for example, *Olsen v. City of Camberwell* [1926] V.L.R. 58, 65–67 per Cussen J.; *Dewar v. Shire of Braybrook* [1926] V.L.R. 201, 205 per Mann J.; *Swan Hill Corporation v. Bradbury* (1936) 56 C.L.R. 746, 764–765 per Evatt J.
16. (1931) 46 C.L.R. 73, 114 per Evatt J.
17. D.J. Mullan, 'Review of Subordinate Legislation on the Merits' in *Report of the Second Commonwealth Conference on Delegated Legislation* (Ottawa: Parliament of Canada, 1983), vol. 2, 233.
18. (1931) 46 C.L.R. 73, 117 per Evatt J.
19. The German procedure of removal is more stringent, requiring a 'constructive vote of no confidence' which is a vote of no confidence which simultaneously elects a successor.
20. Article 80(1) of the *Basic Law*.
21. *Emergency Price Control Case* (1958) 8 BVerfGE 274, quoted from D.P. Kommers, *The Constitutional Jurisprudence of the Republic of Germany* (Durham and London: Duke University Press, 1989), 148.
22. *Ibid.*
23. For further discussion of the German position, see International Commission of Jurists, *The Rule of Law in the Federal Republic of Germany* (The Hague: ICJ, 1958), 7–8.
24. *Re Tracey; Ex parte Ryan* (1989) 166 C.L.R. 518, 580 per Deane J.
25. *Waterside Workers' Federation v. Alexander* (1918) 25 C.L.R. 434, 469–70 per Isaacs and Rich JJ; *R. v. Kirby; Ex parte Boilermakers' Society of Australia* (1955-1956) 94 C.L.R. 254, 267–68 per Dixon C.J. McTiernan, Fullagar and Kitto JJ.; *Attorney-General v. Queen* (1957) 95 C.L.R. 529, 540–41 per Kitto J.
26. *R v. Davison* (1954) 90 C.L.R. 353, 380–81; *Re Tracey; Ex parte Ryan* (1989) 166 C.L.R. 518, 574 per Brennan and Toohey JJ., 579–80 per Deane J.
27. *Boilermakers'* Case (1956) 94 C.L.R. 254.
28. *Harris v. Caladine* (1991) 172 C.L.R. 84.
29. *Hilton v. Wells* (1985) 157 C.L.R. 57.
30. *Huddart Parker & Co Pty Ltd v. Moorhead* (1909) 8 C.L.R. 330, 357 per Griffith C.J.
31. (1956) 94 C.L.R. 254, 279 per Dixon C.J., McTiernan, Fullagar and Kitto JJ.

32. (1954) 90 C.L.R. 353, 368–69 per Dixon C.J. and McTiernan J.
33. (1953) 87 C.L.R. 144, 151.
34. (1926) 38 C.L.R. 153, 178–79 per Isaacs J.
35. (1992) 174 C.L.R. 455, 501 per Gaudron J.
36. See for example, P.H. Lane, *Commentary on the Australian Constitution* (Sydney: Law Book Co., 1986), 334.
37. *R. v. Quinn; Ex parte Consolidated Foods Corporation* (1977) 138 C.L.R. 1, 6 per Gibbs J., 9 per Jacobs J. with whom Stephen and Mason JJ. agreed.
38. (1991) 172 C.L.R. 461.
39. (1989) 166 C.L.R. 518.
40. (1955) 92 C.L.R. 157.
41. (1953) 87 C.L.R. 144.
42. (1954) 90 C.L.R. 353.
43. *Federal Commissioner of Taxation v. Munro* (1926) 38 C.L.R. 153, 178–179 per Isaacs J.
44. See the *Oxford English Dictionary* (Oxford: Clarendon Press 1933) vol.10, 22, cl. 12.
45. *Id.* 22
46. *Id.* vol.4, 602, cl.1 and 3.
47. (1957) 100 C.L.R. 277, 305.
48. (1981) 147 C.L.R. 617, 628.
49. *Ibid.*
50. (1977) 138 C.L.R. 1.
51. (1926) 38 C.L.R. 153, 182 per Isaacs J.
52. *The Shell Company of Australia Ltd v. The Federal Commissioner of Taxation* (1930) 44 C.L.R. 530.
53. 'No free man shall be arrested or imprisoned or disseised or outlawed or exiled or in any way victimised, neither will we attack him, except by the lawful judgment of his peers or by the law of the land.'
54. Art. 9 para. 1 read with Art. 14 para 1.
55. (1977) 138 C.L.R. 1.
56. *Id.* 12.
57. *Id.* 5.
58. Judges of Article III courts serve for life and have guaranteed remuneration under Section 1.
59. *Atlas Roofing v. Occupational Safety and Health Review Commission* (1977) 430 U.S. 442, 450.
60. *Id.* 458.
61. *Northern Pipeline Construction Co v. Marathon Pipe Line Co* (1982) 458 U.S. 50, 69, n. 23.
62. (1991) 172 C.L.R. 501.
63. (1992) 174 C.L.R. 455.
64. (1992) 174 C.L.R. 1.

The Wrongs of a Constitutionally Entrenched Bill of Rights

Gabriël A. Moens[*]

1. Introduction

The republican debate focuses on whether it is possible to transform Australia into a republic without changing the present form of government or substantially redrafting the Commonwealth Constitution. This strategy, which is usually referred to as the 'minimalist approach', involves the idea that it is feasible to examine the proposal to establish a republic without considering other constitutional issues. However, even if a change to a republic eventuates, it can be reasonably anticipated that demands for the constitutional entrenchment of a bill of rights will continue to be heard from time to time. If so, the question whether the Constitution should contain an entrenched (or paramount) bill of rights will remain on the political agenda.

There are many existing overseas models upon which a constitutionally entrenched Australian bill of rights could be based. They include those in national constitutions such as the United States Bill of Rights[1] and the Canadian *Charter of Rights and Freedoms*,[2] and those in international treaties such as the European Convention on Human Rights[3] or the International Covenant on Civil and Political Rights.[4]

In this paper, some conceptual difficulties which are associated with, or pertain to, paramount bills of rights will be discussed. In particular, it will be argued that the entrenchment of an enforceable bill of rights in the Constitution would facilitate a transformation of the role of the Australian judiciary from a judicial one to a quasi-

---

[*] Associate Professor of Law, University of Queensland.

legislative one. This transformation, in turn, would fuel the politicisation of the judiciary and contribute to the elevation, in Australian legal culture, of the philosophy of judicial activism as a rule of constitutional interpretation. As will be seen in the following sections, this judicial philosophy largely destroys the very reason as to why an entrenched bill of rights is adopted by its proponents, namely to protect people against arbitrariness and uncertainty. In the development of this argument, the discussion will draw upon examples from the overseas models mentioned above.[5]

2. Judicial Omnipotence

Vagueness and Subjectivity

Even a perfunctory study of overseas Bills of Rights reveals that their provisions usually consist of vague, indeterminate and ambiguous concepts and phrases. In the main, a bill of rights contains *general* concepts which are deemed capable, by their drafters, of application to specific circumstances. For example, the Fourteenth Amendment to the United States Constitution refers to such inherently ambiguous phrases as 'due process of law' and 'equal protection of the laws'. Since their incorporation in the United States Constitution, these phrases have created difficult problems of interpretation for the Supreme Court. These difficulties arise from the fact that it is possible to attribute quite divergent meanings to these phrases. This diversity of meanings may well have caused the eminent 18th century lawyer Alexander Hamilton to deride 'those aphorisms which make the principal figure in several of our State Bills of Rights, and which would sound much better in a treatise of ethics than in a constitution of government'.[6]

There is, of course, a reason for the adoption of a general, as opposed to a matter-specific, bill of rights. A specific bill of rights, to the extent that it applies only to the situations envisaged by it, would not have the flexibility of a general bill of rights which, at times, may be interpreted as covering situations which are not expressly settled in it. It may even be argued that a matter-specific bill of rights acts as an inhibiting impediment which, because of its inflexibility, restricts rather than expands people's rights. Therefore, as Professor Enid Campbell has remarked, it is difficult, if not impossible, to frame guarantees which are meaningful, but not excessively inhibiting.[7]

The possibility of attributing different meanings to the provisions of a bill of rights creates the potential for judges to read their own biases and philosophies into such a document, especially if the relevant precedents are themselves mutually inconsistent. Indeed, on most rights issues, the relevant decisions overseas are contradictory. For example, rulings on affirmative action,[8] pornography,[9] 'hate speech',[10] homosexual sodomy,[11] abortion,[12] and withdrawal of life supporting treatment[13] vary remarkably. These rulings indicate that judges, when interpreting a paramount bill of rights, are able to select quite arbitrarily their preferred authorities.

The subjectiveness involved in interpreting a bill of rights was recently lamented by Scalia J. of the United States Supreme Court. Commenting on *Roe v. Wade*,[14] in which the Supreme Court gave women the right to seek abortions on demand, he remarked that:

> The point at which life becomes "worthless" and the point at which the means necessary to preserve it become "extraordinary" or "inappropriate", are neither set forth in the Constitution nor known to the nine Justices of this Court any better than they are known to nine people picked at random from the Kansas City telephone directory.[15]

Considering the apparent hostility of sections of the Australian community towards the judiciary, it is more than a little surprising (and perhaps ironic) that many of those same critics appear to wish that decisions by judges on issues of fundamental social importance be given constitutional status. The faith that many advocates of a bill of rights place on judicial decision-making with respect to rights issues, is probably misplaced. At heart, faith in judicial decision-making on such issues stems from a belief that the judges will decide the issue in a way favourable to one's own views, thus putting one's views beyond contradiction by the legislature. This is a hazardous assumption to make. No 'progressive' reformer (and no conservative) should feel at all certain that the courts will decide in ways that he or she will find satisfactory. It is quite possible that the judiciary could in time reverse many of the successes achieved by reformers in the legislative arena - and reverse them permanently. If, however, the indeterminate nature of the provisions of a bill of rights facilitates the adoption by judges of that interpretation which most conforms with their own personal views, then such a document would only heighten the existence of legal uncertainty. Indeed, it would be difficult for people to know what their rights are, even if agreement could be reached on the content of a bill of rights.[16] Such uncertainty may well be identified by the legal community as a destabilising force in society.

Judicial Activism

The subjectivity associated with the interpretation of a bill of rights results in the elevation of the philosophy of judicial activism to a rule of constitutional interpretation. Judicial activism in this context does not refer to the choices which judges have to make when confronted with two or more legally tenable conclusions. Judicial activism should not be confused with the teleological method of interpretation which gives effect to the spirit and the overall scheme of the relevant legal document. Instead, the philosophy of judicial activism refers to the possibility that judges have power to judicialise the most controversial political issues of the day by reading their own preferred ideological or philosophical views into the bill of rights even if they succeed in couching the actual result in legal terms. In this context, it could be speculated that admission, by the judiciary, of the subjectiveness involved in the interpretation of a bill of rights, would substantially increase the transparency of the legal system.

On the surface, judicial activism is an appealing philosophy because it espouses the popular idea that a constitution should be interpreted flexibly to meet new circumstances. A famous example is Lord Sankey's statement that the former Canadian Constitution should be interpreted as 'a living tree capable of growth and expansion within its natural limits'.[17] But judges either lose sight of, or neglect, the qualifying phrase 'within its natural limits' when they take the philosophy of judicial activism to heart. Since a bill of rights will often consist of ambiguous provisions, judges can deliberately and cynically attribute meanings to it which are different from the intentions of those who approved the bill—in Australia's case the electorate.

Sometimes, subjectivity is even encouraged by the bill of rights itself. The bill of rights which is possibly the most admired in Australia, namely the Canadian Charter of Rights and Freedoms, has a clause allowing only such 'reasonable limits' to the rights it confers 'as can be demonstrably justified in a free and democratic society'.[18] This seems to be an express direction that judges should implement the values of a free and democratic society. Since that criteria means essentially nothing in a legal sense, judges are effectively commanded by the instrument itself to give rein to their own moral sensibilities over legal criteria in deciding the validity of legislation. In such circumstances, it is not surprising that in Canada the individual political and social beliefs of the judges are considered more important than the words of the Constitution itself.[19] The principle of legal certainty would not be served if all that really matters is the identity of the judges. This would make it possible for the law to change with the changing of the judges.

The importance of legal certainty and the need to avoid subjectivity in judicial decision-making may be challenged by reference to a statement made by Isaacs J. in *Australian Agricultural Co. v. Federated Engine-Drivers and Firemen's Association of Australasia*:

> Our sworn loyalty is to the law itself, and to the organic law of the Constitution first of all. If, then, we find the law to be plainly in conflict with what we or any of our predecessors erroneously thought it to be, we have, as I conceive, no right to choose between giving effect to the law, and maintaining an incorrect interpretation. It is not, in my opinion, better that the Court should be persistently wrong than that it should be ultimately right.[20]

A similar point was also recently made by the Chief Justice of the United States, Rehnquist C.J., in *Planned Parenthood v. Casey*:

> [S]urely there is no requirement, in considering whether to depart from stare decisis ..., that a decision be more wrong now than at the time it was rendered. If that were true, the most outlandish ... decision could survive forever, based simply on the fact that it was no more outlandish later than when it was originally rendered.[21]

But these statements do not necessarily constitute judicial approval of the philosophy of judicial activism. Both Rehnquist C.J. and Isaacs J. merely convey the point that the judges' duty of maintaining the Constitution sometimes requires them to overrule decisions which were wrongly decided. Certainly, if a decision is plainly mistaken as a matter of fact, it ought not to be necessary to show any greater error than that fact itself. But this duty should not be confused with judicial activism, which involves the substitution, by judges, of their preferred subjective views for the rigour of the doctrine of *stare decisis*. If a bill of rights contained a provision like the one found in the Canadian Charter, judicial activism (and its concomitant subjective decision-making) would be enthroned as a respectable and appropriate philosophy which allows judges to promote their own views of an ideal society.

In the Australian legal system, there is still an expectation that judges will decide cases in accordance with the law, even if the High Court is not bound by its own decisions. Commenting upon Isaacs J.'s statement, Gibbs J. reminds us in *Queensland v. The*

Commonwealth,[22] that it is a generalisation and, as such, it can be misleading. He continued:

> No Justice is entitled to ignore the decisions and reasoning of his predecessors, and to arrive at his own judgment as though the pages of the law reports were blank, or as though the authority of a decision did not survive beyond the rising of the Court. A Justice, unlike a legislator, cannot introduce a programme of reform which sets at nought decisions formerly made and principles formerly established. It is only after the most careful and respectful consideration of the earlier decision, and after giving due weight to all the circumstances, that a Justice may give effect to his own opinion in preference to an earlier decision of the Court.[23]

Those who favour a bill of rights may delight in the vagueness of these documents, for they sometimes assume that this very ambiguity will enable them to achieve, through judicial decision, what they have been unable to achieve through Parliament. This is a dubious assumption to make. It neglects the fact that the vagueness of such a document could just as easily prove advantageous to their opponents, leading ironically to the recognition of constitutionally entrenched rights that they find abhorrent. No one could feel certain about the results of such an instrument for society. It is a constant source of astonishment to hear people confidently predicting the outcome of an entrenched bill of rights. The resulting interpretation simply cannot be accurately predicted until the judges actually decide the cases. Even if the need to have regard to intentions of the bill's framers is written into the instrument, that is no guarantee that judges will not subvert those intentions. The introduction of the interim (unentrenched) bill of rights to test the waters will not change matters. Any unentrenched bill of rights as a prelude to an entrenched bill is unlikely to provide an accurate indication of the effect of the entrenched bill, as Canada's experience readily demonstrates. Proponents of a bill of rights cannot console themselves about the possibly damaging effects of judicial rulings upon their causes by saying that they will not support a bill of rights that gives rise to results such as those in the United States where pornography and racial vilification are sometimes regarded as protected speech. But how can they be sure, given the dependence of rulings on judges' personal preferences under a bill of rights?

The above discussion reveals that a bill of rights can be potentially used as a convenient vehicle for the attainment of social agendas unable to attain majority approval. Such agendas underlie much of the advocacy for a bill of rights. In this context, Sir Harry Gibbs argued:

> Many of the advocates of a Bill of Rights do not merely wish to protect rights already recognised by the law; they often seek, quite openly, to create rights which the law has hitherto denied and hope to achieve that result by securing a favourable interpretation of vague, general phrases which are not specifically directed to the matter which concerns them. In other words, they hope to achieve social change by judicial rather than legislative decision.[24]

The judicialisation of the most controversial political issues of the day has always been a consequence of the Bill of Rights in the United States. Long before the activism of the Warren Court, Alexis de Tocqueville wrote that 'Scarcely any political question arises in the United States that is not resolved, sooner or later, into a judicial question'.[25] In Canada, the Supreme Court is increasingly imposing its own solutions to social issues upon the Canadian Parliament and people, in the absence of a clear constitutional warrant for removing the decision-making from the people and Parliament. Without adequate constitutional guidance this is likely to be a hazardous undertaking. Critics of the Canadian Charter claim that politicians now consider that their major responsibility is to avoid judicial censure rather than to remain accountable to the voters. They also maintain that the only body that now has the privilege of making mistakes is the judiciary. Of course, when that occurs a great deal of time and even greater expense is necessary to see it corrected.[26]

It could be argued that rights issues should be resolved in the branch of government best adapted to solving such problems - the legislature. Such argument is based on the assumption that it is far better for the courts to apply legislatively produced solutions to the great issues of society than for the courts to make their own decisions on society's behalf. If Australia was to adopt a constitutionally entrenched bill of rights, whatever ruling the High Court brought down upon an issue would put the matter beyond the reach of Parliament. Indeed, the decision of the High Court could not easily be overturned since laws that are not compatible with the Constitution would be inoperative or invalid. Any suggestion that the availability of a process for constitutional amendment makes any effective difference to this assessment is disingenuous because of the extreme difficulty of this process. This is a crucial difference from the way in which courts currently deal with controversial social issues. When the judiciary makes errors today about social issues (even if they involve an interpretation of ambiguous statutory concepts), those errors are relatively easy to correct by the adoption of relevant legislation. In contrast, when the judiciary makes constitutional errors under a bill of rights those errors are virtually impossible to correct because of the entrenchment of the bill of rights. After a time, politicians are even likely to acquiesce in this transfer of power to non-representative bodies. When courts possess the law-making opportunities that they do under a bill of rights, parliaments will be tempted to avoid addressing profoundly controversial political issues. They can simply leave such problems to the courts to sort out, thereby enabling intensely controversial social issues to be decided by a few lawyers.[27] It is worth speculating whether such a result involves a violation of the doctrine of separation of powers.

Politicisation of the Judiciary

Political issues already come before the courts in Australia. Sometimes the courts even make political decisions. In particular, the High Court deals with intensely political issues when it determines the division of Commonwealth and State legislative powers. But why should this suggest that society ought to relinquish even *more* political issues to the courts to decide? A review of the relevant literature reveals that courts, when interpreting a bill of rights, deal with the most intensely political issues of our time. In conferring such a jurisdiction upon our courts, judges become quasi-legislators. If judges are turned into quasi-legislators and quasi-policy makers, Australia will inevitably end up with a system that requires the relentless scrutinising of the political views or ideological outlook of potential members of the judiciary.

Politicised 'judicial' decision-making under a bill of rights is thus, in part, a result of the subject matter of a bill of rights. Opinions about the issues raised by a bill of rights tend to be intensely personal and ideological rather than legally based. Politicised decision-making is also, at least in part, a result of the vague wording of bills of rights, which leaves considerable discretion to judges. In this context it is worthwhile to note Brennan J.'s views on this issue. He observed that the interpretation of a bill of rights expressed in vague and general terms would necessarily entail the translation of political and social values into the Constitution. The judiciary's power to override the political branches of government would itself be a political power with the result that 'the judiciary would be politicised'.[28] Brennan J. noted in another context that the High Court would have to weigh competing claims of collective and individual interests in making its decisions. As he said: 'This is the stuff of politics, but a bill of rights purports to convert political into legal debate, and to judicialise questions of politics and morality'.[29] Thus, his wariness of an entrenched bill of rights is largely due to his objecting to the politicisation of the judiciary.

If Australian courts were to decide the constitutional merits of rights issues, they would inevitably become subject to public scrutiny and hostility of such an intensity never before experienced. Sir Anthony Mason has confidently predicted the ability of courts to cope:

> I do not subscribe to the view that, in order to ensure retention of public confidence in the administration of justice, the work of the courts should be confined to non-controversial issues or that its work should be removed from public scrutiny. In the United States the Supreme Court and the lower federal courts decide important controversial issues and their work is subject to close scholarly and public attention. It is significant that in the United States the standing of the courts and the status of law are extraordinarily high. It would be wrong to assume that what is good for the United States is good for Australia. But the American experience indicates that predictions about loss of public confidence in the courts need to be digested with a rather large grain of salt.[30]

Sir Anthony Mason's comments appear, however, to be at variance with the United States' experience, for they ignore the public hostility that regularly surrounds the American Supreme Court when it rules upon a controversial issue—no matter what it decides. For example, the Court's controversial *Roe v. Wade*[31] decision, which gave women the right to seek an abortion on demand, led to serious and even violent conflicts between the proponents of free choice on the one hand, and the opponents of abortion on the other. Whatever the merits of his views upon the abortion issue, Scalia J. has deplored the continuous distortion, by the annual abortion cases, of the public perception of the role the Supreme Court.[32] His Honour alerts us to the fact that the standing of the Court diminishes whatever ruling it issues in this contentious area. He points out that public anger over the issue of abortion is bitterly directed at the Supreme Court rather than at the legislature.[33]

Scalia J.'s warning need not, however, result in a disagreement with Mason C.J. regarding the importance of public scrutiny of the courts. But such an admission is different from claiming that controversial issues should be reserved solely for decision by the judiciary, as they would be, in effect, under a paramount bill of rights. Indeed, it would be strange if the existence of a right was dependent upon the opinions of four (out of seven) Australian High Court judges, or, on the other hand, if the validity of perfectly legitimate restrictions on the exercise of a right were to be dependent upon the assent of four judges.

These views discussed above are particularly interesting because they disclose some disagreement among the present members of the High Court of the desirability of the incorporation of a bill of rights into the Constitution. Such divisions of opinion between judges would increase markedly if the judiciary in Australia was to be given the broad-ranging powers of legislative veto entailed by a bill of rights. The present relative harmony enjoyed by the Australian judiciary could quickly be overtaken by friction and hostility as personal opinions on society's most controversial issues clashed.

Obstruction of Government

It is clear, subject to the validity of the above arguments, that a bill of rights would involve a transfer of legislative power from the legislature to the judiciary. As a consequence, the impact of an entrenched bill of rights upon the orderly working of government is likely to be immense. Gerry Ferguson, commenting on the effect of the Canadian Charter of Rights and Freedoms, remarked:

Like an exploding bomb dropped in the middle of the Canadian legal system, it has destroyed a few laws, shaken up a host of other laws and generated an immense amount of activity and at least some anxiety.[34]

A bill of rights is certainly a powerful incitement to speculative litigation. In Canada, litigious floodgates have been opened and courts have been strained by the overload. As it clearly increases the litigious character of society, the stress upon the judiciary is severe. Dealing with Charter arguments is a very time-consuming process for the Canadian courts. Consequently the backlog of cases in Canada is enormous. Yet while the Charter is one of the factors contributing to the backlog, ironically the right it contains to be tried within a reasonable time[35] has prevented the Crown from proceeding with prosecutions because there has been unreasonable delay in taking the cases to trial. In 1988 alone, in six judicial districts in a single province two hundred and eighty-two prosecutions were stayed under this Charter provision.[36]

Potentially, the most serious detrimental effect of a bill of rights is the chaos it might wreak with the effective enforcement administration of criminal justice. The famous dissent by Byron White J. of the United States Supreme Court to the ruling that no confession was admissible unless the suspect had been informed of the right to remain silent and the right to assistance by an attorney was quite prescient. He said:

> In some unknown number of cases the Court's rule will return a killer, a rapist or other criminal to the streets and to the environment which produced him, to repeat his crime whenever it pleases him. As a consequence, there will not be a gain, but a loss, in human dignity. The real concern is not the unfortunate consequences of this new decision on the criminal law as an abstract, disembodied series of authoritative proscriptions, but the impact on those who rely on the public authority for protection and who without it can only engage in violent self-help with guns, knives and the help of their neighbors similarly inclined. There is, of course, a saving factor: the next victims are uncertain, unnamed and unrepresented in this case.[37]

3. Anti-Majoritarianism

Subversion of Democratic Decision-making

The argument that an entrenched bill of rights results in an omnipotent judiciary implies that such a document is an inherently anti-majoritarian force which subverts the process of decision-making in a democracy. As argued above, in conferring upon the judiciary the power to interpret a constitutionally entrenched bill of rights, controversial social issues are removed from majority decision-making because attempts by the Parliament to overturn such decisions would be frustrated. When the Commonwealth Constitution was drafted the view was taken that such restrictions upon legislative power were undemocratic as involving 'a want of confidence in the will of the people'.[38] Nevertheless, it is often argued by proponents of a bill of rights that decision-making by the majority does not necessarily result in true 'democracy' especially if it involves the imposition, on minorities, of the views of the majority.

The claim that a true democracy does not always equal majoritarianism is not compelling. Democracy, in itself, is partial protection against the introduction and adoption by the legislature of obnoxious and reprehensible legislation. This is so because our political leaders fear being unpopular. Although it is true that democracy is not in every single case served by majoritarian decision-making, it is usually a good indication that society is operating effectively. The proposition that democracy does not always equal majoritarianism often masks an assumption that majoritarianism is *rarely* compatible with 'democracy'. This proposition is based on the assumption that the people themselves, and their representatives in Parliament, cannot be trusted to adopt laws which are in the public interest. Those holding such an opinion generally believe that judges should veto any governmental initiative enjoying majoritarian support if it does not correspond with the idiosyncratic conceptions of democracy of various interest groups in society with which they agree. This view was rejected by the eminent American Supreme Court judge, Frankfurter J., when he said that 'Courts are not representative bodies. They are not designed to be a good reflex of a democratic society'.[39]

Those who regard majoritarianism as inherently flawed overlook the fact that, in overseas jurisdictions, courts have used Bills of Rights to obstruct worthy legislative initiatives. Dissenting to an opinion which held nude dancing in public bars to be a protected form of free speech and hence unproscribable, an exasperated American judge wrote:

It takes little foresight to realize that three-fourths of state legislatures would not ratify a Twenty-seventh Amendment that stated "the right of citizens of the United States to entertain by dancing nude in public shall not be denied or abridged by the United States or by any State". It is a much simpler process for a handful of judges to protect nude dancing as entertainment by calling it speech.[40]

In this context, it is worth mentioning that a Twenty-seventh Amendment has since been ratified by the required number of American States in 1992. As might be expected, it had nothing to do with nude dancing. It concerned restrictions placed on compensation for the services of Senators and Representatives.[41]

Majoritarian decision-making is not an inherently 'bad' thing, given the counter-majoritarian tendencies of a bill of rights. For instance, if rulings under a bill of rights are unacceptable to women, even though they constitute slightly more than half the voting population and can potentially exercise a major influence upon parliamentary majorities, these factors will be of no avail to them, as Parliament cannot usually legislate away the effects of a constitutional ruling that is adverse to women.

Protection of Minorities

One of the claims pressed most strongly by advocates for a bill of rights is that our existing system of majoritarian democracy is inadequate to ensure the protection of minorities. The claim is based on the assumption that a constitutionally entrenched bill of rights will have the effect of protecting minorities.

At the outset, it is not unreasonable to admit puzzlement at this concept of a 'minority'. This byword is used repeatedly by advocates of a bill of rights even though relatively little critical attention has been devoted to the meaning of the concept in a pluralistic society. In a pluralistic society such as Australia there are many groups that might be described as 'minorities' so that a majority of the population can plausibly argue that they are part of a minority. If in some respect a majority of the people are members of a minority in a pluralistic society, the concept of a minority becomes so broad as to be virtually meaningless. The concept of 'discrete and insular minorities' becomes rather indistinct when this realisation is made; there are vast numbers of potential claimants of minority status.[42] A claim that a bill of rights is necessary for the protection of 'minorities' would be conditional upon the establishment of guidelines to ascertain group membership. It could be expected, however, that attempts to draft such guidelines would inevitably lead to claims of over and under-inclusiveness. Thus in reality the concept of minority is meaningless in a pluralistic society because virtually every member of that society is a member of a minority in some respect. If it is impossible to adequately identify minorities in a conceptual sense, how may it be said that a bill of rights is necessary to protect minorities?

To circumvent these severe practical as well as conceptual difficulties one has to consider some minorities to be 'truer' minorities than others, and to attempt the invidious task of identifying just who is to benefit from 'minority' status. This identification may well involve a choice made on the basis of personal preference rather than on the recognition by society of a group as a minority. Recognition of minority status is in essence a vehicle for a claim of special privilege for a group one favours at the expense of a disfavoured group. Furthermore, how can it be said that a bill of rights will protect minorities when, though it may protect one group identified as such, it runs counter to the wishes of the remainder of society, most of whom may be said to be members of minorities themselves? Thus, in the name of protecting minorities, a bill of rights would benefit a 'minority' to the detriment of the *majority* of the minorities existing in society.

Another reason why it should not be assumed uncritically that a bill of rights will ensure the protection of minorities is that such documents have frequently resulted, in overseas jurisdictions, in decisions quite adverse to the interests of groups widely identified as minorities. The American experience is especially instructive. A number of examples may be cited. In 1896, the equal protection of the laws provision of the Fourteenth Amendment to the United States Constitution was interpreted as permitting the segregation of blacks and whites.[43] It was not until 1954 that racial segregation was declared unconstitutional in *Brown v. Board of Education*.[44] Prohibition of slavery was interpreted as deprivation of 'property' without due process of law.[45] During the height of preparation for war, the Supreme Court ruled that the Jehovah's Witnesses could not refuse to salute the American flag despite their strong claim of religious convictions.[46] In fact the flag salute cases suggest that those judges who are members of minorities themselves will not necessarily be more sensitive to minority claims. In explaining his rejection of the plausible free exercise claim of the Jehovah's Witnesses, Frankfurter J., in his dissenting opinion, drew attention to his own membership of a minority at that time subject to genocide:

One who belongs to the most vilified and persecuted minority in history is not likely to be insensible to the freedoms guaranteed by our Constitution. Were my purely personal attitude relevant, I should whole-heartedly associate myself with ... libertarian views. ... But as judges we are neither Jew nor Gentile, neither Catholic nor agnostic.[47]

The Supreme Court also upheld banishment and internment of Americans of Japanese ancestry during the Second World War.[48] Eugenic sterilisation of retarded people was similarly upheld. In this context, the eminent judge, Oliver Wendell Holmes J. commented that 'three generations of imbeciles are enough'.[49]

It is not at all germane that some of these decisions were subsequently reversed. The point is that the Bill of Rights did not protect 'minorities' when they were vulnerable to majoritarian decision-making adverse to their interests. This shows the fallacy of any belief that bills of rights must protect 'minorities'. Thus minority protection under a bill of rights cannot be straightforward, for there will be ready potential for conflicting claims of minority rights. It is thus quite apparent that overemphasis upon the protection of minorities by an entrenched bill of rights will only promote divisiveness in society: 'minority' versus 'majority', 'minority' versus 'minority'. Indeed many proponents of 'minority protection' (protection of the minorities they favour) often achieve only the division of society into ever smaller and more specialised groups of 'victims' of majoritarianism, thereby institutionalising 'pressure group' politics.

4. Is there a Necessity for a Bill of Rights ?

Legislative Protection of Rights

The argument developed in the above sections involves the idea that an entrenched and paramount bill of rights itself carries substantial disadvantages for society. Of course, an analysis of the likely disadvantages of a bill of rights does not provide a sufficiently strong argument against its adoption. Indeed, it is also necessary to consider whether the judicial and legal culture of Australia or its common law adequately protects rights. Introduction of a bill of rights would presumably become necessary or justifiable if existing laws drastically violated rights and freedoms with regularity or if there was a risk that such violations would occur in the future together with a likelihood that a bill of rights could avert such an occurrence. Indeed, if a bill of rights would not defuse any controversial social issue then the argument for introducing such a document is all the weaker. A survey of Australian law reveals that severe abuses of human rights by the legislature are few.

There are very few rights in the Constitution and they generally apply only as against the Commonwealth. States could adopt rights-unfriendly legislation in certain areas and even if a right, for example the right to religious liberty, was protected by the common law, it could be overridden by State legislation. It could, however, be argued that existing Australian laws provide satisfactory protection for rights and freedoms although such laws are not always applauded or welcomed by the people they are supposed to protect. In fact there is already a range of Federal and State human rights legislation, all of which is capable of being easily amended in line with changing social needs. In particular, the Federal and State Parliaments have adopted numerous anti-discrimination laws. The effect of such legislation is hardly insubstantial. The impact of the *Racial Discrimination Act* 1975 (Cth) in the first *Mabo* case[50] and in *Koowarta v. Bjelke-Petersen*[51] shows its potency. Modern administrative law in Australia already provides an unentrenched (and hence flexible) equivalent of American procedural due process.[52] In addition, the Commonwealth Constitution, in providing for responsible government, has made the Government responsible for its actions to the Parliament. Also, the maintenance of a free press could be facilitated by the effective application of Australian competition law, especially by lessening the concentration of media ownership.

Federalism

It is important not to underestimate the protection of rights that is offered by the functioning of a healthy federal system. This has been observed even in the United States where the Supreme Court has only recently stated that State sovereignty is not merely an end in itself but exists for the protection of individuals.[53] Federalism implicitly protects individuals because it prevents an excessive accumulation of power in either level of government. Where there is an adequately functioning balance of power between the State Governments and the Federal Government, the possibility of arbitrary governance by either level of government is greatly reduced.

In Australia governmental power is divided among numerous governments, each of limited powers. Furthermore, the party holding a majority of seats in the Federal and State Lower Houses seldom dominates the Upper House. These institutional factors are powerful limitations upon arbitrary government.[54] Alexander Hamilton recognised this long ago when he wrote that 'the Constitution is itself, in every rational sense, and to every useful purpose, a Bill of Rights'.[55] Thus the absence of a bill of rights in the United States Constitution as originally drafted did not matter because its careful federal division of powers was itself a bulwark against governmental tyranny. The American experience indicates that the incorporation of its Bill of Rights in the Constitution resulted in a weakening of the legislative powers of the States and, hence, served as an anti-federalist device.

Overreaching by the Commonwealth is likely to be challenged by the States. Overreaching by the States in the area of rights is likely to be remedied by paramount Commonwealth legislation. The recent case of *Australian Capital Television v. Commonwealth*[56] provides an instructive example of how a division of powers between the Federal and State Governments protects rights. In that case, the High Court invalidated the Commonwealth Government's prohibition upon electoral advertising on the ground that it violated an implied constitutional right of freedom of communication with regard to the Government of the Commonwealth. The relevant Commonwealth law was successfully challenged by the New South Wales State

Government. Thus, the invalidation of the political advertising ban reflected the healthy working of federalism. Sir Harry Gibbs has expressed the benefits of federalism:

> The most effective way to curb political power is to divide it. A Federal Constitution, which brings about a division of power in actual practice, is a more secure protection for basic political freedoms than a bill of rights, which means what those who have power to interpret it say what it means.[57]

Yet Toohey J. has cast doubts upon the adequacy of a federal division of powers as a safeguard for rights and freedoms:

> Preservation of liberty may be only a fortuitous by-product of that power-dividing process, as the example of the *Australian Communist Party* case well illustrates. Individual rights were sustained by the conclusion that the legislation in question was beyond Commonwealth power; the scheme failed only because it so happened that State Parliaments were not disposed to exercise their power to enact similar legislation.[58]

Nevertheless, the *Communist Party* case provides a good example of why preservation of liberty is *not* a chance benefit of federalism. It is quite possible that a State or States might enact legislation banning the Communist party. However, it is most unlikely that *all* States would enact such legislation. This pluralism is one of the greatest benefits of federalism and is, in itself, an important safeguard. It could be argued that pluralism is one of the designs of federalism, not a 'fortuitous by-product'. Of course, as Toohey J. implies, rights would not always be protected, but to describe this absence of absolute certainty as fortuitous is to misconceive a basic rationale of federalism. A federal structure which provides for the dispersal of power among the many States significantly lessens the likelihood that there will be arbitrary government across the country. If there are infringements of individual liberty by the States, the division of powers as exists in the Australian constitutional system will tend to isolate them.

5. A Bill of Rights: a Safeguard Against Future Infringements?

The Political Landscape

It is often suggested that a bill of rights, even if it is not necessary to protect existing generations, is needed in preparation for future times when human rights could be subject to threat because of social instability. Of course, even if a bill of rights was to be incorporated to protect later generations, as opposed to living people, it would still rule the present probably in ways indicated above. The argument, that a bill of rights protects against *future* infringements, is paternalistic; it assumes that a present generation knows what is best for future generations. The introduction of a bill of rights would be a highly speculative safeguard against a highly speculative situation.

But let us make the assumption, for the sake of argument, that at some future time Australia's respect for rights and freedoms might be rather less than it is today. Having made this rather implausible assumption, it is improbable that a bill of rights could offer real protection in such circumstances. This reluctance to attribute a preventative role to a bill of rights stems from the fact that it is always the political climate that primarily determines whether rights and freedoms will be respected. Indeed, a bill of rights does not guarantee that people will actually enjoy the rights declared in it. The former Soviet Union had a comprehensive and admirable Bill of Rights, but what rights did the people have in that regime? Decisions under the United States' Bill of Rights during the early Cold War era demonstrate that the existence of an entrenched bill of rights is no guarantee that people will be protected against abuses of their rights.[59] These decisions involved, among other things, discrimination against people who were suspected of having Communist sympathies and the dismissal and persecution of Communists. If the political climate and public opinion are sufficiently hostile a bill of rights will be of no avail. Sir Harry Gibbs provides telling evidence:

> Anyone who has seen the film *The Killing Fields* will know that the fact that the Khmer Republic had adopted a bill of rights did not assist the inhabitants of that unhappy country. We are all familiar with the abuses that have occurred in Uganda; that country had a bill of rights on the European model, and had judges who bravely tried to enforce it, but were unable to resist the forces of lawlessness.[60]

Thus, Sir Harry makes the point that it is always open to the courts to reinterpret the bill of rights to condone whatever oppression the legislature wishes to cause to people.

The point that a bill of rights can provide no real protection for liberty when the political climate deserts libertarianism has also been made by Judge Learned Hand. He wrote the following often quoted words:

> I often wonder whether we do not rest our hopes too much upon constitutions, upon laws and upon courts. These are false hopes; believe me, these are false hopes. Liberty lies in the hearts of men and women;

> when it dies there, no constitution, no court, no law can save it; no constitution, no court, no law can even do much to help it. While it lies there it needs no constitution, no law, no court to save it. [61]

Thus, according to Judge Learned Hand the law is unable to protect rights in circumstances where the people themselves do not appreciate or value rights. A similar sentiment was expressed by Sir Harry Gibbs who argues:

> In the end, the stability and justice of society must depend on the wisdom, humanity and self-restraint of its people. If economic stresses, social tensions or revolutionary forces prove too strong and society breaks down, no constitutional guarantees are likely to prove effective.[62]

Sir Harry's reference to the 'self-restraint' of the people alerts us to the demonstrable fact that, in contemporary Australia, there is an obsession with rights. *Duties* hardly rate an honourable mention in rights debates. However, rights always correspond to duties: one person's right is another person's duty. This side of the equation probably needs to be emphasised much more because a concentration on duties as opposed to rights may well make people appreciate the moral consequences of their actions.[63]

Override Clause

A bill of rights would provide only little protection if it was to contain an override clause, unattached to emergency conditions, such as section 33 of the Canadian Charter of Rights and Freedoms. The override clause enables Parliament to opt out of the application of a bill of rights. What real protection additional to the political process is there under such a bill of rights when Parliament can override its application? An override power returns the issue to the decision of a parliamentary majority, which was what the bill of rights was supposed to guard against in the first place. The protection offered by such a bill of rights is thus somewhat illusory. When the override provision is used it offers no more than what the political process would, but with the substantial disadvantage that the presence of a bill of rights could easily lull the population into a false sense of complacency about its liberties.

6. Illiberal Origins of International Instruments

It would be particularly undesirable for an Australian bill of rights to incorporate some of the more illiberal notions from international human rights treaties. Some provisions of these instruments would themselves inhibit rights and freedoms. For example, Article 20(2) of the *International Covenant on Civil and Political Rights* (the 'Covenant') provides that 'any advocacy of national, racial or religious hatred that constitutes incitement to discrimination, hostility or violence shall be prohibited by law'.[64] This prohibition is obviously overbroad, and would have a profound chilling effect upon speech about controversial subjects. Indeed, such a provision in a bill of rights could certainly be used to justify grave interferences with freedom of speech, and it could become a dangerous means of censorship of ideas unpopular with current intellectual orthodoxy. It would be possible for individuals to argue that the bill of rights was violated if the government did not prohibit all 'advocacy of racial or religious hatred' constituting 'incitement' to discrimination. 'Incitement' to discrimination can be a very elastic concept indeed. Article 20(2) of the Covenant, if incorporated in an Australian bill of rights, could undoubtedly be used to inhibit free public debate about an extraordinary range of issues such as affirmative action, immigration and native land title. It is unacceptable in a free society that such devices be used to limit public debate to the expression of opinions that are deemed acceptable by a 'cultural elite'. A provision similar to Article 20(2) of the Covenant would look singularly unattractive in the constitution of a nation, like Australia, that professes its devotion to free expression of ideas. However, other provisions of the Covenant, especially those that make the exercise of rights subject to the maintenance of 'public morality' or 'security' may be accepted by the vast majority of people as a justified restriction on their rights.

In *Australian Capital Television v. Commonwealth*[65] the Commonwealth argued that the Government's ban on paid political speech would have been permissible under the *International Covenant on Civil and Political Rights*. Whatever the merits of his decision in that case, McHugh J. made an interesting response to the Commonwealth's submission. He contrasted the Covenant with the traditional Western conceptions of rights and freedoms. He said that the right to free speech in the Covenant was made subject to the State's power to pass laws restricting free speech. In contrast, the legislative power that the Commonwealth has is subject to the right of free speech which McHugh J. identified in the Australian Constitution—not the other way round. He considered that no valid analogy existed between the Covenant and Australia's Constitution:

> A more valid analogy would be an instrument on which the Commonwealth placed no reliance—the Constitution of the United States

of America. It is a more valid analogy because, like our Constitution, the legislative power of the central government to control elections is subject to the First Amendment guarantee of freedom of speech.[66]

It is difficult to find a more eloquent statement of the contrast between the approach to individual rights of traditional Western Bills of Rights and that of the relatively illiberal approach of the Covenant. The Western conception of rights emphasises the individual and makes State authority subject to individual rights. International law operates on the assumption that individual rights are very much subject to State authority. The restrictions to rights that are permitted by the Covenant are so open-ended and vague that virtually any restriction might be shown to be compatible with its guarantees. As a result, the guarantees the Covenant contains are virtually meaningless. At best they could not provide a secure safeguard, at worst they could be used to justify violations of rights and freedoms.

7. Conclusion

Introduction of a bill of rights would be necessary or justifiable only if existing laws drastically violated rights and freedoms with regularity or if there was a risk that such violations would occur in the future together with a likelihood that a bill of rights could avert such an occurrence. Severe abuses of human rights by the legislature are relatively few in existing Australian law. There is little prospect that, in situations involving serious infringements of human rights, a bill of rights would shield society against the excesses of such a political climate. The great disadvantages that will certainly be consequent upon the introduction of a bill of rights, especially the transfer of legislative power to the judiciary, far outweigh its value as a speculative safeguard against such a situation.

The author gratefully acknowledges the capable research assistance of Mr John Trone, B.A. in the preparation of this article.

Notes

1. Amendments 1 to 10 and Amendment 14 to the United States Constitution.
2. Part I of the *Constitution Act* 1982, being Schedule B of the *Canada Act* 1982 (Imp.) (1982 c.11).

3. *Convention for the Protection of Human Rights and Fundamental Freedoms*, 213 U.N.T.S. 272.
4. (1966) 999 U.N.T.S. 171.
5. This paper does not deal with unentrenched statutory bills of rights such as the New Zealand Bill of Rights 1990 (N.Z.). See P.A. Joseph, *Constitutional and Administrative Law in New Zealand* (Sydney: Law Book Co., 1993), Chapter 26.
6. 'The Federalist', Number 84 in W. Benton (ed.), *The Federalist* (Chicago: Encyclopaedia Britannica, Inc., 1989), 252.
7. E. Campbell, 'Pros and Cons of Bills of Rights in Australia' (June 1970) *Justice* 1, 2.
8. Contrast *University of California v. Bakke* (1978) 438 U.S. 265; *United Steel Workers of America v. Weber* (1979) 443 U.S. 193; *Johnson v. Transportation Agency, Santa Clara* (1987) 480 U.S. 616 with *Richmond v. J.A. Croson* (1989) 488 U.S. 469; *Associated General Contractors of America v. Jacksonville, Fla.* (1993) 61 U.S.L.W. 4626.
9. Contrast *Roth v. United States* (1957) 354 U.S. 476; *Miller v. California* (1973) 413 U.S. 15; *American Booksellers Ass'n v. Hudnut* (7th Circ. 1985) 771 F.2d 323, affirmed (1986) 475 U.S. 1001 with *R. v. Butler* [1992] 1 S.C.R. 452; *Muller v. Switzerland* Series A vol. 133, (1988) 13 E.H.R.R. 212; *Barnes v. Glen Theatre* (1992) 115 L.Ed.2d 504.
10. Contrast *R. v. Keegstra* [1990] 3 S.C.R. 697; *Canada Human Rights Commission v. Taylor* [1990] 3 S.C.R. 892; *Chaplinsky v. New Hampshire* (1942) 315 U.S. 568 with *RAV v. St Paul, Minn.* (1992) 120 L.Ed.2d 305; *Doe v. University of Michigan* (E.D. Mich. 1989) 721 F.Supp. 852.
11. Contrast *Bowers v. Hardwick* (1986) 478 U.S. 186 with *Dudgeon v. United Kingdom* Series A Vol. 45, (1981) 4 E.H.R.R. 149; *Norris v. Ireland* Series A Vol. 142, (1988) 13 E.H.R.R. 186.
12. Contrast *Roe v. Wade* (1973) 410 U.S. 113; *R. v. Morgentaler* [1988] 1 S.C.R. 30 with *Webster v. Reproductive Health Services* (1989) 492 U.S. 490; *Planned Parenthood v. Casey* (1992) 120 L.Ed.2d 674; West German Constitutional Court, Decision of 25 February 1975, 39 BVerfGE 1.
13. Contrast *Cruzan v. Director, Missouri Department of Health* (1990) 497 U.S. 261 with *In Re Quinlan* (1976) 70 N.J. 10, 355 A.2d 647.
14. (1973) 410 U.S. 113.
15. *Cruzan v. Director, Missouri Department of Health* (1990) 497 U.S. 261, 293.
16. The Electoral and Administrative Review Commission of Queensland, however, confidently states in its *Report on Review of the Preservation and Enhancement of Individuals' Rights and Freedoms*, August 1993, 380 that 'The declaration in a Bill of Rights of the rights and freedoms

of people in Queensland will serve the purpose of clarifying what those rights are. It will demystify appeals to the common law or the heritage of English law and make it possible for everyone to know their rights.'

17. *Edwards v. Attorney-General (Canada)* [1930] A.C. 124, 136.
18. *Canadian Charter*, s.1. See similarly *New Zealand Bill of Rights Act 1990*, s.5.
19. D. Beatty, 'Human Rights and Constitutional Review in Canada' (1992) 13 *Human Rights Law Journal* 185, 194.
20. (1913) 17 C.L.R. 261, 278.
21. (1992) 60 U.S.L.W. 4795, 4829; 120 L.Ed.2d 674.
22. (1977) 139 C.L.R. 585.
23. *Id.* 599.
24. Sir H. Gibbs, 'A Constitutional Bill of Rights?' in K. Baker (ed.), *An Australian Bill of Rights: Pro and Contra* (Melbourne: Institute of Public Affairs, 1986), 40.
25. A. de Tocqueville, *Democracy in America* (1835, repr. ed. P. Bradley, New York: Vintage, 1945), I:288.
26. G. Sturgess and P. Chubb, *Judging the World: Law and Politics in the World's Leading Courts* (Sydney: Butterworths, 1988), 62-63.
27. Sir H. Gibbs, 'Law and Government' (October 1990) 34 *Quadrant* 25, 29.
28. Sir G. Brennan, 'Courts, Democracy and the Law' (1991) 65 *Australian Law Journal* 32, 38.
29. Sir G. Brennan, 'The Impact of a Bill of Rights on the Role of the Judiciary: an Australian Response', Paper presented to the Human Rights Conference, Canberra, 16 July 1992, 10.
30. Sir A. Mason, 'A Bill of Rights for Australia?' (1989) 5 *Australian Bar Review* 79, 84-85.
31. (1973) 410 U.S. 113.
32. *Webster v. Reproductive Health Services* (1989) 492 U.S. 490, 535.
33. *Ibid.*
34. G. Ferguson, 'The Impact of an Entrenched Bill of Rights: the Canadian Experience' (1990) 16 *Monash University Law Review* 211, 213.
35. *Canadian Charter*, s.11(b). See *R. v. Askov* [1990] 2 S.C.R. 1199.
36. Ferguson, *supra* note 34, 218.
37. *Miranda v. Arizona* (1966) 384 U.S. 436, 542-3.
38. O. Dixon, *Jesting Pilate and Other Papers and Addresses* (Melbourne: Law Book Co., 1965), 102.
39. *Dennis v. United States* (1951) 341 U.S. 494, 525.
40. *Miller v. Civil City of South Bend* (7th Circ. 1990) 904 F.2d 1081, 1132 (Manion J. dissenting).
41. See (1993) *Encyclopaedia Britannica Book of the Year* 16.
42. See *United States v. Caroline Products* (1938) 304 U.S.144, 152, n. 4.

43. *Plessy v. Ferguson* (1896) 163 U.S. 537.
44. (1954) 347 U.S. 483.
45. *Dred Scott v. Sandford* (1857) 60 U.S. (19 How.) 393.
46. *Minersville School District v. Gobitis* (1940) 310 U.S. 586, overruled by *West Virginia Board of Education v. Barnette* (1943) 319 U.S. 624.
47. *West Virginia Board of Education v. Barnette* (1943) 319 U.S. 624, 646–7.
48. *Hirabayashi v. United States* (1943) 320 U.S. 81; *Korematsu v. United States* (1944) 323 U.S. 214.
49. *Buck v. Bell* (1927) 274 U.S. 200, 207.
50. *Mabo v. Queensland (No. 1)* (1988) 166 C.L.R. 186.
51. (1982) 153 C.L.R. 168.
52. R.D. Lumb, *Australian Constitutionalism* (Sydney: Butterworths, 1983), 104.
53. *New York v. United States* (1992) 60 U.S.L.W. 4603; 120 L.Ed.2d 120.
54. B. Galligan, 'Parliamentary Responsible Government and the Protection of Rights' (1993) 4 *Public Law Review* 100, 112.
55. 'The Federalist', Number 84, *supra* note 6, 253.
56. (1992) 177 C.L.R. 106.
57. Sir H. Gibbs, 'Courage in Constitutional Interpretation and its Consequences: One Example' (1991) 14 *University of New South Wales Law Journal* 325, 326.
58. J. Toohey, 'A Government of Laws, and Not of Men?' (1993) 4 *Public Law Review* 158, 169.
59. *Dennis v. United States* (1951) 341 U.S. 494; *Wilkinson v. United States* (1961) 365 U.S. 399.
60. Sir H. Gibbs, *supra* note 24, 38.
61. Learned Hand in I. Dilliard (ed.), *The Spirit of Liberty* (New York: A.A. Knopf, 1952), 189–190.
62. Sir H. Gibbs, *supra* note 24, 38.
63. R. Butt, 'This Bill's Light Tax on Duty', *The Times*, 19 December 1985, 12.
64. See similarly Article 4 *International Convention on the Elimination of All Forms of Racial Discrimination* (1966) 660 U.N.T.S. 195.
65. (1992) 177 C.L.R. 106.
66. *Australian Capital Television v. Commonwealth* (1992) 177 C.L.R. 106, 240–241.

The Status of Aborigines and Torres Strait Islanders in an Australian Republic

*Frank Brennan SJ**

1. The Minimalist Position

The Report of the Republic Advisory Committee notes that the hereditary office of the monarch as Head of State is the only element of the Australian system of government which is not consistent with a republican form of government. In its summary of conclusions and options, the Committee stated, 'The only constitutional change therefore required to make Australia a completely republican system of government is to remove the monarch'. If the monarch were removed there would then be a need to establish the office of a new Australian Head of State, outlining the powers of the Head of State, and providing ongoing arrangements for those States which maintained the monarchy.

None of this is likely to impact upon Aborigines and Torres Strait Islanders any more than on other citizens. Neither would one expect any greater unanimity among Aborigines and Torres Strait Islanders about the desirability of a republic rather than a monarchy than one would find in a populace generally. However, there may be slightly more republican sentiment given the history of dispossession of indigenous Australians at the hands of British authorities.

---

* Visiting Fellow in Law, Research School of Social Sciences, Australian National University, and member of the Constitutional Centenary Foundation.

The Republican Advisory Committee had no special regard for the interests of Aborigines and Torres Strait Islanders except when it came to a consideration of the preamble of the Constitution. The Committee noted that a number of submissions had 'stressed the need for recognition of prior ownership, and inclusion of a specific power for the Commonwealth to legislate for the benefit of Aboriginal and Torres Strait Islander people'.[1]

The majority of Torres Strait Islanders living on Torres Strait Islands are members of the Anglican Church in Australia and some could be expected to have some residual interest in the monarch remaining the head of the Church. For these, there may be appeal in retaining the monarch as Head of State also. Many Aborigines whose ancestors were dispossessed and dispersed under authority of the British Crown could be expected to see Australia's transition to republican status as a desirable historical development marking the end of colonial dispossession and the commencement of fully fledged recognition within a nation state priding itself on the hallmarks of a pluralist democracy making a special place for its indigenous citizens.

Many Aborigines emphasise that Lieutenant James Cook failed to honour his instructions from the British authorities who commissioned him, 'You are also with the consent of the natives to take possession of convenient situations in the country in the name of the King of Great Britain'. Wholesale extinguishment of native title occurred on the Australian continent between 1788 and 1975 without provision for compensation nor consent. Since 1975 the Commonwealth *Racial Discrimination Act* 1975 has required in accordance with the High Court's 1992 decision in *Mabo v. State of Queensland*[2] that native title holders not be treated in a racially discriminatory way when the Crown comes to deal with their interests in land for public purposes.

Indigenous Australians did not consent to the acquisition of their lands by the Crown or by third parties. Neither did they agree to their new status as British subjects. At the time of Federation, no Aborigine in Western Australia or Queensland was eligible to vote. In other colonies, though eligible, most Aborigines were not in a position to exercise the right. Upon passage of the *Nationality and Citizenship Act* 1948, all persons born in Australia after 26 January 1949 and all existing natural born and naturalised British subjects then living in Australia became Australian citizens. All

Aborigines and Torres Strait Islanders born after 1 January 1921 were natural born British subjects. It was not until 1965 that all Australian jurisdictions removed disqualifications on Aborigines from voting, on the basis of their race.

In the post-*Mabo* era, it is no longer an option for Australian governments to disregard Aboriginal interests and it is in everyone's interests that there be processes and legal rights which can be explored systematically providing the opportunity for indigenous groups to be assured a 'fair go' in litigating and negotiating rights and interests with certainty. The recognition of Aboriginal rights is not necessarily contrary to the national interest or the common good. A just and proper settlement requires better leadership from Aborigines, industry and government. It also requires a better informed community able to transcend its prejudices and accommodate its diverse groupings with their different world views and aspirations. It also requires changes to our constitutional framework so that Australia's indigenous people may enjoy the full benefits of citizenship without discrimination or threat of involuntary assimilation, and with due acknowledgement of their history, culture and place in this land.

Though there may be a case for specially allocated seats, especially in the Senate, for indigenous Australians, there is no compelling argument for the Head of State necessarily being an indigenous person. Obviously it would be intolerable to exclude access to Australia's highest office by an indigenous Australian. Especially following the recent revelations by Sir Garfield Barwick regarding the events of November 1975, it is now inconceivable that a Head of State would seek and obtain formal advice from High Court justices without first obtaining the consent of the Prime Minister. Whether or not the reserve powers are to be codified, it may be desirable to constitute a council of persons such as retired chief justices and State Governors, Premiers and Prime Ministers who could provide advice as required to the Head of State on the exercise of the reserve powers. If so, there could be provision for some indigenous representation on such a Council.

If the transition to a republic were to be marked by an adoption of the minimalist position, there would be little more to discuss regarding the status of Aborigines and Torres Strait Islanders other than consideration of their specific inclusion in any new preamble of the Constitution. The preamble of the Imperial Act to constitute the Commonwealth of Australia claims that the people 'have agreed to unite in one indissoluble federal Commonwealth under the Crown of the United Kingdom of Great Britain and Ireland'. If all reference to the Crown were to be omitted, there would be a need to draft a new preamble. This could be done in conjunction with a referendum for the repatriation of the Constitution from a schedule of an Imperial Act to the expressed legislated will of the Australian people. The preamble of the new Constitution could acknowledge the place of Aborigines and Torres Strait Islanders as other Australians in these terms:

> Whereas the territory of Australia has long been occupied by Aboriginal peoples and Torres Strait Islanders whose ancestors inhabited Australia and maintained traditional titles to the land for thousands of years before British settlement;
>
> And whereas many Aboriginal and Torres Strait Islanders suffered dispossession and dispersal upon exclusion from their traditional lands by the authority of the Crown;
>
> And whereas Aboriginal and Torres Strait Islanders, whose traditional laws, customs and ways of life have evolved over thousands of years, have a distinct cultural status as indigenous peoples;
>
> And whereas the people of Australia now include Aboriginal people, Torres Strait Islanders, migrants and refugees from many nations, and their descendants seeking peace, freedom, equality and good government for all citizens under law;
>
> And whereas the people of Australia drawn from diverse cultures and races have agreed to live as one indissoluble federal Commonwealth under the Constitution established a century ago and approved with amendment by the will of the people of Australia;
>
> Be it therefore enacted:

Omission of the Crown may also require a reconsideration of who or what holds the radical title to all lands in the Commonwealth. The owners of freehold and other Crown grants including leases presently hold title from the Crown. If the radical title were in the name of the traditional owners, there would be no threat to existing interests and there would be the basis for a truer appreciation of the history of dispossession which has occurred.

2. Sovereignty

In its Report the Republican Advisory Committee has boldly asserted, 'Australia is a State in which sovereignty derives from the people'.[3] The Committee here is following the recent line of political and constitutional theory enunciated by the High Court in cases relating to rights implied in the Constitution. In *Australian Capital Television Pty Ltd v. Commonwealth of Australia*[4] Mason C.J. said, 'The very concept of representative government and representative democracy signifies government by the people through their representatives. Translated into constitutional terms, it denotes that the sovereign power which resides in the people is exercised on their behalf by their representatives'.[5] Mason C.J. said:

> [T]he representatives who are members of Parliament and Ministers of State are not only chosen by the people but exercise their legislative and executive powers as representatives of the people. And in the exercise of those powers the representatives of necessity are accountable to the people for what they do and have a responsibility to take account of the views of the people on whose behalf they act.[6]

Sovereignty imports the supreme internal legal authority within a nation state. In Australia it is vested in the legislature, executive and judiciary of the Commonwealth, States and Territories, subject to the supreme law of the nation which is the Constitution which broaches no limitation on Commonwealth and State powers except the limits set down in the Constitution and those limits which are necessarily implied. Many Aboriginal groups continue to press for recognition of their own distinctive sovereignty. In 1973, the Senate Standing Committee on Constitutional and Legal Affairs made it clear in its bipartisan report that politicians had little interest in such a notion. The Committee concluded, 'That as a legal proposition, sovereignty is not now vested in the Aboriginal peoples except in so far as they share in the common sovereignty of all peoples of the Commonwealth of Australia. In particular they are not a sovereign entity under our present law so that they can enter into a treaty with the Commonwealth'.[7]

There is no way that Aborigines can agitate the issue of separate sovereignty in Australian courts. In *Mabo*, Brennan J. (with Mason C.J. and McHugh J. concurring) took as his starting point the principle stated by Gibbs J. in the *Seas and Submerged Lands* case:[8]

'The acquisition of territory by a sovereign state for the first time is an act of state which cannot be challenged, controlled or interfered with by the courts of that State'. Brennan J. went on to say, 'The recognition is accorded simply on the footing that such a prerogative act is an act of state the validity of which is not justiciable in the municipal Courts'.[9] Deane and Gaudron JJ. said, 'The assertion by the Crown of an exercise of that prerogative to establish a new colony by "settlement" was an act of State whose primary operation lay not in the municipal arena but in international politics or law. The validity of such an act of state (including any expropriation of property or extinguishment of rights which it effected) could not be challenged in British courts'.[10] They went on to say, 'The result is that, in a case such as the present where no question of constitutional power is involved, it must be accepted in this Court that the whole of the territory designated in Phillip's commissions was, by 7 February 1788, validly established as a "settled" British colony'. Toohey J. said, 'A sovereign can, by a positive act, seize private as well as public property in the act of acquiring sovereignty and the seizure is non-justiciable'.[11]

All judgments in *Mabo* make it clear that the Crown's acquisition of sovereignty over the several parts of Australia cannot be challenged in an Australian municipal court. There is no party with standing who could agitate the issue of sovereignty before the International Court of Justice in relation to the mainland of Australia. The only possible proceedings in the International Court could relate to disputed boundaries such as Portugal's pending action relating to the Timor Gap Treaty.

Though there has been much academic speculation about the jurisprudential tangents which may develop from *Mabo*, Mason C.J. has made it clear in *Coe v. Commonwealth of Australia* [12] that *Mabo* is more a tight window of opportunity rather than a floodgate for Aboriginal claims to sovereignty and self-determination. In passing, it should be noted that our courts are yet to consider a case which determines the limits of any fiduciary duty or duty of trust owed by government to Aborigines prior to the issue of Aboriginal land grants.

After *Mabo*, Isabel Coe on behalf of the Wiradjuri Tribe initiated proceedings against the Commonwealth of Australia and New South Wales in the High Court. In pressing her sovereignty claim, she pleaded:

The Wiradjuri are a sovereign nation of people. In the alternative, the Wiradjuri are a domestic dependent nation, entitled to self government and full rights over their traditional lands, save only the right to alienate them to whoever they please. In the further alternative, the Wiradjuri are a free and independent people entitled to the possession of those rights and interests (including rights and interests in land) which as such are valuable to them.[13]

In striking out the statement of claim, Mason C.J. restated the effect of the *Mabo* decision 'that the Aboriginal inhabitants of Australia had rights in land which were recognised at common law'.[14] But on the sovereignty issue, he quoted with approval the earlier judgment of Gibbs J. in the 1979 case brought by Isabel Coe's brother, Paul: 'The contention that there is in Australia an Aboriginal nation exercising sovereignty, even of a limited kind, is quite impossible in law to maintain'.[15] Mason C.J. said:

> *Mabo (No. 2)* is entirely at odds with the notion that sovereignty adverse to the Crown resides in the Aboriginal people of Australia. The decision is equally at odds with the notion that there resides in the Aboriginal people a limited kind of sovereignty embraced in the notion that they are "a domestic dependent nation" entitled to self-government and full rights (save the right of alienation) or that as a free and independent people they are entitled to any rights and interests other than those created or recognised by the laws of the Commonwealth, the State of New South Wales and the common law.[16]

For these reasons Aboriginal sovereignty is not a legal claim. It is at best a political claim which is unlikely to be furthered by the consideration of options in the republic debate. By asserting the continuation of their sovereignty, Aborigines are presumably seeking a legal basis on which to exercise power over land and resources and increase control of their lives as individuals and communities. That basis will not emerge from any court declaration of sovereignty, nor is it likely to be embodied in any popularly endorsed constitutional referendum in the foreseeable future.

The recognition and protection of those elements of control implied by Aborigines using the rhetoric of sovereignty could be assured by some parliamentary acknowledgement of Aboriginal entitlements to internal self-determination backed by legal machinery for recognition and enforcement. Such legal machinery may even be constitutionally entrenched. If it were to result from constitutional amendment, the Constitution as the supreme law of the land would be more than a symbolic way to recognise the special place of Aborigines within the life of the nation, sharing in the sovereignty of the people of the nation without forfeiting their claim to special recognition as the indigenous people of the country being prior owners of the land and the primary custodians of the only culture unique to the nation.

3. A Bill of Rights and Indigenous Peoples

As Australians discuss the merits of a republic, inevitably attention will turn to the desirability of a bill of rights. Aborigines and Torres Strait Islanders will have significant contributions to make to this debate not only because of their concerns about individual rights which they ought to enjoy without discrimination but also because of their assertion of collective rights to self-determination, self-management and self-government so that they might avoid the evil of assimilation within the mainstream of post-colonial society.

Much of the Australian legal heritage including the development of the common law comes from the United Kingdom which now being part of the European Community has a legal system which is being increasingly influenced by the European *Charter of Rights and Freedoms*: '20% of the cases taken to the European Commission on Human Rights under the charter to the end of 1989 have involved the United Kingdom and approximately 75% of those cases have resulted in a finding against the British Government'.[17] Clearly the common law and its application have required some adjustment to bring each into line with best European instruments and practice.

After the fanfare of the introduction of the Canadian *Charter of Rights and Freedoms*, there are a number of warning bells which have been sounding. By early 1990, there had been over four thousand Charter cases in Canada, over a hundred of which were decisions of the Supreme Court of Canada.[18] Prior to the introduction of the Charter, the average for a reserved judgment in the Supreme Court of Canada was four months. By 1986 it had ballooned to over ten months. 'In 1980 and 1981 combined, only two judgments took more than 12 months to deliver, while in 1984 and 1985 combined, 33 judgments took 12 months or more to be delivered.'[19]

The Canadians have found that the Charter impacts not only on relations between citizens and the state but on activities of citizens which can adversely impact on other citizens especially those who are poorer and enjoy less political power. The *Big M* case is illustrative. In that case, a corporation was charged with contravention of the *Lord's Day Act* 1906 which prohibited the conduct of business on Sundays. As one commentator has put it, 'A law called the Lord's Day Act is an absurdity in 1986. The principle that we should have one day in the week free of some of the excesses of commercialism is not. But the Supreme Court believed that Big M's freedom to pedal its wares seven days a week was more important'.[20] In the *National Citizens Coalition* case,[21] the court removed limits on corporate political activity which had been supported in Parliament by all three political parties. Accordingly, 'The right of the many—the average non-rich Canadian voter—gave way to the rights of the few—those with pots of money to spend on elections'.[22] Professor Hammond has lamented that the Charter has placed 'an extraordinarily heavy burden on government and government departments who have the very difficult task of trying to ascertain what is presently in conformity with the Charter and what is not'.[23] He tried to caution New Zealanders that in the late twentieth century what was needed was not 'nineteenth century small 'l' liberalism from a small group of Judges'.[24] He thought there might be a better way of trying 'to create something that might have some hope of leading to a better balanced, more open and civilised form of government in the twenty-first century'. He recalled Lord Radcliffe's 1954 Reith Lectures: 'Constitutional regimes are all very well but their shapes can be seen to be performing the strangest dances unless those inside them have a very real idea of the purposes to which they were intended to be put'.[25]

In many instances the articulation of rights can serve to set limits on action by the state impinging upon the liberty of the subject. Such limits are unobjectionable. However, there are also cases when the articulation of rights effects a new distribution of power and new incidences of relationships between subjects, or a redistribution of the balance between private interests and the public interest, between individual expectations and the common good. A child's right to life if enforced by third parties may be said to be interfering with the mother's right to privacy. The enforcement of one's right to privacy may be said to be the defeat of another's right to free speech. The right of peaceful assembly can be an interference with the right of shopkeepers to conduct their business and the rights of shoppers to have access to shops. In these instances a policy decision, striking the balance, has to be made. In 1986 Sir Gerard Brennan of the High Court of Australia made the observation:

> I am sure that Australians wish the courts to protect important individual rights and freedoms. I am not sure whether Australians would wish judges to be the final arbiters between the public interest as the legislature perceives it and private interests, if judgment is to turn on individual judges' appreciation of where the balance is to be struck. We have developed neither a jurisprudence of social values nor a calculus of social priorities which might serve to govern the drastic power of judicial review of legislation on the ground that the legislation infringes individual rights. Of course, the common law is permeated by values that are fundamental to our society and effect is given to them, but in the final result it is for the Parliaments of the Commonwealth, the States and the Northern Territory to say whether the public interest should prevail.[26]

Recent debates about High Court decisions on rights highlight the problems which exist in trying to effect the public consultation necessary to re-distribute power from the legislature to the judiciary in order to re-shape not only power relationships within the community but also the way we describe ourselves as a community, enshrining those things we hold most dear. The United States heritage prizes the individual, including life, liberty and the pursuit of happiness. Those of the common law tradition prize the collective good including peace, order, welfare and good government.

In 1988, Sir Anthony Mason informed a National Conference of Barristers that his previously adverse view to a bill of rights had changed, 'not to the point of enthusiastically embracing a Bill of Rights, but at least to the point of recognising that it has much more virtue' than he had perceived initially.[27] He thought a bill of rights could deter Parliament from abrogating the rule of law, and that it could help stop the majority in Parliament from overriding the rights of minorities and individuals. Appreciating that individual and minority rights can be infringed by institutions and pressure groups that enjoy access to government, Sir Anthony Mason now sees a bill of rights as providing a basis for principled and reasoned decision making, as reinforcing the legal foundations of society, and as enhancing the role of law and educating citizens about human rights. For Mason, the political question is whether the added protection for minorities through a bill of rights is worth the price to be paid for it by the majority. Like other High Court justices who have contributed to the debate, he has expressed no definitive view on such a political question. In a later interview, Sir Anthony Mason said:

> The majority of countries in the western world do subscribe to a Bill of Rights on the basis that individual minority rights often need protection, and that the only effective protection is by a Bill of Rights. If we don't adopt a Bill of Rights, I am inclined to think that we will stand outside the mainstream of legal development in the western world. These are factors which tend to make me favour a Bill of Rights.[28]

Since then New Zealand has enacted a Bill of Rights leaving Australia as the only major Western common law jurisdiction without such an instrument. International human rights law is impinging more on the development of the Australian common law as interpreted and made by judges and on the formulation of legislation so as to ensure State compliance with instruments enjoying Australia's accession. Most recently, Australia has ratified the first Optional Protocol to the *International Covenant on Civil and Political Rights*. This now means that if an Australian citizen has exhausted all domestic remedies and is still aggrieved by an infringement of a civil and political right as defined by the Covenant, the citizen has access to the Human Rights Committee of the United Nations which can call the offending Federal or State Government to account. It now makes sense for all levels of government in Australia to ensure the due recognition of civil and political rights, including the right of members of indigenous minorities 'in community with the other members of their group, to enjoy their own culture, to profess and practise their own religion, or to use their own language'.[29] We might then avoid the needless expenditure of time and resources by the citizen and the needless exposure to the international community in guaranteeing redress of grievances based on government's failure to give due recognition to such rights. It would be folly to view the International Covenant itself as a substitute bill of rights for Australia.[30]

Since Sir Anthony Mason's qualified endorsement of a bill of rights, the High Court has given its decision in *Mabo v. State of Queensland* (No.2).[31] Brennan J. (with Mason C.J. and McHugh J. concurring) observed:

> The opening up of international remedies to individuals pursuant to Australia's accession to the Optional Protocol to the International Covenant on Civil and Political Rights brings to bear on the common law

the powerful influence of the Covenant and the international standards it imports. The common law does not necessarily conform with international law, but the international law is a legitimate and important influence on the development of the common law, especially when international law declares the existence of universal human rights. A common law doctrine founded on unjust discrimination in the enjoyment of civil and political rights demands re-consideration.[32]

This judicial creativity which effects a direct influence by international instruments on the development of common law regarding civil and political rights may lessen the need for statutory domestic recognition of such rights. However, given the bulk of legislation and subordinate legislation enacted in Australian Parliaments nowadays and the delay in the development of the common law by the High Court as the second and last appellate procedure to which access is gained only by the grant of special leave, there may be a strong case for an Australia-wide bill of rights which, at least in the New Zealand fashion, ensures that wherever an enactment can be given a meaning that is consistent with the rights and freedoms contained in the bill, that meaning is preferred to any other meaning.[33]

At a Human Rights Conference in 1992, Sir Gerard Brennan, the only other serving High Court Justice to discuss the merits of a bill of rights at any length, raised the question, 'We could introduce a bill of rights and have it administered by our existing courts, but would Australians wish that to be done?'[34] He said that as a judge he did not propose to answer, the question being 'essentially political and should be answered by reference to the political needs that might be satisfied by an entrenched bill of rights and the burdens which might be imposed by its introduction'.[35] Brennan J. made the observation that an entrenched bill of rights would require the development of new judicial skills. He said, 'Once the right is defined, the court must weigh the collective interest against the right of the individual. This is the stuff of politics, but a bill of rights purports to convert political into legal debate, and to judicialise questions of politics and morality'.[36] An entrenched bill of rights would require judges to adduce evidence of how government practices impact upon the exercise of individual rights and the collective interest of other citizens. This could be a time consuming exercise which undermines the legitimacy of the judiciary. As Brennan J. says, 'It is no light thing to strike down a law or an executive act which one of the political branches of government, armed with information and experience much wider than the court can muster, has deemed to be justifiable'.[37]

Another concern is the cost of constitutional litigation. Though bills of rights are designed to protect the rights and interests of individuals, few individuals are in a position to afford litigation all the way to the High Court to determine the limit of their rights. Experience in Canada has shown that rights cases can become all absorbing in the court lists with the result that the ultimate court of appeal is less available to determine ordinary appeals, having then to be more strict in granting special leave to appeal in routine cases. Even before the fallout over the *Mabo* decision, Brennan J. made the observation:

> A new judicial role under a bill of rights has attractions not only for those who would challenge the actions of government, but for government itself. There are some issues which, in a pluralist and divided society, are the subject of such controversy that no political party wishes to take the responsibility of solving them. The political process may be paralysed. If governments can create a situation where such issues are submitted to curial decision, political obloquy can be avoided by governments, though it is sometimes transferred to the courts.[38]

The passage of a bill of rights inevitably requires judges to make political, social and ethical decisions affecting the whole community. This may require different procedures for the training and selection of judges. Aborigines buoyed up by their success in High Court cases from *Koowarta*[39] to *Mabo*[40] may have a distinctive view on the question of Brennan J.: 'Whether the arming of the courts with an additional constitutional weapon is desirable to assist in the creation and maintenance of a free and just society'.[41]

The recent 'Rights' survey by Professors Galligan and Fletcher indicates that private citizens are far more likely than members of the political and legal elites to look to judges rather than Parliament for the protection of their basic rights and liberties. In answer to the question, 'On the whole, do you think Australians are well protected against unfair government action, or are they not well protected?', 53.6% of citizens surveyed answered that they believed rights were not well protected. Another 49.7% of citizens said they were very concerned that a State Government could pass laws limiting basic rights and freedoms. Some 40.8% thought that additional safeguards were needed and that putting political pressure on members of

Parliament was not sufficient to protect adequately their rights. Only half the citizens surveyed had heard of proposals to create a bill of rights for Australia. But 72.6% of citizens were in favour of a bill of rights when answering the question:

> As you may know, a bill of rights sets out certain basic rights and freedoms for citizens. It includes the sorts of guarantees we've been talking about, such as freedom of speech and religion, freedom from discrimination, and various legal rights. Generally speaking, are you for or against the idea of a bill of rights for Australia which provides these sorts of guarantees, or don't you have an opinion either way?

Galligan and Fletcher also surveyed legislators from the major political parties. Only 15–24% of legislators thought that rights were not presently protected in Australia. Some 84.5% of National Party members surveyed thought that rights were well protected. Only 8.6% of National Party members were concerned about infringement of rights by State Governments. Some 40% of Australian Labor Party (ALP) members were so concerned but that was still 10% less than the general population. Although 79.7% of ALP legislators thought that rights were generally well protected in Australia, 89.1% of them were still in favour of a bill of rights. But on the other side of the chamber, only 13.3% of Liberals and 14.3% of Nationals were in favour. All persons surveyed were told that 'having a bill of rights would mean that many of the decisions about basic rights now made by Parliament would be decided by the courts instead'. They were asked 'who do you think should have the final say in deciding upon issues of basic rights and freedoms—Parliament or the courts?'

Some 61.1% of citizens thought the final say should rest with the courts; whereas the politicians from the various major political parties varied from 18.6% to 20.6% thinking that the final say should rest with the courts. The researchers concluded that only 8% of the general population were opposed to any bill of rights, 58% of them being doctrinaire or persuadable entrenchers of such a bill of rights. But 34% of the legislative elite opposed all bills of rights and only 19% of them were doctrinaire or persuadable entrenchers, while 26% of the legal elite were opposed to all bills of rights and 27% were persuadable or doctrinaire entrenchers.

More needs to be done to listen to citizens rather than elites in determining the need for and content of any bills of rights. Also we have to expect that once a bill of rights is on the political agenda, it is likely to be strongly supported by ALP legislators and strongly opposed by Liberal and National Party legislators. Such partisan division is unlikely to result in any constitutional referendum entrenching a bill of rights even though the majority of citizens prior to the public debate are of the view that the final say on such rights issues should rest with the courts rather than Parliament.

Community mistrust of new constitutional arrangements and protections would be heightened with any bill dealing with issues enjoying no community consensus. Professors Fletcher and Galligan in their Australian Rights Project found that 73.1% of citizens surveyed thought it 'important for the well-being of Australian society that the aspirations of Aboriginal people be recognised'. Another 58.7% also thought that Government had a responsibility to grant land rights to Aborigines. A further 46.7% thought land claims settlements with Aboriginal people should be reached before using their land for economic purposes, although a majority thought this should not be a reason for postponing major development projects. Some 43.2% of those surveyed said they were 'basically in favour of a treaty with Aboriginal people', having been told, 'there has been quite a lot of discussion recently about a treaty with Australia's Aboriginal peoples, which would recognise their unique rights as the original people of Australia'.

Some 85.6% of ALP legislators were in favour of such a treaty whereas only 9.9% of National Party legislators were so in favour. Another 39.3% of citizens surveyed thought that in the long run it would not be best for Aboriginal people to be completely assimilated into Australian society. While less than 20% of ALP legislators were pro-assimilationist, the majority of Liberal and National Party legislators were. (National Party by two to one.) While 73.5% of citizens surveyed thought Aborigines should be able to decide for themselves their own way of life, only 19.2% thought 'the Constitution should specifically recognize the right of Aborigines to self-government'. While only 6.3% of Liberal Party legislators surveyed supported such a notion, there was not one National Party legislator in support. Only 5.7% of citizens generally supported a strong notion of Aboriginal self-government without the setting of limits 'as long as their system of government conforms with the principles of Australian democracy'.

In August 1993, the Queensland Electoral and Administrative Review Commission (EARC) published its *Report on Review of the Preservation and Enhancement of Individuals' Rights and Freedoms*.

EARC recommended the passage of a bill of rights which would include enforceable civil and political rights and an affirmed set of economic, social, community and cultural rights. Though the latter rights would not be enforceable, the proposed bill of rights contains a clause stating that: 'The Parliament urges the Queensland community generally to observe (these) rights ... and encourages persons to assert the rights in ways that do not involve the legal process or proceedings'.[42] The rights enunciated in EARC's Bill read like the shopping list of present day interest groups. They include a laudable wishlist of rights to adequate standard of living, the right to gainful work, the right to a safe society, as well as the more fashionable right to personal autonomy over reproductive matters, the right to adequate childcare, the right to culture, the right to environmental protection and conservation, and the right to ecologically sustainable development. For example, 'A person has the right to promote ecologically sustainable development in the interests of current and future generations. A person has the right to object to development that is not ecologically sustainable and to expect that government will accept and act on a reasonable objection'.[43] Such a bill of rights can only result from the pressures exerted by various interest groups on the politicians who then are charged with the task of educating the unknowing public.

Such a bill is inconsistent with any notion of power and sovereignty moving from the people to the elected representatives and then to Government. It is not a Parliament's role to urge the citizens generally to observe rights or to encourage citizens to assert rights in ways that do not involve the legal process or proceedings. It is rather for Parliament to observe those rights and to provide ways in which those rights may be protected particularly in the interests of disempowered or minority groups within the community. A bill of rights, if it is to be justified, has to be tailored such that the rights it enunciates are accepted by the general community, rather than by particular interests groups, as so fundamental that they may not be overridden by elected representatives seeking a mandate, because in all conceivable circumstances the discharge of their responsibility to take account of the views of the people on whose behalf they act would require that they forbear from legislating in such a way as to interfere with such rights. A Parliament exercising the sovereign power vested by the people will act within the constraints set down by the people by referendum. Within those constraints, the Parliament can legislate for or against particular rights. If Parliaments fail to provide a judicial remedy for the protection of a particular right, there is no symbolic, educative or substantive value in the Parliament urging the community generally to observe such 'rights' in ways that do not involve the legal process or proceedings.

The value of a bill of rights is in setting limits on the exercise of legislative power by the representatives of the majority so as to protect the interests of minorities. Such constraints can then arm the courts with the power of judicial review. As Brennan J. said in *Nationwide News Pty Ltd v. Wills*:

> The Courts are concerned with the extent of legislative power but not with the wisdom or expediency of its exercise. If the courts asserted a jurisdiction to review the manner of a legislative power, there would be no logical limit to the grounds on which legislation might be brought down.[44]

It is not appropriate for an elected Parliament to urge the sovereign people to observe rights which the Parliament, deriving its sovereignty from those people, has failed to protect through judicial review. For a bill of rights to be effective, and to be more than a bureaucrat's utopian vision of how the masses should conduct themselves, the rights capable of judicial protection against parliamentary abuse must be sufficiently defined so that courts can perform their judicial function without judges being so pilloried for political decisions that the public could lose faith in the courts.

Queensland's Electoral and Administrative Review Commission in its Bill of Rights report has recommended an expansive statement of indigenous rights, which though affirmed would not be enforceable. Under the heading 'Community and Cultural Rights', the EARC Bill provides:

> Aboriginal People and Torres Strait Islanders have the following collective and individual rights—
>
> (a) the right to revive, maintain and develop their ethnic and cultural characteristics and identities, including—
>   (i) their religion and spiritual development;
>   (ii) their language and educational institutions;
>   (iii) their relationship with indigenous lands and natural resources;
>
> (b) the right to manage their own affairs to the greatest possible extent while enjoying all the rights that other Australian citizens have in the political, economic, social and cultural life of Queensland;

(c) the right to obtain reasonable financial and technical assistance from government to pursue their political, economic, social and cultural development in a spirit of co-existence with other Australian citizens and in conditions of freedom and dignity.[45]

Though these provisions may be politically unacceptable to present governments because they are too open-ended on issues of land rights and self-determination, the specific recognition of Aboriginal rights is essential in a contemporary Australian bill of rights, provided such recognition in this form is sought by Aboriginal groups. If there were to be no recognition as requested, we would be denying a bill of rights operation in one of the fields central to its rationale. We need legal rights and processes which Aborigines can invoke, confident that they will be accorded justice according to law which is respectful of their cultural heritage.

In its report on consolidation and review of the Queensland Constitution, EARC also gave consideration to the status of indigenous people. Given the uncertainty of future jurisprudential development in the light of the *Mabo* decision, the increasingly insistent demands of Torres Strait Islanders for self-government in their discrete territory, and the controversy regarding the entitlement of indigenous persons to special status under a constitution, EARC could not see its way clear to making any recommendation other than that any proposed Constitutional Convention consult with Aborigines and Torres Strait Islanders before drafting any constitutional changes.

The Canadians have spent much time considering the limits of what 'can be demonstrably justified in a free and democratic society'. In the end we have to decide whether that matter is best resolved in individual cases by unelected judges or officials of a Human Rights Commission or in the generality of cases by elected politicians, police and public servants. Legislative protection and promotion of civil and political rights is possible through discrete pieces of legislation which deal with the relevant issues. It may even be desirable to have a Bill of Rights Act by which other future legislation is assessed for compliance with those rights. As the 1988 referendum taught us, 'rights' talk in the political forum is mistrusted by those who think they have something to lose in changes to the *status quo*, knowing that they have no guaranteed control over the outcomes of the new processes which are contemplated.[46]

If a bill of rights is not to be an exhaustive statement of rights especially for those who are the poorest, most disempowered and least enfranchised, it will be only a selective piece of window-dressing which does nothing to effect greater protection for those who most need it. Any bill of rights transfers power from Parliaments to judges. It also politicises the role of the judiciary. A bill of rights may have an educative function but it is no guarantee of a better citizen or a better society. Its only guarantee is restrictive power for elected legislators and increased power for unelected judges for the benefit, if sought, of the sovereign people, especially those whose rights are most likely to collide with the interests of the majority. Aborigines and Torres Strait Islanders who do not have their own representatives in our Parliaments, whose aspirations for land rights and self-determination are not assured majority support, and whose claims to non-discrimination and non-assimilation find support in universal principles of human rights law may have much to gain by the application of judicial method to their grievances assessed against statutory standards for individual and collective rights.

4. Overseas Experience

The Dominion of Canada, the Commonwealth of Australia and the Dominion of New Zealand were all parties to the negotiations before the *Statute of Westminster* 1931. The constitutional development of each country since then has been very different especially regarding bills of rights and the recognition of indigenous rights. The other two countries have enacted a constitutional *Charter of Rights and Freedoms* (Canada) and an unentrenched *Bill of Rights* (New Zealand) respectively. Canada has negotiated numerous land claims settlements, constitutionally recognised existing Aboriginal treaty rights, proposed an inherent power of Aboriginal self-government and called Aboriginal representatives to the negotiating table even in constitutional discussions. New Zealand has reactivated the 1840 Treaty of Waitangi with a Waitangi Tribunal which has power to recommend the recognition of Maori rights to government; and New Zealand has also given legislative recognition, of the treaty principles, which has enabled the courts a role to play in supervising government development programmes which impinge on traditional Maori activities.

Meanwhile in Australia, we have passed the *Australia Act* 1986 (Cth) 'to bring constitutional arrangements affecting the Commonwealth and the States into conformity with the status of the Commonwealth of Australia as a sovereign, independent and federal nation'. But we have not entrenched citizens' rights generally, let alone the distinctive rights of indigenous peoples. Our Governments and Parliaments have been very wary about expanding the scope for court involvement on issues of Aboriginal rights. The intransigence of the Northern Territory Government and its unlimited legal aid budget has allowed the development of a High Court jurisprudence on land rights resulting from the large number of cases appealed to the Court from the Aboriginal Land Commissioner and the Federal Court. Also the Commonwealth's *Racial Discrimination Act* 1975 has provided the Court with fertile ground for a jurisprudence of discrimination in cases such as *Koowarta v. Bjelke Petersen*,[47] *Gerhardy v. Brown*[48] and *Mabo v. Queensland* (No. 1).[49]

Experience in Canada and New Zealand shows that legislative recognition of collective Aboriginal rights, permitting court litigation and tribunal hearings, and negotiations with indigenous citizens need not be open-ended and they are not necessarily contrary to the national interest.

(a) Canada

The Canadians have been doing much constitutional soul-searching in recent years, not only trying to accommodate the aspirations of their Aboriginal peoples but also to accommodate Quebec's demand for status as a 'distinct society' and to redistribute powers between the Federal Government and the Provinces. On 26 October 1992, a draft of constitutional reforms was rejected and the politicians returned to the drawing board. But in the Consensus Report accompanying the Charlottetown Accord there was an acknowledgement that Aboriginal peoples were 'the first peoples to govern this land' and that 'their governments constitute one of the three orders of government in Canada'.[50]

Since 1991, the Canadians have been conducting a Royal Commission on Aboriginal Peoples. It is still due to run another couple of years. It is chaired by George Erasmus, former National Chief of the Assembly of First Nations, and Rene Dussault, a Judge of the Quebec Court of Appeal. In February 1992, that Commission put forward a suggestion 'to smooth the path to constitutional reform'. They recommended constitutional recognition of the right of Aboriginal self-government which would be recognised as inherent in nature, circumscribed in extent, sovereign within its sphere, justiciable immediately, adopted with the consent of the Aboriginal peoples and consistent with the view that section 35 of the Constitution may already recognise a right of self-government.[51]

The Commissioners were adamant that the 'inherent' right sprang 'from sources within the Aboriginal nations, rather than from the written Constitution', Aboriginal governments providing Canada 'with some of its deepest and most resilient roots in the original traditions of this land'. This rhetoric is not far removed from some of the statements by Michael Mansell and his Aboriginal Provisional Government. Recently, the respected economist Professor Russell Mathews with a lifetime of experience with the Grants Commission put forward proposals of Aboriginal self-government of Aboriginal territories within the Commonwealth.[52]

Though no country would wittingly want to emulate the present constitutional turmoil of the Canadians, we would do well to concede their contribution through the legal and political processes to greater Aboriginal self-determination. The Canadians have now finalised arrangements for Nunavut, the self-governing territory of the Inuit which comprises one-fifth of the Canadian land mass (what was the eastern part of the Northwest Territories). By 2000, the Inuit who are the majority resident in the region will be running their own affairs, enjoying provincial powers within the federation. The Canadians have been even bolder with their Yukon First Nations self-government agreements. In the Yukon Territory, there are 14 non-contiguous First Nation groupings which are 'in different stages of readiness in terms of embracing self-government'.[53] So far the governments of the Yukon Territory and Canada have negotiated agreements with four groups. The hope is that self-government will lead to a decrease in welfare dependency. The risk is that the nation state which has been built on the dispossession and marginalisation of these people will abandon them to self-government before the communities themselves have the requisite commercial skills for the affairs of modern government.

A further risk is that racial distinctions and historic identifications will become so entrenched that there will be less prospect of people building upon their shared sense of nationhood so as to contribute to the well-being of all groups. I do not espouse the Canadian solutions as ideal recipes for Australia. But the boldness of the Canadian initiatives does highlight how unwilling we Australians have been to experiment and to heed the calls of Aboriginal groups to do their thing on their terms on their lands.

(b) New Zealand

In 1992 the New Zealand Government finalised an agreement with Maori negotiators whereby the Crown would provide Maori with capital to participate in a joint venture to purchase Sealord Products Ltd which held 26% of the nation's fishing quota. In return the Maori agreed to government proposals for amendment of the *Fisheries Act 1983* (NZ) thereby extinguishing fishing rights under the Treaty of Waitangi and reducing the Waitangi Tribunal's jurisdiction over fishing matters. Under the memorandum of understanding, the parties acknowledged the need for a just settlement of Maori fishing claims' and that the settlement would 'mark the resolution of an historical grievance'. When some Maori opposed to the deal unsuccessfully took court action to prevent passage of the necessary legislation, Sir Robin Cooke, President of the Court of Appeal, said in *Te Runanga o Wharekauri Rekohu Inc v. Attorney-General*:

> The proposal of the Crown and the Maori negotiators to endeavour to obtain a substantial Maori interest in Sealord is thoroughly consistent with the approach of this Court in previous cases. .... If there are shortcomings in the drafting of the deed and it might possibly turn out in the long term not to satisfy all understandable Maori aspirations, it is nevertheless an historic step. The Sealord opportunity was a tide which had to be taken at the flood. A failure to take it might well have been inconsistent with the constructive performance of the duty of a party in a position akin to partnership.[54]

With the rebirth of the Treaty of Waitangi, there has been a move from political protest to judicial process and now to negotiation. The Waitangi Tribunal has power only to make recommendations to Government upon completion of claim hearings. There have been over three hundred and thirty claims registered and the Tribunal is equipped to conclude only about five claims a year.[55] One commentator has observed that in the 1980s:

> [T]he Tribunal practised another mode of thought than the reparative, one which nevertheless co-existed with it on easy terms. ... The other mode was one not of retrospection for the reparation of past wrongs but of prospection for future, just distributions. It looked to distribution in terms

of need, especially, and of equalization of opportunities to lead satisfying lives. Sometimes it was simply prospection with a view not to justice at all, but to other ends like the avoidance of violence and discord, and like the attainment of peace, tranquility, concord and the maximization of fulfilment for individuals and groups: prospection was for policy goals. Whether aiming at justice or other policy goals, though, prospection was the mode that made possible moderation, compromise, accommodation, conciliation and mildness. It was their conceptual foundation.[56]

In Australia, this has been the role of the Council for Aboriginal Reconciliation. The problem with the *Mabo* debate has been that some think a letter of the law implementation of *Mabo* will resolve all problems of living together in the future. The implementation of *Mabo* is about equal protection of the rule of law for those Aborigines who have maintained their connection with their land in jurisdictions where there is not yet a claims process. While conceding the justice of that process, we as a nation also need to listen to the claims of Aborigines for living conditions favourable to Aboriginal self-identification within a pluralist society whose history is marked by cavalier disregard for Aboriginal perspective and just claims. New Zealand lawyer, Carrie Wainwright claims that:

> While the Waitangi Tribunal has played a very important role in achieving recognition of the Treaty of Waitangi, to the extent that Maori have made real strides in their move towards a stake in the country's asset base, those strides have come about primarily as a result of actions brought in the ordinary courts of the land.[57]

When the New Zealand Government instituted their policies of corporatisation and privatisation of state-owned enterprises, it had to consider how to accommodate the principles of the Treaty of Waitangi. It was one thing for Maori interests to co-exist with the Government's access to, and use of, public assets including lands. It was another to determine the hierarchy of rights when a public asset was to be alienated to a private corporation. The Parliament sought to paper over the problem by legislating that the principles of the Treaty be complied with in any such dealings.[58] This provision cast a responsibility on the courts to oversee all such dealings at the request of affected Maori. Sir Robin Cooke has said: 'The principles of the Treaty have to be applied to give fair results in today's world'.[59] He has constantly restated that the Treaty has created an enduring relationship of a fiduciary nature. He says, 'In the end no doubt only the Courts can finally rule on whether or not a particular solution accords with the Treaty principles. But in this kind of issue judicial resolution should be very much a last resort'.[60] The costs and delays of litigation have now convinced both Maori and Government of the need to negotiate rather than litigate. Chief Judge Eddie Durie, of the Maori Land Court has offered this assessment:

> Final settlements, attractive to Government but the bane of Maori iwi when based on the current state of research, may not in any event accord with the Court's findings, in its Treaty jurisprudence, recognising continuing and on-going responsibilities between the Treaty partners. In the meantime the just resolution of Maori claims that are fair and reasonable, not only between the partners but amongst Maori themselves, presents the greatest challenge to the claims process. Despite some opinion that the settlement of claims is a political matter, the courts may need to have a continuing role in the search for a proper solution, and this for the protection of the Crown as much as anyone else.[61]

One of the most outspoken Maori critics of the Sealord fishing deal, Donna Awatere Huata, has said:

> From the outset, the four Maori Crown negotiators were appointed by the Crown. Now, when is it a partnership when one partner decides who will negotiate on behalf of the other partner? If you steal my car, and then you appoint, against my wishes, my neighbour as my negotiating agent, if you two decide that you will buy me a pushbike, you can hardly cry foul when I object to your procedures and to your full and final settlement.[62]

She says it is not possible to effect a full and final settlement of any treaty matter 'without every *iwi*, and through them every *hapu*, being directly involved in the extinguishment of their own rights'. Huata has given Pakeha the choice of dancing alone or together in the new partnership:

> When they open up the political arena for partnership, when the laws that are made are based on two cultures, and when the courts or their new equivalents suit both of us, and not just one of us. When the whole gamut of cultural underpinnings and not just the icons of Maori people are those of the Pakeha, when restoration of our property is made. When these matters are put right in a spirit not hampered by mean spirited carping. Then we will be dancing together.[63]

5. Conclusion

The Canadian and New Zealand experiences highlight that there is no perfect answer to questions about process or outcomes. Even less so, can we simply transpose their methods to Australia. All jurisdictions confirm that these are ongoing issues requiring continued commitment of imagination, energy and resources. They are questions which are an integral part of the national conversation about identity. They are pointers to a just distribution of the national patrimony and political power amongst those on the opposite sides of a long-time historical conflict which is central to the nation's history. The present generation has the capacity to demonstrate good will on both sides, thereby creating the capacity for ongoing components of a just and proper settlement being melded by those committed to the common good and the national interest.

The republic debate provides the next opportunity for Aborigines and Torres Strait Islanders to agitate their cause for special status within the life of the Australian nation. Their greatest gains will be if there is broadly based support for a bill of rights. Such a bill would then include some provision for recognition and entrenchment of Aboriginal collective rights as well as according non-discriminatory recognition to their individual rights. If a bill of rights were not to be part of the republican package, the review of the Constitution would still require some recognition of special Aboriginal claims.

Political protest, court litigation and realistic negotiations all have a part to play. It is not a matter of undoing the innumerable wrongs of the past; we need to demonstrate a shared national commitment to designing national institutions and processes which take seriously the various perspectives of life within the nation, whether of indigenous persons, descendants of long time migrant stock or the most recent refugees. There will never be any substitute for trust, humour and knowledge of each other.

At the 1993 New Zealand Law Conference, there was a panel of Maori speaking on treaty issues. They disagreed publicly and intelligently with each other before a predominantly Pakeha and foreign audience. One Maori lawyer was musing about the Canadian *Charter of Rights and Freedoms* which includes recognition and protection of Aboriginal and Treaty rights and the *New Zealand Bill of Rights Act* 1990 which omits all reference to Maori and Treaty rights. The New Zealand Government had recommended that the Treaty of Waitangi be included as an integral part of such a Bill of

Rights. Maori were opposed. The Maori lawyer opined that if the Government had recommended its omission, Maori more than likely would have agitated for its inclusion. There is not necessarily any right answer. There may be much to be said for the main options being considered at any time. It is essential that members of the indigenous minority are not excluded from the real decision making processes and that their leaders have the integrity and resources to negotiate only once they have consulted at length with those who most justifiably are mistrustful of the political process and who are most jealous to protect their cultural heritage and their historic claims to justice at the hands of those who have profited most from their dispossession.

If the republican debate is reduced to a minimalist consideration of the need for a change of Head of State, Aborigines and Torres Strait Islanders like other citizens will be expected to express a variety of viewpoints. If the consideration of the Headship of State leads to deeper considerations of the nature of our constitutional machinery, we can expect that significant groups of Aborigines and Torres Strait Islanders will plead for some special status within the Australian nation while necessarily foregoing claims to separate sovereignty. If we countenance a bill of rights, they will insist on a non-discriminatory enjoyment on equal terms of individual rights but may want to pursue the less certain areas of collective rights and the machinery necessary for determining the correct balance between individual rights of indigenous citizens wanting to assert human rights according to international standards and the collective community rights to self-determination and self-government according to traditional law which is not necessarily in sympathy with international norms.

At the very minimum, Aborigines and Torres Strait Islanders can be expected to insist upon recognition of their place in our history and in our future, that place being set down in the preamble of the Constitution. However that symbolism will ring hollow unless it is accompanied by substantive provisions for the recognition of their right of self-determination within the Australian nation. The *Mabo* debate has ensured that never again will our politicians exclude Aborigines from the political processes in determining laws which will be applicable to them. However, failing guaranteed membership of the House of Representatives or the Senate, Aborigines and Torres Strait Islanders will still be left dependent on major political parties making space for indigenous representatives finally to take their place in the elected assemblies so that the constitutional machinery may more adequately reflect the reality of the citizenry, thereby affirming that sovereignty is vested in all the people and that our democratic republican institutions draw their legitimacy from the sovereign people, none of whom is excluded from the political processes nor from any office of any organ of government. Such an outcome would enhance the political status of Aborigines and Torres Strait Islanders within an Australian Republic. Even if we were to retain the monarchy, we would still need to consider these matters as the political consciousness and power of indigenous peoples increase in Australia as elsewhere.

Notes

1. The Report of the Republic Advisory Committee, *An Australian Republic: The Options* (Canberra: A.G.P.S., 2 vols., 1993), vol.1, 140.
2. (1992) 175 C.L.R. 1.
3. Republic Advisory Committee Report, *supra* note 1, vol.1, 1.
4. (1992) 177 C.L.R. 106, 137.
5. *Id.* 593.
6. *Id.* 594.
7. Senate Standing Committee on Constitutional and Legal Affairs, *Two Hundred Years Later* (Canberra: A.G.P.S., 1983), 50.
8. (1975) 135 C.L.R. 337, 388.
9. (1992) 66 A.L.J.R. 408, 437.
10. *Id.* 438.
11. *Id.* 484.
12. (1979) 53 A.L.J.R. 403, 408.
13. *Coe [The Wiradjuri Tribe] v. The Commonwealth* (1993) 118 A.L.R. 193, 197–8.
14. *Ibid.*
15. *Coe v. The Commonwealth* (1979) 53 A.L.J.R. 403, 408.
16. *Coe [The Wiradjuri Tribe] v. The Commonwealth* (1993) 118 A.L.R. 200.
17. EARC Issues paper No. 20, *Review of the Preservation and Enhancement of Individual's Rights and Freedoms*, 1992, 46, para. 4.12.
18. G. Ferguson, 'The Impact of an Entrenched Bill of Rights: the Canadian experience' (1990) 16 *Monash University Law Review* 211, 217.

19. *Id.* 218.
20. R. Martin, 'A bad idea to give judges wide Charter powers' [1987] *New Zealand Law Journal* 136.
21. *National Citizens' Coalition Inc. v. Attorney-General for Canada* (1984) 11 D.L.R. (4th) 481.
22. Martin, *supra* note 19.
23. R.G. Hammond, 'The Bill of Rights and the Canadian experience' [1987] *New Zealand Law Journal* 132, 133.
24. *Id.* 134.
25. *Ibid.*
26. F.G. Brennan, 'Judicial qualities of a different kind' (1986) 60 *Law Institute Journal* 654, 655.
27. A. Mason, 'A Bill of Rights for Australia?' (1989) 5 *Australian Bar Review* 79.
28. G. Sturgess and P. Chubb, *Judging the World: Law and Politics in the World's Leading Courts* (Melbourne: Butterworths, 1988), 70.
29. Article 27, *International Covenant on Civil and Political Rights*.
30. See C. Chinkin 'Using the Optional Protocol: the practical issues' in *Internationalising Human Rights: Australia's accession to the first Optional Protocol* (Melbourne: Centre for Comparative Constitutional Studies, 1991), 6.
31. (1992) 175 C.L.R. 1.
32. *Id.* 42 per Brennan J.
33. *New Zealand Bill of Rights Act* 1990 (NZ), s.6.
34. F.G. Brennan, 'The Impact of a Bill of Rights on the Role of the Judiciary: an Australian Response', Human Rights Conference, 16 July 1992, University House, Canberra, A.C.T., 3.
35. *Ibid.* Samuel Griffith Society members John Stone and Peter Connolly QC have claimed that Brennan J. is in favour of a bill of rights. Mr Connolly, referring to the July 1992 paper, said Brennan J. was 'on record as saying, with apparent enjoyment, that a Bill of Rights would bring the courts "into the political process as a new and dominant force"'. He continued, 'One cannot help asking oneself how the enthusiasm of judges (presumably of the High Court for I should not think that Mr Justice Brennan would venture to speak for other judges) for a Bill of Rights squares with the obvious lack of concern of the Court for the interests of Australians generally'. See 'The High Court of Australia in *Mabo*' (Leederville: Association of Mining and Exploration Companies, 1993), 11–12.
36. *Id.* 10.
37. *Id.* 12.
38. *Ibid.*
39. *Koowarta v. Bjelke Peterson* (1982) 153 C.L.R. 168.
40. (1992) 175 C.L.R. 1.

41. Brennan, *supra* note 33, 22.
42. Bill of Rights, cl. 5(2), EARC, *Report on Review of the Preservation and Enhancement of Individuals' Rights and Freedoms* (August, 1993) A6.
43. *Id.* cl. 45, A19.
44. (1992) 108 A.L.R. 681, 701.
45. EARC Report, *supra* note 41, A17–18, cl.41.
46. For example, see F. Brennan, 'The 1988 Referendum—A Lost Opportunity For An Australian Declaration On Religious Freedom' (1992) 69 *Australasian Catholic Record* 205.
47. (1982) 153 C.L.R. 168.
48. (1985) 159 C.L.R. 70.
49. (1988) 166 C.L.R. 186.
50. *Consensus Report on the Constitution*, 3.
51. Royal Commission on Aboriginal Peoples, Press Release, 13 February 1992.
52. R. Mathews, *Towards Aboriginal Self-Government*, CEDA Public Information Paper, No. 46 (July 1993).
53. T.J. Courchene, 'Aboriginal Self-Government in Canada', Occasional Lecture, Australian Senate (19 April 1993), 13.
54. [1993] 2 N.Z.L.R. 301, 306–307.
55. C. Wainwright, 'Leverage Through Litigation: the new Maori Politics', 1993 New Zealand Law Conference, Conference Papers, vol. 2, 294, 307.
56. A. Sharp, *Justice and the Maori—Maori Claims in New Zealand Political Argument in the 1980s* (Oxford University Press, 1990), 142.
57. Wainwright, *supra* note 54, 311.
58. *State Owned Enterprises Act* 1986 (NZ), s.9.
59. *Tainui Maori Trust Board v. Attorney-General* [1989] 2 N.Z.L.R. 513, 529.
60. *Id.* 529.
61. E. Durie, 'Politics and Treaty Law', 1993 New Zealand Law Conference, Conference Papers, vol.2, 75, 83.
62. D. A. Huata, 'Indigenous Peoples' Rights', 1993 New Zealand Law Conference, Conference Papers, vol.2, 84, 87.
63. *Id.* 90.

APPENDIX I
THE REPORT OF THE REPUBLIC ADVISORY COMMITTEE[*]
SUMMARY OF CONCLUSIONS AND OPTIONS

The Committee's Terms of Reference require it to produce an 'options paper' describing the minimum constitutional changes necessary to achieve a viable federal republic of Australia while maintaining the effect of our current conventions and principles of government. The Committee was asked specifically not to make recommendations but did come to a number of conclusions about matters relevant to consideration of those options. Those conclusions, along with the options identified, are summarised below.

Australia is a state in which sovereignty derives from the people. The hereditary office of the monarchy is the only element of the Australian system of government which is not consistent with a republican form of government. The only constitutional change therefore required to make Australian a completely republican system of government is to remove the monarch. All the essential elements of our system of government—federalism, responsible parliamentary government, the separation of powers and judicial review of legislation and government action—would be unaffected by such a change. So would all the important institutions of Australian government—the States, Parliament, including the Senate, and the High Court.

In order to replace the monarch with a republican head of state, the Constitution would need to be amended in only three substantive ways:
- establishing the office of a new Australian head of state (including the method of appointment and removal);
- providing for the powers of the head of state; and
- providing for the States.

---

[*] *An Australian Republic: The Options* (Canberra: A.G.P.S., 2 vols., 1993), vol.1., *The Report*, 1.
Commonwealth of Australia copyright reproduced by permission.

The Office of head of state[1]

The Committee concluded that:
- While there are arguments for dispensing with the office of head of state, to do so would involve a major departure from our existing system of government—there is much to be said for a national figure who can represent the nation as a whole, both to Australians and to the rest of the world;
- While the functions of a new head of state are likely to be similar to those of the Governor-General, the new head of state would occupy a more important and prominent role in Australian life simply because he or she would not be just a representative of the Queen, but Australia's head of state in his or her own right;
- establishment of a new office of head of state would provide an opportunity to consider the manner in which the functions are to be carried out and to determine what is appropriate for Australia;
- the title 'President' is the one most commonly used for the head of state in a republic but there are other practical and acceptable options, particularly 'Governor-General' and 'Head of State';
- apart from the requirement that the head of state be an adult Australian citizen and not hold any other remunerated position while in office, there would appear to be no particular formal qualifications essential for the office, although a number could be considered;
- the term of office should be specified, and anywhere from four to seven years is considered reasonable, with a limitation on reappointment; and
- it is necessary to provide for acting arrangements when the head of state is absent or the position is vacant; options include using the senior, available State Governor, using another office-holder, or creating a separate office of deputy head of state.

---

[1] See Chapter 4 of the Report. Chapters 1, 2 and 3 of the Report deal with the Committee and the consultation process, our way of government, and the concepts of 'republicanism' and 'minimalism', respectively.

Appointment of the head of state[2]

In considering the many and varied options for appointing and removing (if necessary) the head of state, the Committee took into account the view commonly expressed that the office should be 'above politics' and that the occupant be, and be seen to be, impartial.

The Committee concluded that there are four main methods of selecting the head of state, with a number of options within these. The methods are outlined below.

Appointment by the Prime Minister

Leaving the appointment of the head of state to the Government of day is the option which most closely reflects the current practice. Although Prime Ministers would no doubt continue to appoint appropriately qualified individuals, and those appointees would similarly carry out the functions of the office in an even-handed fashion, the *process* of appointment may be viewed as a partisan one if left to the Prime Minister alone.

Appointment by Parliament

Involving the people in the appointment process through their parliamentary representatives is a democratic process and, depending on the particular method selected, can ensure that the person selected has the support of all major parties. Moreover, it would, through the Senate, reflect the federal nature of the Commonwealth.

There are a number of issues to be resolved. These include:
- whether the Houses should vote separately, thereby risking deadlock, or whether the members should vote in a joint sitting;
- whether the vote should require a simple majority of members or whether a 'special majority' should be required to ensure that the person selected would have not only the support of the Government members, but also of a substantial number of non-Government members; and
- whether a single nomination by the Prime Minister or a bipartisan nominating panel should be considered, or a number of nominations from other sources.

---

[2] See Chapter 5 of the Report.

A joint sitting of the Houses would be in keeping with the importance of the occasion and could provide a symbol of unity appropriate for the appointment of a head of state who would represent the nation as a whole.

Requiring only a simple majority in each House, or indeed of members of both Houses in a joint sitting could, depending on the relative size of the Government's majority in the House of Representatives and its representation in the Senate, see the Government determine the outcome without the support of any other party, or with the support of a small number of non-Government Senators.

Adopting a voting procedure which would necessarily require the support of members of more than one political party would discourage the nomination of individuals who were not likely to gain that support and would encourage prior consultation on nominees.

A single nomination by the Government would have the advantage of avoiding parliamentary discussion on the relative merits of the candidates which could be seen as divisive and detrimental to the office . Moreover, if a two-thirds majority were required, prior consultation with other parties could be expected. An alternative to a Government nomination would be nomination by an independent commission or group of eminent people with membership on an *ex officio* basis (such as the Chief Justice of the High Court, the Prime Minister and the Leader of the Opposition) or made up of Australians outside the political process.

If having only a single nomination was considered too restrictive, multiple nominations could be allowed, possibly by a specified number of members of Parliament or by a nominating commission. A two-thirds majority requirement would ensure a bipartisan result in the end.

Popular election

The head of state could be elected by the people in a direct election. The argument in favour of such a method is that it is entirely democratic and would give Australians a direct voice in the process.

Another argument made to the Committee is that a direct election would prevent a political appointment, as could occur if the matter was left to politicians. This may not turn out to be the case in practice — indeed a direct election could ensure that the person elected is the nominee of one or other of the major political parties which have the expertise and resources to mount nationwide political campaigns. A popular election might ensure that the head of state is not a 'political' appointment, but it may well result in the person elected being a 'politician'.

The Committee considered two options to reduce the partisan nature of a popular election — a ban on political parties endorsing candidates for the head of state and excluding former politicians. It is doubtful whether such provisions would be effective in freeing the election from political campaigning and they may be seen as unduly restricting political freedoms.

The Committee considered that, while the option of popular election of the head of state is one which appears to have significant public support, it should be recognised that it would be expensive (particularly if held separately from a parliamentary election), would almost certainly involve political parties in the endorsement of candidates, and by its nature could discourage suitable candidates from standing. Moreover, the process of popular election may encourage the head of state to believe that he or she has a popular mandate to exercise the powers of that office, including the ability to make public statements and speeches, in a manner which could bring the head of state into conflict with the elected Government.

The Committee is therefore of the view that if popular election is selected as the appropriate method of selecting the head of state, then, if the effect of our current conventions and principles of government is to be maintained, the Constitution should be amended so as clearly to define and delimit the powers of the head of state so that the Australian people know precisely the powers and duties of the head of state they are being called upon to elect.

Appointment by electoral college

Several federal nations with non-executive heads of state establish electoral colleges to appoint their heads of state. Typically, the electoral college is made up of representatives from the national and State parliaments. The case for including representatives of the States and Territories in the process for selecting the Commonwealth head of state this way is not, in the view of the Committee, a compelling one.

It would be possible to design a special body with representatives drawn from outside the Commonwealth, State and Territory Parliaments with the task of electing the head of state. Reaching a consensus in the community as to which groups or individuals should participate in such an electoral college would, to say the least, not be a straightforward task.

Removal of the head of state[3]

In determining what procedure should be followed for removing the head of state, the Committee considered two main issues:
- whether the method for removal should reflect the method of appointment; and
- whether specific grounds for removal should have to be established.

Unless there were practical reasons for *not* doing so, the Committee considered that the method of removal should reflect the method of appointment and that the arguments for requiring proof of grounds were less strong where the method of removal required an expression of general dissatisfaction in the head of state, such as a two-thirds vote of Parliament.

Removal where appointment by the Prime Minister

The Government alone could remove the head of state, as is in practice the case with the Governor-General (although the Queen formally exercises the power). Although not generally regarded as a disadvantage of the current system, it could be regarded as jeopardising the impartiality and independence of the office, particularly if the head of state was to have more than a ceremonial role. Another option would be to have an independent tribunal establish the grounds before the Government could take action.

Removal where appointment by Parliament

There would seem to be no practical reasons why a head of state appointed by Parliament should not be removed in the same way. The same considerations arise as those for appointment—i.e. the

---

[3] See Chapter 5 of the Report.

majority required, whether the Houses sit together or have separate functions, and how the process should be initiated. An additional issue is whether the Constitution should provide that Parliament be assisted in its deliberations by an independent tribunal.

There are particular advantages in having a joint sitting for the purpose of removing the head of state, to avoid both a deadlock and undesirable delay.

Requiring a majority which virtually guaranteed that removal could occur only if support were forthcoming form non-government members (two-thirds or even three-quarters if that were the majority necessary for appointment) would be in keeping with the principle that the office of head of state be kept free of partisan political considerations to the greatest extent possible.

As to the grounds of removal, there is an argument that, if two-thirds of the members of Parliament in a joint sitting resolve that the head of state should cease to hold office, that expression of dissatisfaction should be cause in itself for the head of state to be removed without proof of any particular misbehaviour or incapacity.

Removal of a popularly elected head of state

There are a number of practical reasons why it may not be appropriate to remove a popularly elected head of state by popular vote (particularly if it involves consideration of sensitive issues such as mental or physical capacity). Removal by the Parliament by a special majority on the basis of demonstrated unfitness may be one way of providing the necessary degree of protection to a popularly elected head of state.

Removal where appointment by an electoral college

Removal of a head of state selected through an electoral college process by the same process appears to be the logical option but, if the practical problems associated with reconvening such a specially constituted body are judged to be substantial, removal by the Commonwealth Parliament, upon proof of unfitness for office, could be considered.

Powers of the head of state[4]

Options which 'maintain the effect of our current conventions and principles of government' would see a new head of state continue to exercise the same kind of 'governmental' functions on the advice of the Government of the day as are presently exercised by the Governor-General. In order to eliminate any uncertainty, the Constitution should provide that in the exercise of these powers the head of state acts on ministerial advice.

Options which eliminate the 'reserve powers' might be regarded as a substantial change to our way of government, which leaves for consideration the issue of how the reserve powers, and the unwritten constitutional conventions which govern the exercise of those powers, should be dealt with in the Constitution so as to maintain the effect of those conventions.

The Committee considered the following options for dealing with the issue of the reserve powers:

- leaving the powers in the same form as are presently set out in the Constitution, but stating in the Constitution that the existing constitutional conventions will continue to apply to the exercise of those powers;
- leaving the powers in the same form as are presently set out in the Constitution with the constitutional conventions formulated in an authoritative written form, but not as part of the Constitution;
- leaving the powers in the same form as are presently set out in the Constitution and providing that Parliament can make laws (possibly by a two-thirds majority) to formulate the relevant constitutional conventions in a legislative form; and
- 'codifying' the relevant constitutional conventions by setting out in the Constitution the circumstances in which the head of state can exercise the reserve powers.

The last option can be done in one of two ways:

- by setting out the most important (and generally agreed) conventions and providing that the remaining (unwritten) conventions are otherwise to continue (i.e. partial codification); or

---

[4] See Chapter 6 of the Report.

- by setting out in the Constitution all the circumstances in which the head of state can exercise a reserve power and stating expressly that in all other circumstances the head of state is to act on ministerial advice (i.e. full codification).

The Committee has considered the possibility of leaving the provisions conferring powers on the head of state in their present very broad terms, saying nothing about the constitutional conventions and simply assuming that they will continue to apply. The Committee does not regard this to be a viable option and believes that some provision should be made in the Constitution in relation to the exercise of the head of state's powers (whether simply expressly applying the existing conventions or through some form of codification). It is clearly possible to do so in a way that preserves the essential elements of Australian democracy and maintains the present balance between the Government and the head of state.

The Senate, supply and the reserve powers

Any attempt to codify the reserve powers of an Australian head of state must deal, in one way or another, with the question of the Senate and supply. The Committee considered several approaches to the issue of the powers of a head of state faced with the blocking of supply by the Senate:

- leave the issue to be governed by the existing conventions, thus preserving the uncertainty of the current situation;
- rely on a codification provision which allows the head of state to dissolve the House of Representatives if the Government is breaching the Constitution (as would happen if the Government spent money that had not been lawfully appropriated) and also dismiss the Prime Minister, and therefore the Government, if the breach continues;
- provide for an automatic double dissolution in such circumstances; or
- remove the Senate's power to reject or delay these kind of bills.

At least the last two of these approaches may be regarded as a substantive change to our way of government—to remove the uncertainties surrounding this issue involves a more fundamental question about the relative powers of the House of Representatives and the Senate.

How a republic can be achieved[5]

The changes to the Constitution (which requires agreement of the people in a referendum) necessary to achieve a republic in Australia would involve provisions:
- terminating the Queen's role as head of state and establishing the office of a new Australian head of state;
- dealing with the appointment and removal of the new head of state and other matters relevant to the new office;
- dealing with the powers of the new head of state;
- dealing with the positions of the States and their links with the Crown; and
- making consequential changes and inserting transitional provisions.

The Committee has considered three important legal issues in this regard and is satisfied, on the basis of advice from the Acting Commonwealth Solicitor-General, that:
- the referendum process provided in section 128 of the Constitution can be used to make the necessary changes to the Constitution;
- apart from section 9 (i.e. the Constitution itself), the *Commonwealth of Australia Constitution Act 1900* does not need to be amended in order for Australia to become a republic; and
- if it is considered appropriate to amend that Act in any event (for instance, to remove references to the Crown), it can be done as part of the change to a republican Commonwealth of Australia.

The States[6]

There are implications for the States in a move to a republic as the Queen is head of state in the States as well as the Commonwealth. Views differ about what might be the legal effect on the States of Australia becoming a republic and the Committee accepts the conclusion of the Acting Solicitor-General that, in order to

---

[5] See Chapter 7 of the Report.

[6] See Chapter 8 of the Report.

minimise legal debate, it would be desirable for amendments creating a republic to deal specifically with the position of the States.

If all States decided to follow a national decision in favour of a republic, there are a number of ways in which the Constitution could be amended (possibly along with the *Australia Act 1986*) to achieve this outcome.

While it might appear anomalous, particularly after a referendum in which a majority of Australians in a majority of States expressed a desire for Australia to become a republic, it would be legally possible for the Constitution to allow a State to retain the monarch as its head of state (assuming that the Queen would agree to such an arrangement). The method for dealing with the States in the Constitution would depend on whether that outcome was considered acceptable. If a State were to be left free to retain the monarchy, it would be advisable, for avoidance of legal doubt, to include a provision in the Commonwealth Constitution which ensured that it could do so. If this outcome were not considered acceptable, the Constitution could be amended so as to extend a republican form of government to all of the States.

Other issues relevant to becoming a republic[7]

A number of other issues were considered by the Committee including:

- whether a change to a republic necessarily involves a change to the name 'Commonwealth of Australia'—the Committee concluded that it does not, and that there does not appear to be a strong case for such a change;
- whether a change to the preamble of the *Commonwealth of Australia Constitution Act 1900* would be necessary or desirable if Australia were to become a republic—the Committee concluded that it is not necessary, as a matter of law to change the preamble, but that the change to a republic might be an appropriate time to assess the statements about Australia which are included in the preamble;

---

[7] See Chapter 9 of the Report.

- whether the specific references in the text of the Constitution to the Queen and the Governor-General would have to be removed —the Committee concluded that generally they would; and
- what should be done to the 'royal prerogatives'—the Committee concluded that the powers and rights of the Commonwealth and State governments which derive from the common law prerogatives of the Crown could and should be preserved.

The Committee also concluded that:
- consideration would have to be given to other aspects of the law and our legal system such as the laws and practices relating to royal charters etc., offices at present filled by commissions from the Crown, and transitional and consequential changes to replace references in legislation to the Governor-General etc; and
- a change to a republic need not have any implications for Australia's membership of the Commonwealth of Nations.

Conclusion[8]

The Committee's task was to outline what a change to a republic in Australia might involve so as to allow for informed judgements to be made about whether a republic is what Australians want. Having considered the issues at length, the Committee is satisfied that it is both legally and practically possible to amend the Constitution to achieve a republic without making changes which will in any way detract from the fundamental constitutional principles on which our system of government is based.

The Report will, the Committee hopes, assist in clarifying the issues associated with a change to a republic. The major issues are few—how should the head of state be appointed (and removed if necessary); what sort of powers and functions should the head of state have; what will be the effect on the Queen's role in the States if Australia were to become a republic; and finally, what changes to the Constitution need to be made to achieve this outcome. The Report demonstrates that there are a number of practical and workable options for addressing these issues.

---

[8] See Chapter 10 of the Report.

APPENDIX II

THE STATES AND A REPUBLIC

A LEGAL OPINION BY SIR HARRY GIBBS AND THE LEGAL COMMITTEE OF AUSTRALIANS FOR CONSTITUTIONAL MONARCHY IN RESPONSE TO THE REPUBLIC ADVISORY COMMITTEE REPORT[*]

The Republic Advisory Committee, in the conclusion to its report, expresses the view that 'the legal complexities (associated with a change to a republic) are readily soluble'. This statement carries optimism too far. In order to show how wrong it is to say that these complexities are readily soluble, it is sufficient to consider the position of the States.

The *Australia Act* was passed, in 1986, as a result of agreement reached between the Commonwealth, the States and the United Kingdom. The Act is a great constitutional document which finally brought all constitutional arrangements affecting the Commonwealth and the States into conformity with 'the status of the Commonwealth of Australia as a sovereign, independent and federal nation'.

The *Australia Act* recognises that Her Majesty's representative in each State shall be the Governor.

If Australia were to become a republic it would be necessary to affect the position of the State Governors as representatives of the Queen. The suggestion that Australia might become a republic, while some States remained constitutional monarchies, is simply absurd, since the whole purpose of the change is intended to be symbolic.

The position of the State Governors would create no difficulty if all State Parliaments would agree to the change. The *Australia Act* may be amended by an Act of the Commonwealth Parliament passed at the request or with the concurrence of the Parliaments of all the States. It is clear, however, that at the present time not all

---

[*] An Australian Republic: The Options (Canberra: A.G.P.S., 2 vols., 1993).

State Parliaments would agree to the change—at least two State Premiers have said that they oppose it.

There is only one other way in which the *Australia Act* might be amended. If a referendum is passed in the future giving the Commonwealth Parliament power to amend the *Australia Act*, it seems that the Parliament might subsequently pass an Act amending the *Australia Act* even if all States did not agree.

However, there is a strong argument that a referendum in any way affecting the Constitution in relation to a State cannot be passed unless a majority of electors voting in that State vote in favour of the law proposed at the referendum. If that argument is correct, a referendum enabling the Commonwealth to abolish the position or status of State Governors would have to be approved in all States. Whether the argument is correct depends on the proper construction of the ambiguous words of section 128 of the Constitution, and is a disputed question which only the High Court can decide.

There is another, deeper question, of political principle as well as of law. The peoples of the Australian colonies agreed to unite under the Crown. It was the basis of the union that Australia should be a constitutional monarchy. The Crown was the tie that bound the peoples of the various colonies in the union. If that bond is severed, a new basis of union must be found, or in other words, there must be a new agreement to unite.

The Republic Advisory Committee itself recognised that as a political proposition there was force in the suggestion that a change of this nature 'cannot be forced on the States' and that the Commonwealth 'cannot alter the fundamental character of the parties to the compact without requiring the renegotiation of the entire agreement'. For any such renegotiation to be effective a majority of the people of each State would have to agree to the change. However, the Republic Advisory Committee considered that as a matter of law the change could be forced on the States against their will. There is no decision of the courts that supports that opinion.

We consider that, as a matter of law, it is by no means clear that there is any constitutional means whereby the basic monarchical character of the Constitution could be destroyed, unless the Parliaments or peoples of all the States supported the change. It would not be possible, in this short statement, to canvass the convoluted legal arguments on which the Republic Advisory Committee relied. Put very briefly, there is a strong argument that the Commonwealth was created by the *Constitution Act*, and not by the Constitution, which governed the Commonwealth and the States once the Commonwealth was created. It may further be strongly argued that the power given by section 128 of the Constitution allows amendments to be made to the Constitution itself, but not to the *Constitution Act*, and that no amendment could validly give the Commonwealth Parliament power to amend the *Constitution Act*. If these arguments are correct this radical change could not be forced on the States or the people of the States. The questions raised are novel, free from authority and shrouded in doubt.

So far from being readily soluble, the legal complexities associated with the change to a republic involve difficult questions that go to the very heart of federation.

Sir Harry Gibbs, former Chief Justice of the High Court of Australia.

The signatories to this opinion are the members of the Legal Committee of Australians for Constitutional Monarchy:

Professor Ivan Shearer, Professor of International Law at Sydney University,
Justice Ken Handley, New South Wales Court of Appeal,
J D Heydon QC, former Professor of Law at Sydney University,
Jack Lee QC, former Judge of New South Wales Supreme Court,
David Yeldham QC, former Judge of New South Wales Supreme Court,
Alan Loxton, senior solicitor,
Josephine Kelly, barrister,
Arthur Emmett QC,
Lloyd Waddy QC,
Jeffrey Phillips, barrister.